Reimagining
Zion

A History of the Alliance of Baptists

D0890610

Andrew Gardner

© 2015

Published in the United States by Nurturing Faith Inc., Macon GA,

www.nurturingfaith.net.

Library of Congress Cataloging-in-Publication Data is available.

ISBN 978-1-938514-80-7

Foreword

"Perhaps Zion is wherever the people of God reside." So Andrew Gardner concludes this excellent history of the Alliance of Baptists, some thirty years after the movement's founding. That single sentence portrays the "Alliance story" insightfully. Born of intense internecine divisions within the Southern Baptist Convention, Alliance-related churches and individuals have shaped an interfaith-ecumenical-justice-pursuing-Baptist identity. The courage present in the movement's beginnings endures in concerns for peace and justice; racial, sexual and gender equality; creation care, and mission engagement. Gardner surveys all that and more as he recounts the history of the Alliance. The metaphor of Zion reflects a theological and ecclesial relocation from the nurture, identity, and traditions of the Southern Baptist Convention, to a new network of congregational and spiritual engagement. Andrew Gardner captures that journey with sensitivity and thoroughness.

Those who did not experience "the Controversy" in the Southern Baptist Convention (SBC) during the 1970s and 1980s may not fully grasp the intensity of the struggle for "the soul" of America's largest Protestant denomination. From 1979 to roughly 1990, Southern Baptist "Moderates" and "Conservatives" challenged each other over theological differences and denominational control. The annual denominational gatherings drew huge crowds of "messengers" from participating churches, empowered to vote for Convention presidents who would use their appointive power to name trustees with specific agendas for affirming or redirecting the nature of the SBC itself. The Controversy probably reached its apex in 1985 in Dallas when some 45,000 messengers showed up to vote for or against Atlanta pastor Charles Stanley for president. Stanley's election convinced many Moderates that new strategies beyond continued confrontation were essential and achievable. Some new coalition was necessary to respond to the shifting directions of the old denomination. The Southern Baptist Alliance, later to become the Alliance of Baptists, was born of that insightful, and in those days courageous, decision.

Courage is an operative word for the origins of the Alliance of Baptists. Once again, those who did not experience the Controversy in the SBC cannot know how courageous it was in 1986 to suggest an alternative approach to responding to the divisions and reshaping Baptist identity in response to transitions in American denominations and culture. Gardner's history retells that story with clarity, naming names of those who shaped the fledgling movement, forming new coalitions and ministries, many of which continue to this day.

One of those early coalitions contributed to the founding of a new theological seminary, Baptist Theological Seminary, Richmond, Virginia, (BTSR) another courageous response to the times that became a long term contribution to theological education in the United States. Thirty years later it is all too easy to forget how daunting it was to begin a new seminary among a Baptist constituency in the South. With the exception of Southeastern Baptist Seminary, whose faculty offered immediate resistance to the right-ward movement of the SBC, the other five SBC-related theological schools were still "intact" and many Moderates insisted that a new school was not necessary. Nonetheless, Alliance supporters anticipated the future and BTSR was yet another sign of something new and courageous, born of and beyond the Controversy.

Such courage was no flash in the pan. As Gardner shows, Alliance churches were from the beginning, strong advocates of women in ministry, not only through ordination, but as essential participants in pastoral minis-try in congregations, chaplaincy, and other callings inside and outside the church. Likewise, as the movement took shape, the Alliance courageously affirmed the presence and voice of LGBT persons and their families in congregations and communities across the nation. Gardner reminds us that the report of the Task Force on Human Sexuality (1994), facilitated perhaps the first public dialogue regarding same-sex issues among Baptists in the South. Such a prophetic response and "fervent discussion" was not with-out controversy then and now, but that once again, Alliance congregations responded to persons and issues in advance of many other Baptist and non-Baptist communions.

Spiritual formation, concern for peace and justice—evident in the close relationship with the Baptist Peace Fellowship—and missional endeavors such as those forged with Cuban Baptists reflect Alliance "witness" nationally and globally. The invitation to PhD student and Millennial Andrew Gardner to write the history of the movement evidences the Alliance's commitment to and anticipation of the future.

To study Gardner's text is to get a sense of Baptist freedom from a group of persons and churches that responded to an ecclesiastical crisis but moved beyond it. His final chapter demonstrates the diversity and energy of several Alliance-related congregations, ministering with care and conscience in the communion of saints and in the naked public square. Andrew Gardner is quite correct, for the Alliance of Baptists, Zion is a moveable feast.

Bill J. Leonard
The School of Divinity
Wake Forest University

Preface

Reimagining Zion: A History of the Alliance of Baptists was not a project I conceived of for myself. While I identify as a budding church historian and a member of the Alliance of Baptists, when I was a student in divinity school the thought of writing a history for a national religious body never emerged on my radar. It was not until Paula Dempsey, Alliance director for partnership relations, approached me about writing a history in February of 2014 that the idea took form. She explained that the Alliance of Baptists had a desire to have its story captured. I did not yet have a topic for my third-year project at Wake Forest School of Divinity, and considering that the Alliance archives were housed on campus, I thought the idea was a perfect match.

I learned that the thought of writing an Alliance history was not a new idea. Alan Neely, the first interim executive director of the (then) Southern Baptist Alliance, wrote a brief history for a book edited by Walter Shurden in 1993, *Struggle for the Soul of the SBC.* The chapter was expanded in the early 2000s as Neely began writing a full history of the organization. Neely's death in 2003, however, halted the project.

Prior to Neely's death, Mahan Siler, a fellow founder of the Alliance, promised Neely that he would find a way to finish the history. Siler and Dempsey both approached Stan Hastey and Richard Groves about writing a history, but for various reasons, both declined. Ultimately, Dempsey asked me, and I accepted with enthusiasm.

In many respects, I question why I would have been asked in the first place. My only formal connection to the Alliance of Baptists at the time was that I served as summer staff at Metro Baptist Church in New York City through the Alliance and the United Church of Christ's Summer Communities of Service program. I attended an Alliance church, Knollwood Baptist in Winston-Salem, North Carolina, but I had never attended an annual Alliance gathering. I find that this says something both about Alliance people and the organization itself. They were willing to let me hold and craft their story despite my newness to the organization.

I was not new, however, to Baptist life. I grew up in a Baptist church just outside of Yorktown, Virginia, in a little town called Poquoson. The church was known as the "liberal" Baptist church in town, but in some ways that really just meant we had female deacons. It was not until I attended The College of William and Mary in Williamsburg, Virginia, that I began to think about my faith in new ways. Perhaps the first time I ever heard of the Alliance of Baptists was in a freshman seminar class taught by Don Polaski, a longtime Alliance member. At the time, I thought the Alliance sounded a little bit more progressive than I felt comfortable with, but my feelings would change.

I participated in the Baptist Collegiate Ministries (BCM) at William and Mary for four years, during three of which I had the privilege of leading a family group Bible study known as "The Inklings." For some strange and bizarre reason, I attracted the more progressive students. At the time, I found it a bit confusing why my Bible study attracted these students, but in reality I was excited that people were coming. Over the course of my studies at William and Mary, I eventually came to identify myself as a progressive and even, dare I say, liberal Baptist.

While leading this Bible study, I met and became good friends with a number of people who attended and, by association, became known as "Inklings." One of these individuals was Alex. He was a year behind me and became my roommate during my junior year. By the time I was about to graduate, Alex applied to be on the Baptist Collegiate Ministry coordinating team as social outreach chair during his senior year. This was a perfect position for Alex because of his personality and commitment to justice. The rest of the organization thought so as well, and he was elected to the position with no apparent opposition.

A few weeks after his election, Alex participated in a panel called "Rainbow and Religion" for the wider campus as a gay man who happened to also be a member of BCM. News of this reached the Virginia Baptist Mission Board, which funded and staffed our campus ministry. Individuals from the state office asked Alex to step down from his position of leadership. If I had had any reservations about accepting LGBT persons within ministerial leadership positions, upon hearing of Alex's requested resignation, all of these reservations were clarified. Not only was Alex hurt, but so was I. Alex was a dear friend, and the idea that I could serve God in a position of leadership but Alex could not seemed antithetical to the gospel. In addition, for a larger Baptist body to usurp the students' ability to elect their own officers seemed antithetical to what it meant to be Baptist.

As an incoming student at Wake Forest School of Divinity, I began to investigate the types of organizations that would allow me to invest in a friendship like the one I had with Alex without fearing that the organization would limit that friend's capacity to serve. I came upon the Alliance of Baptists.

As I have come to identify more fully with the Alliance of Baptists, I have continually been reminded that this is the right religious body for me. I feel at home in this organization, and many other Alliance members echo similar sentiments.

In this work, I claim my biases. I am a member of the Alliance of Baptists. At the same time, I attempt to share an accurate history of the organization. I hope to exemplify the Alliance's fifth point of its covenant — a *"respect for open inquiry and responsible scholarship."* I hope not only to provide a history of the Alliance that is of interest to those within the academic community, but to provide a history that is of value to the Alliance.

Many individuals were responsible for helping make this work a reality. First and foremost, I must thank Paula Dempsey for asking me to work on this project. She provided much support and encouragement throughout the process. Bill Leonard (my advisor at Wake Forest), Relma Hargus, Richard Groves, Mahan Siler, Ken Meyers, Jeanette Holt, and John Roberts all read various parts of the history, providing valuable editorial support and feedback. I must also thank the Wake Forest University Archives and the community at Wake Forest School of Divinity for their help and encouragement. Lastly, this work would not have come to fruition without the encouragement of my mom and dad, Susie and Brad Gardner.

Contents

Introduction

Marked by their beginnings in the early 17th century, Baptists are a strange and diverse denomination within the Christian faith. The Southern Baptist Alliance, founded in 1987, began with the intention of providing a space for Southern Baptists disillusioned by their denominational body. Eventually changing its name to the Alliance of Baptists, this organization created a space for theologically marginalized Baptists to participate and thrive in denominational life. The organization's history is permeated with an inclusiveness and hospitality that reaches out in partnership to disenfranchised female ministers, members of the gay, lesbian, bisexual, and transgender (LGBT) community, radical Baptists in Cuba, after-school programs in the South Side of Chicago, and many more.

Such expansive inclusiveness and hospitality often caused people to develop misconceptions of the Alliance. These misconceptions often arose because of characterizations that focused on one particular aspect of the organization's identity — particularly the inclusiveness of LGBT individuals. In a 2009 graduate seminar, historian Aaron Douglas Weaver acknowledged an overemphasis within Baptist life on the Alliance's support for LGBT rights and individuals. Weaver said, "Historians should be careful not to neglect the Alliance for their contributions on behalf of equality, ecumenism, interfaith dialogue and innovative missions work."[1]

While Weaver accurately recognized the diversity of the Alliance's focus and scope, he wrongly pegged the intentionality of the Alliance. According to Weaver, the organization has, throughout its history, "found a small niche in Baptist Life as the most progressive or liberal Baptist body in the United States."[2] Such a statement, however, fails to acknowledge the complexity and diversity both within the Alliance and within Baptist life more broadly. The Baptist Peace Fellowship of North America and the Association of Welcoming and Affirming Baptists also occupy the more progressive wing of Baptist life. Beginning with the assumption that the Alliance is the most progressive Baptist body in 21st-century religious life neglects the long history and journey the Alliance took to get to the 21st century. In addition, this assumption wrongly assesses the left wing of Baptist life as a spectrum rather than a cluster or community of organizations. Parsing out which of these organizations is the "most liberal" would be a rather pointless task.

This work serves distinctly as *a* history and not *the* history of the Alliance. While this work may be the sole book-length history of the organization, it by no means accounts for everything the Alliance accomplished until 2015. Instead, it seeks to be an introduction not only to the history of the organization, but to its identity as well.

Rather than approaching the story of the Alliance through a lens of being a progressive or liberal body, this work seeks to understand the Alliance through the circumstances and meaning of the organization's founding. As an organization disgruntled with the theological trajectory of the Southern Baptist Convention of the 1980s, the Alliance was founded on the premise of leaving its former denomination. It was reactive. Over the course of the Alliance's history, however, the organization has been remarkably receptive to reimaging the status quo of what it means to be Baptist. It has been proactive.

To illustrate the duality of this reactive and proactive identity, the metaphor of "Reimagining Zion" has been used as a framing tool for the work. This metaphor draws from a history of academic scholarship on the Southern Baptist Convention. Rufus Spain's 1961 work *At Ease in Zion: A Social History of Southern Baptists 1865-1900* used the metaphor of "Zion" to describe how Southern Baptists understood both their denomination specifically and the South generally in the post-Civil War era. Spain concluded that this period witnessed a convergence of Southern Baptist religion and southern culture. According to Spain, Southern Baptists became complacent with the status quo of their religion and society — they became at ease in this southern Zion.[3]

Echoing Spain's work, Barry Hankins' *Uneasy in Babylon: Southern Baptist Conservatives and American Culture* recounts the history of Southern Baptist conservatives in the second half of the 20th century. These conservatives came to dominate the theological, social and political agenda of the Southern Baptist Convention by the 1990s. Drawing upon a similar metaphor to Spain's, Hankins suggests Southern Baptist conservatives (referred to also as inerrantists or fundamentalists) were discontented with the trajectory of their society and their denomination.[4] To combat the "Babylon" of secular society, Southern Baptist conservatives believed they needed to purify their convention by purging any remnant of "liberalism."[5]

This work addresses the story of the moderate or progressive Baptists from whom the conservatives wrested control of the Southern Baptist Convention. Those members of the Southern Baptist Alliance and other moderate Baptists lost their denominational home in this resurgence, or take-over. They grappled with the question of whether they could remain in the Southern Baptist Convention: could they remain in "Zion?" An even more pressing question for members of the Alliance was: Did the Southern Baptist Convention ever resemble Zion in the first place? Were their understandings of Zion flawed from the very beginning? Should they leave, rebuild, or, perchance, reimagine Zion?

I contend that the history and identity of the Alliance is concurrently one of leaving Zion and of reimagining Zion. The Alliance embodied a history and a desire to leave the perceived Zion in the Southern Baptist Convention, as well as a history and a desire to reimagine that perceived Zion. For in the process of leaving, the Alliance recognized, and more importantly was able to acknowledge, that the conception of Zion was flawed from the beginning. There remained, however, an opportunity to reimagine what a Baptist denominational institution could look like.

This history is composed of three parts: Leaving Zion, Reimagining Zion, and Living Zion. Part I — Leaving Zion — provides a chronological historical overview from Baptist beginnings in Chapter One to a history of the Southern Baptist controversies that led to the birth of the Alliance in Chapter Two. The final chapter in Part I provides a summative history of the Alliance from its formation in 1987 to its life and ministry in the second half of the 21st century.

Part II — Reimagining Zion — provides a more detailed and topical history of the Alliance of Baptists. Chapter Four provides a brief history of the creation of the Alliance Covenant, which serves as the framework for the seven subsequent chapters. Each of those chapters addresses a particular tenet of the covenant and the ways in which the Alliance of Baptists "lived into" these covenant principles. These chapters are as follows: Chapter Five — The Freedom of the Individual; Chapter Six — The Freedom of the Local Church; Chapter Seven — The Larger Body of Christ; Chapter Eight — Servant Leadership; Chapter Nine — Theological Education; Chapter Ten — Proclamation of the Good News; and Chapter Eleven — The Free Church in a Free State.

Part III — Living Zion — changes trajectory from a traditional source-based methodological perspective to a more ethnographic perspective. Within this section are brief congregational studies that examine the Sunday morning services and experiences of eight Alliance congregations from eight states. These studies attempt to provide a description of how Alliance congregations operate, rather than a birds-eye view of the organization's history. They also showcase some of the diversity and similarity within Alliance congregations. The congregations are First Baptist Church, Greenville, South Carolina; Glendale Baptist Church, Nashville, Tennessee; Ginter Park Baptist Church, Richmond, Virginia; Woodbrook Baptist Church, Baltimore, Maryland; Oakhurst Baptist Church, Decatur, Georgia; Metro Baptist Church, New York, New York; Pullen Memorial Baptist Church, Raleigh, North Carolina; and Lakeshore Avenue Baptist Church, Oakland, California.

These three sections hopefully provide a comprehensive overview of the history and identity of the Alliance of Baptists.

Part I: Leaving Zion

Chapter 1

From Dissent to Establishment

Discussing the state of religion in America in 1978, historian Martin Marty writes, "It is possible to speak of the Southern Baptist Convention as being 'the Catholic Church of the South,' so pervasive is its influence in so many dimensions of the culture."[1] Less than ten years later, the Southern Baptist Alliance, now called the Alliance of Baptists, organized within the Southern Baptist Convention as a reaction against the internal political struggles between a faction of "inerrantists" and a faction of "moderates" — struggles that would eventually fragment this southern religious "catholicity."

Although the Southern Baptist Alliance was organized in 1987, its history must be connected to the larger history of Baptists generally and Southern Baptists particularly. The Southern Baptist Alliance looked toward Baptist history for inspiration and motivation as it attempted to create something new within the landscape of Baptist life. To understand the creation of the Southern Baptist Alliance necessitates an understanding of how the massive denominational entity known as the Southern Baptist Convention emerged from a small, dissenting minority religious tradition.

Most scholars will agree that Baptists are a second-generation reformation group that emerged out of a separatist tradition within the English Reformation. However, some scholars will suggest a connection between this separatist tradition and the continental Anabaptist tradition that emerged in the first wave of reformation in Germany, Switzerland and Austria in the 16th century.[2] The first Baptist congregation generally agreed upon by scholars, however, stemmed from a separatist congregation in Gainsborough, Lincolnshire, in the early 17th century. Led by John Smyth and funded by Thomas Helwys, a group from this congregation fled to Amsterdam in 1607 to escape the strict regulations of the Church of England.

In Amsterdam, these early Baptists found a number of theological similarities with a congregation of Anabaptists known as Waterlander Mennonites. This early congregation of Baptist separatists was convinced, like most Anabaptists, that baptism ought to be scripturally understood as a practice reserved for adult believers. Having practiced adult baptisms in his congregation, Smyth was surprised to find that these Waterlander Mennonites had been practicing adult baptism for many years. In 1610, Smyth and others left their Baptist congregation with the intention of joining this Anabaptist sect within the Mennonite tradition. Helwys and the rest of this newly formed Baptist congregation, however, identified some distinctions between these Waterlander Mennonites. Choosing not to join the Mennonite tradition, Helwys and the remaining members returned to England in 1612.[3]

These early Baptists were characterized by an Arminian rather than a Calvinistic understanding of the atonement, believing that Jesus Christ died for all people and not just the elect. In one of the earliest confessions of faith, *Propositions and Conclusions concerning True Christian Religion*, these Baptists affirmed "That infants are conceived and born in innocency without sin, and that so dying are undoubtedly saved."[4] This belief in the blamelessness of children and the rejection of the doctrine of original sin, along with other scriptural interpretations, guided Baptists to believe that baptism was reserved for "penitent and faithful persons."[5] This position not only supports an understanding that individuals were free to choose God's grace, but also that this choice should only be made according to the conscience of independent adults.

Another distinction present within early Baptist thought was a belief that God created humans with the ability to make individual choices regarding belief or unbelief without interference or compulsion from other individuals and, particularly, governmental authorities. Because of this belief in freedom of conscience, Baptists espoused some of the earliest forms of religious liberty by suggesting that "the magistrate is not by virtue of his office to meddle with religion, or matters of conscience, to force or compel men to this or that form of religion."[6] Prior to his death in prison, Helwys wrote *A Short Declaration of the Mystery of Iniquity* in which he declared, "The king is a mortal man, and not God, therefore has no power over the immortal souls of his subjects, to make laws and ordinances for them, and to set spiritual lords over them."[7] Religious freedom was an essential distinction of these early Baptists, who occupied the margins of religious life in England. As early as 1612, they sought the protection to believe as they chose not only for their own community, but for non-Christian religious minorities and even non-religious individuals.

By the 1640s, a group of Baptists emerging within England espoused a more Calvinistic understanding of the atonement. Known as Particular Baptists, they believed that Christ died for particular members of the elect.

Spanning this large theological gap, Baptists with a more Arminian view of the atonement became known as General Baptists. Particular Baptists emerged through a split within a Puritan congregation over a rejection of infant baptism and a belief that "dipping" was the most biblical mode of administering this ordinance. While some General Baptist congregations began baptizing adults by affusion (pouring water over the baptismal candidate), immersion (or dipping) quickly became the normative mode for baptism throughout most of Baptist life.[8]

Because Baptist congregations were understood and organized as independent churches and because the authority of belief resided in the individual, historically there was no hierarchical church governance. Baptist churches practiced a congregational, democratic polity, and would group together in "associations." Both Particular and General Baptists created associations as a means of cooperative engagement. Some associations were more centralized, while others remained loose. These associations would often adopt confessions of faith that most often served as guidelines to clarify Baptist positions rather than as strict tenants of belief.[9]

Baptists from the very beginning held numerous opinions regarding the role of women within the church. Some held closely to the scriptural passage from I Corinthians 14, "women should be silent in the churches. For they are not permitted to speak, but should be subordinate, as the law also says."[10] Others, however, made room for women to preach. General Baptist minister Edmund Chillenden argued that some women ought to be permitted to preach in "extraordinary" conditions. Because of such opinions by Chillenden and others, early Baptist women were able to exercise a level of religious authority through preaching. As Baptists became more and more organized and established within society, however, this window of authority was slowly closed to women. Most explicitly, ordination would eventually be regarded as for men only.[11] Nonetheless, women participated as leaders within the early Baptist movement and, like men, were persecuted for their beliefs.[12]

The established English authorities viewed these early Baptists with suspicion and often would whip and imprison them for their radical religious views. Baptists were persecuted not only for being a new religious sect, but also because of their desire to separate secular authority from religious authority. Their belief in the individual's freedom of conscience led them to support the rights of all people to believe according to the dictates of conscience, regardless of religious affiliation or non-affiliation, which made them unpopular with established religious traditions, such as the Anglican

Church in England. This rejection of governmental religious establishments also served as the motivation for the origin of Baptist life in the American colonies.

In 1631, Roger Williams and his wife, Mary, emigrated from England to the Massachusetts Bay Colony. While in England, Williams had been an ordained Anglican clergyman who became a Puritan Separatist after growing disenchanted with the Anglican Church. He traveled to the Massachusetts Bay Colony, where the colonial government had constructed an oppressive religious establishment that functioned similarly to the Anglican Church in England, differing only in certain beliefs and practices. After leading churches in Plymouth and Salem, Williams began to disagree with some of the colony's Puritan establishment. Williams believed the colonial government in Massachusetts should have been more accepting of religious minorities within the colony, particularly those who believed in the practice of adult baptism.[13]

As a consequence of his rejection of the Puritan establishment, the Massachusetts colony exiled Williams, who founded Providence, Rhode Island, in 1635 as "a shelter for persons distressed of conscience."[14] Rhode Island thereby became one of the only colonies to provide religious liberty to those holding minority viewpoints.[15] In 1638, Williams, as well as other Baptist colonists, established the first Baptist church in America. A year later, John Clarke established another Baptist church in Newport, Rhode Island. From these two congregations, Baptists established numerous churches throughout New England, including one in Boston, Massachusetts, in 1665. In the process of expanding, Baptists found the middle colonies, and particularly Pennsylvania, to be more hospitable to expansion because of Quaker influences that also afforded religious liberty to some of the more marginalized faith traditions in the colonies. In 1707, the first Baptist association in the United States was formed in Philadelphia. In the southern colonies, the Anglican establishment complicated Baptist expansion throughout the region, but by the 1690s Baptists had developed a significant presence in and around Charleston, South Carolina.[16]

By the beginning of the 18th century, Baptists were still a small denominational group within the colonies. It was not until what scholars call the First Great Awakening that Baptists began to see a sizeable increase in adherents. During this period of growth, Baptists also diversified. The revivals of the First Great Awakening led to schisms between what would become known as Regular Baptists and Separate or "New Light" Baptists. Regular Baptists, also called "Old Light" Baptists, remained committed to strict

Calvinistic doctrine. Regular Baptists were organized with the approval of the Philadelphia Confession in 1742, a confession of faith with significant Calvinistic overtones. Separate Baptists embraced revivalistic tendencies that included more spontaneity and emotionalism within worship. Smaller sects in American Baptist life also emerged during this period, including Old Regular Baptists, Seventh-Day Baptists and Free Will Baptists.[17]

Throughout the 18th century, Baptists — still a religious minority within the colonies — remained committed to religious liberty. In New England and Virginia, Isaac Backus and John Leland fought the Puritan and Anglican establishments, respectively. In Virginia, ministers had to be approved by the state, and many Baptist ministers were jailed because they refused to submit to the colonial law that forbade non-Anglican ministers from preaching. The colony's preaching restriction led some Baptist ministers to conduct services from their jail cells, speaking to crowds gathered outside. Under the leadership of John Leland, Baptists in Virginia were instrumental in pressuring statesmen such as James Madison and Thomas Jefferson to incorporate religious liberty into America's founding documents, including the Bill of Rights and the Virginia Statute for Religious Freedom.[18]

The role of women within the church remained a topic of debate during the 18th century. The recorded minutes of the Philadelphia Convention reveal that this topic was often discussed, but typically the local church was responsible for deciding the place of women in the congregation. Regular Baptists characteristically adhered to strict modes of authority, which limited the role of women. Many Separate Baptists and some Regular Baptists created the role of deaconess as a position of authority for women. A few women such as Martha Stearns Marshall, Margaret Meuse Clay and Hannah Hall found pulpits to fill within the Separatist tradition. Clay and Hall were arrested and tried for preaching.[19]

During America's formation, and particularly throughout the Revolutionary War, Baptists found themselves on both sides of the conflict. Ministers Richard Furman of South Carolina and Samuel Stillman of Boston were among the clerical supporters of the break from England. Many Baptists served in the colonial militia as well, but some remained loyalists and even fled the colonies. Second Baptist Church in Newport, Rhode Island — which was occupied and later burned during the war — was among the congregations that lost their meetinghouses. Studies also show that the Revolution stunted Baptist growth; however, in the years after the Revolution and into the 19th century, Baptists became one of the largest denominations in the new nation.[20]

The birth of America and the early ante-bellum period brought what many scholars call the Second Great Awakening. During this stage of American history, society experienced the unparalleled growth of both the Methodist and Baptist denominations, which soon became the two largest Protestant religious bodies in the United States. Religious revivals that lasted for days, like the 1802 Cane Ridge Revival in Kentucky, became the primary means of drawing individuals into the church. Scholars debate, however, how Christianity functioned in the framework of the new nation. Some suggest there was a "democratization" of Christianity that drew upon Baptist principles of church autonomy, priesthood of all believers, and individual freedom of conscience. Other scholars drawing upon Baptist principles of religious liberty suggest that Christianity should not be understood as a "democratizing" agent. Instead, these scholars argue that Christians in the ante-bellum period established a hierarchical order within the separate sphere of the church in response to their skepticism about the extensive freedoms granted in the new country's constitution. Although both interpretations have strengths and weaknesses, Baptists remain a key ingredient in both arguments. Baptist proliferation during this period turned this once small sect of Christianity into one of the most important groups in American religious history.[21]

At the same time that Baptists were growing exponentially in America, the missionary movement was also developing rapidly. Many state mission societies formed to support missionaries to the American frontier as early as the late 18th century, but it was not until 1810 that American Congregationalists formed the first national missions society — the American Board of Commissioners for Foreign Missions. Adoniram Judson, Ann Hasseltine Judson and Luther Rice were commissioned as missionaries by the organization and sent to India in 1812. While traveling to India, however, they became convinced of the practice of believer's baptism. All three were baptized by immersion and became Baptists. Luther Rice, returning to the United States, drew support from Baptists across the American geographic divide to create a national organization to support foreign missionaries. In 1814, "The General Missionary Convention of the Baptist Denomination in the United States for Foreign Missions" was founded in Philadelphia. This organization would hold national meetings every three years and became known as the Triennial Convention.[22]

Baptists across the United States had different understandings of how this new Triennial Convention should function, and not all of them supported the convention. Anti-Missionary Baptists believed that missionary efforts of the Triennial Convention attempted to usurp God's sole authority to bring individuals to salvation. For those who did support missionary efforts, however, understanding how the convention should operate was a different question. Some, including Rice, desired that the organization become a comprehensive denominational body, while others wished the organization would remain a loose collection of societies — what became the organizational model known as the society method. This debate was largely a technical one regarding the best method of cooperation. Some individuals feared that certain methods of cooperation would supplant congregational polity. At the second meeting of the Triennial Convention, John Mason Peck and James E. Welch were appointed to missionary efforts in Missouri. The 1820 meeting of the Triennial Convention, however, stopped supporting Peck's mission efforts in order to solely support foreign missions.[23]

Eventually, the centralized and comprehensive denominational structure failed to defeat the society method that emerged within Baptist life. In 1824, the Baptist General Tract Society was formed, and in 1832, the American Baptist Home Mission Society was created to support home missionaries like Peck. While there was a concerted effort on the part of some individuals to create a more centralized denominational structure, the society method provided an organizational intermediary between local associations and a centralized convention.[24]

As the nation progressed into the sectional conflict preceding the Civil War, Baptists in the North and South also argued about their stances on slavery and the appointment of missionaries. By the start of the 19th century, many within evangelical groups like the Baptists and Methodists were involved in the anti-slavery movement. Once these groups gained positions of prominence within the South, however, slavery became a necessary evil and, by the 1830s, a "positive good."[25] Many Baptists in the South also remained committed to the plan of colonization, which sought to transport free blacks back to Africa and remove the entire population of black people from the United States. Contrary to Baptists in the South, northern Baptists increasingly found the practice of slaveholding antithetical to the gospel. The decentralized organization of the Triennial Convention, however, allowed for cooperation between anti-slavery Baptists in the North and pro-slavery Baptists in the South.[26]

By the 1830s, the slavery issue was so pronounced within the larger society that the Triennial Convention began to receive pressure from pro-slavery and abolitionist sides of the debate. William Lloyd Garrison's abolitionist newspaper *The Liberator*, coupled with a revolt led by enslaved Baptist minister Nat Turner in Southampton County, Virginia, in 1831, set the tone for this decade. While some Baptists like Francis Wayland sought to maintain a moderate position within the convention, by 1840 abolitionist Baptists formed the "American Baptist Anti-Slavery Convention." The following year, the Triennial Convention and the Home Mission Society both passed compromises that promoted a position of neutrality regarding the institution of slavery. In 1843, the Anti-Slavery Convention created a separate board to support foreign missions.[27]

The following year, the Triennial Convention and the Home Mission Society reaffirmed their respective positions on neutrality. Anglo-Baptists in the South, however, remained anxious. Shortly after this 1844 meeting in Philadelphia, the Georgia Baptist Convention recommended James E. Reeves to serve as a missionary to Cherokee Indians. Reeves was a slave-holder in Georgia and was put forward to test the denomination's position of neutrality. Shortly after Georgia recommended Reeves, the Alabama State Convention sent a letter to the Triennial Convention requesting that the foreign mission agency grant the same privileges to slaveholders that were afforded to non-slaveholders. The Home Mission Society then voted seven to five against appointing Reeves, a slaveholder. In like manner, the Triennial Convention responded to the Alabama resolution by stating: "If any one should offer himself as a missionary, having slaves, and should insist on retaining them as his property, we could not appoint him."[28] These two responses gave Anglo-Baptists in the South the motivation to break away from these missionary societies and create something new and more sympathetic to their practice of slaveholding.

At the request of the Virginia Foreign Mission Society in May of 1845, a group of 328 individuals representing churches across the South met in Augusta, Georgia, and formed the Southern Baptist Convention. Rather than maintaining a societal organizational structure, the founders of the Southern Baptist Convention created a centralized and connective organization that would oversee the boards of all aspects of the denomination — foreign missions, home missions, publications and more. While these boards were all connected under the umbrella of the Southern Baptist Convention, they retained a society method of funding. Individuals, churches, associations and state conventions all remained autonomous entities, but because of the centralization, each had a closer relationship to one another than previously experienced within the Triennial Convention.[29]

Historians have had difficulty articulating the reasons for the formation of the Southern Baptist Convention. Some scholars claim that the convention was formed over slavery, while others claim that it was formed over missions.

Both have a grain of truth. In reality, the task of separating the desires of those within the Southern Baptist Convention to retain their black slaves in the slaveholding South with their desires to sponsor missionaries might be impossible. Still others considered a commitment to southern regionalism as the primary motivator for the convention's creation.

From the beginnings of the Civil War, the Southern Baptist Convention supported the formation of the Confederate States of America. From the minutes of the 1861 annual meeting, the convention resolved "That we most cordially approve of the formation of the Government of the Confederate States of America."[30] Baptists were also very supportive of the war and many ministers served as chaplains, although some Baptist associations like the Georgia Baptist State Convention opposed funding these chaplains with public money.[31]

The war also placed Christian denominations at odds with one another. Chaplains from different denominations often saw the task of evangelizing soldiers as a competition between denominations. During this period, and even more so after the war ended, competition arose between northern and Southern Baptists. Not only were northern Baptists allowed to assume control of occupied Southern Baptist churches during the war, but afterwards they remained present in the area through their efforts to missionize freedmen. At the 1866 annual meeting of the Southern Baptist Convention, the body resolved regarding the missionizing of ex-slaves: "While we are not opposed to any right-minded man aiding in this important work, it is our decided conviction, from our knowledge and character of these people, and of the feelings of our citizens, that this work must be done mainly by ourselves."[32] The convention was clear in claiming that freedmen fell within the jurisdiction of the South, and any missionizing of these people ought to be the work of Southern Baptists.

After the Civil War, Southern Baptists came to prominence within southern society, and in many ways their status engendered social and political clout as well as religious. The emergence of the Cult of the Lost Cause in the post-war South also brought with it a civil religion. As historian Charles Wilson has argued, since the Confederate political experiment failed, the civil religion of the South coalesced around the question of cultural identity rather than political identity.[33] Religion became a tool for southerners as they attempted to form a collective distinctiveness. This is not to completely neglect the multiplicity of roles religion played in an individual's life, but it does offer an explanation as to why the "Southern" Baptist tradition became such an entrenched denominational body.

As scholars like Rufus Spain have shown, it became difficult to determine whether Southern Baptists influenced southern culture more or the other way around. Recognizing the creation of the Southern Baptist Convention in 1845, Spain argued that the South molded Southern Baptists in its own likeness. He wrote:

> Southern Baptists defended the status quo. Their final attitudes toward political, social, economic, and other problems of Southern society coincided with the prevailing attitudes of Southerners in general . . . their importance as a social force was in supporting and perpetuating the standards prevailing in society at large.[34]

Southern Baptists were not held hostage by the greater society, but instead relinquished their prophetic voice to unify and perpetuate the identity of this southern society. They had moved from dissent to establishment.

Spain titled his study of the post-bellum Southern Baptist Convention *At Ease in Zion*, for all was "at ease" in the life of what was slowly becoming the largest Protestant denomination in the United States. For Anglo-Baptists in the South, their religious identity became wedded to southern cultural identity, and their collective, prophetic voice became complacent with the larger, dominant society. As the denomination continued to grow into the twentieth society, the Southern Baptist Convention achieved a place of privilege and power surpassing anything early English Separatists could have conceived for their descendants. The convention blurred the lines between religion and cultural order in the American South, something its Baptist forebears strove to avoid.

The historical stream that traces Southern Baptists particularly from this dissenting religious minority to a culturally entrenched religious majority greatly influenced the formation of the Southern Baptist Alliance. The Alliance sought to return to early Baptist principles like freedom of conscience and local church autonomy. Support of these principles turned figures like Thomas Helwys, Roger Williams, Martha Stearns Marshall and others into the sources of the organization's inspiration. The Alliance saw itself as a course correction, returning to the principles that its members understood to be distinct within Baptist life. While the Alliance did not form until 1987, its founding connected to the larger historical stream of Baptist life, a stream marked by a transition from a culturally marginalized religious group that fought for the rights of all religious traditions to a hegemonic religious institution. Without the creation of this Southern

Baptist establishment, conceiving of the formation of a "course correction" like the Alliance of Baptists would be impossible. This "course correction" stemmed from a history of conflict and controversy within the Southern Baptist Convention that culminated in the "Holy War" of the 1980s between "inerrantists" and "moderates."

Chapter 2

Trouble in Zion

By the start of the 20th century, the Southern Baptist Convention was well on its way to becoming a religious powerhouse, but all was not at ease in this cultural and religious "Zion."[1] Throughout the history of the convention, various controversies threatened the stability and, in some cases, the existence of the denomination. While many controversies were avoided or quelled, the historical stream of these difficulties culminated in a struggle between "moderates" and "inerrantists," beginning in 1979. This struggle, known as the "Fundamentalist Takeover" by theological moderates and the "Conservative Resurgence" by biblical inerrantists, led to the birth of the Southern Baptist Alliance in 1987. Recognizing the history of these struggles contextualizes the motivations behind the formation of the Alliance and the conception of the Alliance Covenant, which came to hold the organization together from its earliest years into the second decade of the 21st century.

To understand the history of struggle within the Southern Baptist Convention, it becomes necessary to recognize the ways in which the denomination was an amalgam of multiple traditions of Baptists. Baptist historian Walter Shurden termed this amalgamation "The Southern Baptist Synthesis."[2] While other traditions have since been added to this synthesis, the original four Shurden identified in the founding of the Southern Baptist Convention were the Charleston Tradition, the Sandy Creek Tradition, the Georgia Tradition, and the Tennessee Tradition.

The Charleston Tradition was composed of predominantly "Regular Baptists" who practiced formalized, liturgical worship and espoused a strict Calvinism. "Separate Baptists" helped to establish the Sandy Creek tradition that featured a less formal style of worship and was characterized by revivalism and a modified form of Calvinism. The Georgia Tradition and the Tennessee Tradition emphasized, respectively, regional identity and exclusivity, which when paired together created an idea that the Southern Baptist Convention was the one, true church.[3] The distinctive qualities of each of these traditions not only fueled many struggles throughout the 20th century but were also the historic qualities that the Southern Baptist Alliance rejected, redefined, and retained through its formation.[4]

Southern Baptist seminaries were frequently a hotspot for theological controversy. The flagship seminary, Southern Baptist Theological Seminary, was founded in 1859 in Greenville, South Carolina, and moved after the Civil War to its present location in Louisville, Kentucky. One early member of the faculty, Crawford Toy, studied in Germany and supported scholarship that utilized forms of biblical higher criticism. Through the use of textual and historical methods, Toy concluded that the book of Isaiah was a compilation of writings by multiple authors rather than one work by a single author. This view caused enough debate among Southern Baptists that Toy resigned from his position to take another post at Harvard University.

Not long after Toy's resignation, a church historian named William Whitsitt caused another controversy. His publication in the mid-1890s regarding the origins of baptismal immersion countered the views of one particular sect within the Southern Baptist Convention. Whitsitt argued that not only were early Baptists products of English Separatism, but that they practiced baptism by affusion rather than by immersion. This scholarship directly countered the successionist beliefs of J.R. Graves and others within the Tennessee Tradition, who were also referred to as Landmarkists. They believed that Baptists could trace their lineage in succession from John the Baptist. Their name, Landmarkists, stemmed from the Proverbs 23:10 verse, "Remove not the old landmark . . . "[5] Enough state Baptist newspapers and individuals rallied against Whitsitt and his scholarship that, in 1899, he resigned as professor of church history and president of Southern Seminary. He spent the rest of his life teaching at the University of Richmond.[6]

Both Toy and Whitsitt were academics of the finest degree, and their scholarship created the first wave of controversy within the great sea of theological perspectives present in the Southern Baptist Convention. By 1925, however, conflict within Southern Baptist higher education was coupled with the organization's financial troubles. In this year, the nation was buzzing with the fundamentalist-modernist controversy encapsulated in the Scopes Monkey Trial.[7] At the same time, the convention was struggling with its own fundamentalist-modernist debate. Beginning in the early 20th century, J. Frank Norris, a fundamentalist from Texas, began putting pressure on the convention to halt the growing popularity of Darwinian evolution. Led by Norris, a faction of fundamentalists forced the resignation of five professors from Baptist schools. They were unable, however, to remove Wake Forest College president and evolutionist William Poteat.[8]

While the debate regarding evolution raged, the convention also faced a drastic financial deficit. In 1919, the 75 Million-Dollar Campaign challenged churches to raise money to offset the convention's deficit. Despite promising pledges ($92.6 million), the total raised amounted to only $58 million. In an effort to find a more financially stable model for funding both state and national organizations, the convention adopted the Cooperative Program as a singular and unified method for funding.[9] This program reversed the earlier decision that the convention retain a societal method of funding. The committee recommendation for the Cooperative Program concluded:

> . . . the only way of liquidating our debts and creating an adequate financial support of all of our institutions and activities under God is to commit ourselves thoroughly to our Co-Operative Program, taking the nucleus of regular and systematic givers and the wholly or partially enlisted churches and the great body of the unenlisted members, and week by week and month by month, build them into a great and mighty host of never-failing supporters of Kingdom causes.[10]

With the adoption of the Cooperative Program, the Southern Baptist Convention now possessed a unified mechanism to fund all of its institutions, agencies, and ministries. Over the years, the Cooperative Program worked exceedingly well, growing to more than $350 million by 1990.[11]

The internal fundamentalist-modernist controversy and the financial crisis caused the convention to move to adopt its first confession of faith — The Baptist Faith and Message (1925). The committee that recommended this confession of faith believed that it would serve as "a reaffirmation of Christian fundamentals" and "remove some causes of misunderstanding, friction, and apprehension."[12] The financial instability within the denomination necessitated a confession to quell the tensions between fundamentalists and modernists that might threaten the unity of the convention. Along with the Cooperative Program, the statement of faith brought the convention together theologically, financially and administratively.

The Baptist Faith and Message was drawn from the 1833 New Hampshire Confession of Faith, with a few modifications. A small fundamentalist faction attempted to amend the Faith and Message to claim that "man came into this world by direct creation of God and not by evolution;" however, the motion failed.[13] Some individuals, like W.J. McGlothlin, were opposed to the adoption of the Baptist Faith and Message because they believed Baptists should not be in "the business of creed building."[14] The confession essentially became a compromise between the fundamentalists who desired a more rigid doctrinal consistency within the denomination and modernists who remained committed to a less creedal religious expression.

This compromise held fundamentalist- and moderate-leaning Southern Baptists together for thirty-eight years until a controversy surrounding the use of the historical-critical method in scholarship led to a revision of the Baptist Faith and Message. Beginning in 1958, during Duke McCall's presidency at Southern Baptist Theological Seminary, the board of trustees dismissed thirteen faculty members who were frustrated with the administration.[15] Several of these faculty members took positions at the newly founded Midwestern Theological Seminary in Kansas City, Missouri, and at Southeastern Theological Seminary in Wake Forest, North Carolina. Joining the professors at Midwestern Seminary was Ralph Elliott, a professor of Old Testament and Hebrew who had previously taught at (and graduated from) Southern Seminary.[16]

Elliott's faculty advisor from his student days at the seminary suggested that the two work together on a commentary for the book of Genesis to be published through Broadman Press, the Southern Baptist publishing house. After Elliott quickly churned out a manuscript, his advisor recommended that he publish the volume independently. In July 1961, Broadman Press published *The Message of Genesis*. Reflecting years later on the publication, Elliott wrote,

> The book was a rather conservative effort. A considerable amount of digression was spent in upholding the historicity of the patriarchs. This was a deliberate disassociation from much of the scholarly position at the time. . . . Quite in contrast to Julius Wellhausen, with whose brush I was often painted, I made it clear that the Hebrew heritage was *not* something initiated and concocted to fit a late priestly scheme, but was wrought by God in the history of a people, including and prior to the time of Moses.[17]

The book was not received as a "conservative effort." Not only were letters sent within the year to Midwestern requesting Elliott's immediate dismissal, but Baptist periodicals questioned his beliefs about the divinity of Jesus.[18]

The public reception of *The Message of Genesis* was influenced drastically by the climate surrounding Midwestern Theological Seminary. A rivalry existed between Midwestern and Southern Seminary, where many of the new seminary's faculty had taught prior to being dismissed in 1958. Central Theological Seminary, an American Baptist school in Kansas City, also put pressure on Midwestern to produce scholarship within the bounds of certain theological parameters. The subsequent response of those opposed to Elliott's scholarship revolved around using Midwestern Theological Seminary's board of trustees to have Elliott dismissed.

At the 1962 annual meeting of the Southern Baptist Convention in San Francisco, messengers confronted "allegations of liberal theology among faculty members of two Convention seminaries" — Midwestern and Southern.[19] A group of messengers from Oklahoma had been pressuring the Sunday School Board to halt the printing of Elliott's book, but they were also pressuring the convention's Committee on Committees to appoint individuals to Midwestern's board who supported removing Elliot from the school's faculty. This strategy proved effective. The board of trustees dismissed Elliott five months after the annual meeting, and *The Message of Genesis* was transferred from Broadman Press to Bethany Press.[20]

Elliott's dismissal led to a revision in the Baptist Faith and Message at the convention's annual meeting in 1963, and although the revision included a statement on academic freedom and responsibility, the damage had already been done.[21] (After the convention that reared and educated him turned its back on him, Elliott joined the American Baptist Churches USA.) Revising the Baptist Faith and Message helped calm things for the immediate future, but the "Genesis Controversy" revealed something no one at the time recognized.[22] Using the Committee on Committees to appoint trustees to Southern Baptist institutions and agencies proved quite affective in removing a theological "moderate" like Elliott from the Midwestern faculty. To use the Committee on Committees in this way, however, required the election of like-minded convention presidents for a period of roughly ten years to ensure "like-minded" trustee majorities in all major Southern Baptist institutions.

By 1977, state appeals court judge Paul Pressler had become fed up with the direction of the Southern Baptist Convention. For more than ten years, Pressler and pastor Paige Patterson had been frustrated with more progressive forms of theology being taught in the denomination's seminaries. By 1977, after conversations with Bill Powell, an employee of the Home Mission Board, and students from Baylor who felt they were being taught liberal theology, Pressler began planning to "take back" the convention.[23]

Historian David T. Morgan explains that histories of this period often overlook Powell's role. Powell was an active conservative in the 1970s who helped found the Baptist Faith and Message Fellowship and the *Southern Baptist Journal,* both of which served the fundamentalist-leaning or "inerrantist" wing of the convention.[24] Morgan explained that Powell worked out the strategy Pressler used to change the direction of the convention — the sequential election of convention presidents who would then influence the appointment of inerrantist trustees to various convention agencies and seminaries.[25] Powell, Pressler and Patterson pointed to the 1979 Houston meeting as the first year for their "conservative resurgence."[26]

Through the power of the presidency, Pressler and Patterson could influence the appointment of members to the Committee on Committees. This appointment process then would influence the Committee on Nominations, which was confirmed by the messengers at the annual meetings. The Committee on Nominations nominated the trustees of various institutions. The voting messengers had little power to influence this process, but they also never historically tried. As sociologist Nancy Ammerman writes, "power was at issue when people met for their annual meeting; they just never noticed it because they accepted the legitimacy of the leaders who governed and the staff who executed policy."[27] Certainly small-scale politics had taken place prior to the 1980s in steering agencies and institutions toward a theological position, but nothing to the magnitude and scale of what Pressler and Patterson envisioned.

At the 1979 convention, the Pressler/Patterson coalition's nominee for president, Adrian Rogers of Memphis, Tennessee, was elected with 51.36 percent of the vote, with the next closest candidate garnering 23.39 percent.[28] The election shocked many of the convention's "old guard." Prior to the election, Rogers delivered a sermon at the Pastor's Conference, a conservative event held in tandem with the annual convention, where he warned against theological liberalism and raised up the doctrine of inerrancy. After Rogers' sermon, W.A. Criswell, a self-described fundamentalist and former convention president, rose to speak and endorsed Rogers' candidacy for president. As historian Bill Leonard writes, "Denominational statesmen, in a gentlemen's agreement, previously considered it unbecoming for a former SBC president formally to endorse a candidate for office . . . things had changed in the SBC."[29] Despite the stunning election, many of the "old guard" believed that Rogers' election was a fluke or perhaps part of a five- to seven-year swing in the convention that would eventually move back toward the more moderate center.[30]

The moderate faction failed to form any response to Rogers' election at the 1980 annual convention meeting, and another Pressler/Patterson candidate, Bailey Smith, was elected. A few months after the meeting, however, a Pressler address at Old Forest Road Baptist Church in Lynchburg, Virginia, spurred moderates to respond. Pressler announced that conservatives of his stripe, often marked as fundamentalists, were "going for the jugular" and were "not going to sit there like a bunch of dummies and rubber stamp everything that's presented to them."[31] Pressler's address sounded the alarm for moderates like Cecil Sherman, who organized a group of moderate pastors to meet in Gatlinburg, Tennessee, in November. The participants returned to their churches with a plan to urge attendance at the 1981convention in Los Angeles and to create a network of moderate churches with which to organize.[32]

The Pressler/Patterson coalition proved too strong at the Los Angeles meeting, and the moderates were defeated handily. Since Bailey Smith was the incumbent running for his second and final term, wresting control of the convention from the declared inerrantists proved difficult, as was the case for moderates when challenging incumbent presidents throughout the period of conflict. At the Los Angeles meeting, the moderates also attempted, via a motion from the floor, to limit the presidential power to appoint the Committee on Committees, but the motion failed.[33]

The following year (1982), Duke McCall, former president of Southern Baptist Theological Seminary, ran as the moderate candidate. He lost to Jimmy Draper, pastor of First Baptist Church in Euless, Texas. Importantly at this meeting, conservatives were able to carry the convention's resolutions.[34] The convention had traditionally supported the 1962 decision of the Supreme Court in *Engel v. Vitale* to ban prayer in public schools, but in 1982 the convention, by a three-to-one majority, voted to support a constitutional amendment that would reintroduce organized prayer into public schools. This decision came only two hours after James Dunn of the Baptist Joint Committee on Public Affairs spoke against President Ronald Reagan's proposed amendment to allow prayer in public schools.[35]

While there was certainly a theological as well as internal struggle for power within the Southern Baptist Convention, there was also a national political struggle influencing the controversy. Stan Hastey, former *Baptist Press* correspondent in Washington, D.C., and the first executive director of the Southern Baptist Alliance, claimed in 1993 that "it is more than coincidental that the rise of the fundamentalist party to power in the SBC paralleled the domination of the national scene by . . . the New Christian Right."[36] Many members of the Pressler/Patterson coalition also served as leaders in new national political organizations such as the Moral Majority.[37]

Ed McAteer, a member of Adrian Rogers' church in Memphis, founded the Religious Roundtable in 1979, which included eleven Southern Baptists. While the Pressler/Patterson coalition focused on influencing the institutional machinery of the convention, McAteer focused on pushing the convention resolutions in a more conservative direction, affecting the convention's voice in the public sphere. These goals, while separate, often worked in tandem. In many respects, attempting to disentangle the two would be impossible.[38] Perhaps what brought them together was a common enemy — self-identified moderates within the Southern Baptist Convention who were neither iner-rantists nor supporters of the new Religious Right. Leading the banner for this loose moderate coalition was James Dunn. When "People for the American Way" was founded in 1981 to directly counter the "Religious Right," Dunn served on the organization's board of directors.[39] By 1984, members of the Pressler/Patterson coalition made their first attempt to defund the Baptist Joint Committee on Public Affairs (BJC), of which Dunn was the executive director. The attempt failed, but it would not be long before the Southern Baptist Convention was no longer one of the then nine Baptist bodies that supported the work of the BJC.[40]

After another loss at the 1984 annual convention, the moderate faction finally began to form a more unified coalition. Three seminary presidents — Russell Dilday, Roy Honeycutt and Randall Lolley — began decrying the tactics of the "fundamentalist takeover." In a convocation address at Southern Baptist Theological Seminary in August 1984, Honeycutt preached a sermon titled "To Your Tents, O Israel," in which he declared the conflict within the denomination a "Holy War." Honeycutt said, "Those of us who are free by the grace of God in Jesus Christ are free forever, for us there is no turning back to a limited legalism untouched by the grace of God. There is no turn-ing back. No turning back."[41] Leading the charge, the seminary presidents helped to bring the more moderate coalition together for the upcoming 1985 annual convention meeting in Dallas.

More than 35,000 messengers had preregistered to attend the Dallas meeting, and by the time the presidential vote took place, more than 45,000 were in attendance. Previously, the largest attendance for any Southern Baptist meeting had barely surpassed 22,000.[42] By this point, the moderate coalition had a two-year-old institutional framework for organizing. The publication of a newspaper (*Southern Baptists Today*), the founding of Southern Baptist Women in Ministry, and the beginning of the Baptist Forum (a reception to rival the more conservative Pastor's Conference) all were designed to help elect a moderate convention president.[43]

This young infrastructure proved ineffective, however, and moderate candidate Winfred Moore lost to the incumbent, inerrantist Charles Stanley. After Stanley's re-election, moderates offered a new slate of nominees to the Committee on Committees. Initially, moderates were required to issue their recommendations one nominee at a time, but after an afternoon break, business resumed in the evening to a new ruling reported by Stanley that the convention must rule on the presidential slate of nominees as it stood, without alterations. The inerrantist slate was subsequently elected. Moderates were forced to try again at Atlanta in 1986, but they met the same fate — another victory for the Pressler/Patterson coalition.[44]

After the 1986 convention, a group of moderates met in August in Macon, Georgia. They were split regarding whether or not to keep struggling within the convention or to focus their energies on the formation of something new. This was the first inkling of the Southern Baptist Alliance. A purpose statement was crafted, and in December an initial planning meeting for the Southern Baptist Alliance was held at Meredith College, the North Carolina Baptist Women's College located in Raleigh.[45] Between these meetings, the convention's Home Mission Board voted to withhold financial support to churches with female pastors, and Southern Baptist seminary presidents issued the "Glorieta Statement," which declared that the Bible was "not errant in any area of reality."[46] The statement was interpreted by some moderates as a concession to the inerrantist coalition.[47]

In September, however, prior to the "Glorieta Statement," "Concerned Southern Baptists" met at Meredith College. Many ideas were voiced regarding what type of organization moderates needed. Larry Coleman, pastor of Bellewood Baptist Church in New York, questioned the idea of creating an organization around support for the Baptist Joint Committee and religious liberty, fellowship, and theological forum. There was concern as well regarding how a new organization would relate to other small organizations in Georgia and North Carolina that primarily existed to affect the elections in Baptist state conventions. Jim Strickland proposed the formation of the "Southern Baptist Heritage Fellowship," but a purpose statement was crafted that would guide the organization's name to eventually become "The Southern Baptist Alliance." The purpose statement described the group as "An alliance of individuals and churches dedicated to the preservation of historic Southern Baptist principles, freedoms, and traditions, and the continuance of its ministry and mission."[48] The group appointed committees to discuss identity, communication, fellowship, education and publications, with the intention of meeting again in January.[49]

There may have always been a history of conflict and compromise within the Southern Baptist Convention, but the conflict of the 1980s was of a different variety. The coalition of inerrantists under the leadership of Paige Patterson and Paul Pressler was bent on removing any hint of liberalism or unorthodoxy from the convention and its agencies and institutions. By the latter part of the 20th century, these conservatives were struggling to make sense of the decreasing religious identity of American and especially southern society, and reclaiming the Southern Baptist Convention became a step for them to differentiate themselves from the rest of irreligious America. As historian Barry Hankins suggests, conservative inerrantists had become "Uneasy in Babylon." They sought to purge and cleanse Zion from those less rigid in their understanding of orthodoxy. The Southern Baptist Convention needed to be completely set apart from the Babylon of secular mainstream society.[50]

For more moderate Southern Baptists who had grown up in this southern Zion, seeing the denomination of their childhood "taken over" was nothing short of heartbreaking. Many continued the fight to try to see the convention return to its former "glory," but they would fail. A few, however, never saw or experienced the Southern Baptist Convention as all that glorious to begin with. After all, Ralph Elliott was fired when moderates were "in control." These individuals, who had always felt left out of the convention because of their beliefs, began the journey toward something new. They questioned why they should keep fighting for the return of a convention that had always marginalized them and wondered at what point the self-avowed moderates would start to look like their enemy.

Witnessing all this trouble in Zion led the left wing of the Southern Baptist Convention to consider reimagining its identity as Southern Baptists. Initially, this new "alliance" remained within the convention, providing a home and a safe place for the weary and wounded as well as for those who did not desire to participate in the political turmoil. As time progressed and the inerrantists began purging institutions of moderate influence, however, the Southern Baptist Convention looked less and less like Zion for members of the Southern Baptist Alliance. When this process was all but complete, the Southern Baptist Alliance broke away and began to set its own course — free from the establishment that birthed it. This trouble in Zion forced members of the Alliance to pursue a more true and more faithful way of being Baptist in the quickly approaching 21st century.

Chapter 3

An Exodus People

February 12, 1987, marked the official founding date of the Southern Baptist Alliance. However, this was not the day the Alliance broke its relationship with the Southern Baptist Convention. On this day, the Alliance leadership pledged to work within the convention in non-political ways to provide a space for moderates who were tired of fighting with the inerrantists. Four years later, in 1991, the Southern Baptist Alliance had emancipated itself from its commitment to work within the convention, and by 1992 the organization had changed its name to the Alliance of Baptists. In reality, however, the 1987 founding marked the beginning of the Alliance's exodus not just from the Southern Baptist Convention, but from all oppressive religious and denominational structures — an exodus that is ongoing.

After the 1986 meeting that established a purpose statement for the organization, the first official meeting of the Southern Baptist Alliance took place in December of that year. The meeting resulted in a general consensus of desires for the new organization. Those who attended divided into three groups — an "Affirmations Group" to examine writing a covenant, a "Structure Group" to create an organizational configuration, and a "Plans and Program Group" to discuss the possibility of issuing statements, holding gatherings and establishing support networks.[1]

These three groups reconvened on February 2-3, 1987. Over the course of the two days, the Southern Baptist Alliance adopted the Alliance Covenant, the organization's founding document. In addition to the covenant, the leadership agreed on membership dues, a pro-tem board, organizational officers, an organizational newsletter to be delivered through *SBC Today* (a moderate newspaper), and the dates for the first convocation, to be held in the middle of May at Meredith College in Raleigh, North Carolina. Less than two weeks later, on February 12, the Alliance held press conferences in Charlotte, Raleigh and Atlanta to announce its formation.[2]

State organizations quickly began to form, the first in Kentucky.[3] Despite the quick establishment of these state chapters, however, by the mid-1990s the only active state associations were in Georgia, North Carolina, and Virginia, and in the second decade of the 21st century no formal state chapters were operating.

At the first convocation on May 15, three months after the Alliance's formation, the membership was just over 800 members.[4] The meeting was attended by nearly 600 individuals, and those present appointed Henry Crouch as president, Susan Lockwood as vice president, Richard Groves as secretary, and Bruce Morgan as treasurer. A month later, when the board of directors met during the Southern Baptist Convention's annual meeting in St. Louis, the Alliance membership was more than 3,000.[5]

At the fall board meeting in September of 1987, the Southern Baptist Alliance began addressing issues ranging from when "an executive director will need to be hired" to the Home Mission Board, the Baptist Joint Committee, Southern Baptist Seminaries, the need for moderate Sunday School material, and much more.[6] There was a great need for financial support and new infrastructures. The Southern Baptist Convention no longer served as a denominational option for moderate Southern Baptists like those affiliating with the Alliance — a number that was growing.

During a November meeting, Crouch reported that the organization had more than 12,000 members (1,700 individual members and 19 churches with more than 10,600 members).[7] Despite its growing membership, the Alliance wondered what role it might play if moderates won the presidency of the Southern Baptist Convention at the 1988 San Antonio meeting. Most leaders agreed on the continuing need for the Alliance, but at this point the organization had no full-time staff and was unsure about its financial longevity.[8]

At the meeting, the Alliance also discussed the recent "takeover" of Southeastern Theological Seminary. The seminary, located in Wake Forest, North Carolina, was the first of the Southern Baptist seminaries to have an inerrantist majority appointed to its board of trustees. This resulted in the resignation of the president and the dean, with many faculty and students leaving in the subsequent years. The Alliance leadership responded by examining the possibility of establishing its own school for theological education. In addition, the Alliance came to the financial aid of the Southeastern faculty by approving $5,000 to support the legal fees of those who attempted to retain some control over their teaching positions.[9]

After thirteen months, the Alliance membership totaled 25,362 (2,106 individual members, with the rest accounted for in 40 churches).[10] In March, a second annual convocation was held at Mercer University in Macon, Georgia. The membership elected John Thomason as president and moved to hold the following year's convocation at Furman University in Greenville, South Carolina.[11]

After the 1988 Southern Baptist Convention's annual meeting in San Antonio resulted in the loss of another moderate candidate for president, the Alliance moved to hold a listening session in Nashville, Tennessee, in September for moderates to discuss issues within the convention.[12] While in Nashville, the board of directors approved financial requests for the Alliance's first ministry partners and agreed to continue investigating the possibility of founding a school for theological education.[13]

In 1989, the Alliance hired Stan Hastey and Jeanette Holt to serve as executive director and associate director, respectively. Both were former employees of the Baptist Joint Committee on Public Affairs.[14] With their employment, the Alliance moved its offices to Washington, D.C. The first convocation under the leadership of Hastey, Holt and Alliance president Anne Thomas Neil took place at First Baptist Church in Greenville, South Carolina, after Furman University became leery of hosting the Alliance. (The school still received money from South Carolina Baptists and did not want to jeopardize its funding.) At First Baptist Greenville, the Alliance moved forward with its decision to found Baptist Theological Seminary at Richmond in hopes of providing an alternative seminary for moderate Baptist students.[15]

At the 1990 Alliance convocation in St. Louis, Missouri, Richard Groves was elected president for a two-year term. At the gathering, the Alliance passed a statement apologizing for the role the Southern Baptist Convention played in perpetuating the institution of slavery.[16] A few months later, the Alliance board recommended striking the statement within the organization's covenant that said that the organization would work within the Southern Baptist Convention. The recommendation was approved in 1991 at the convocation at Grace Baptist Church in Richmond, Virginia. The Alliance subsequently detached itself from the Southern Baptist Convention and began to seek a relationship with the American Baptist Churches USA as well as the Progressive National Baptists Inc.[17] In addition, at the 1991 convocation the Alliance began a partnership with its first international ministry partner — the Fraternity of Baptists in Cuba.

In 1990, the Alliance raised almost $25,000 for its first Global Missions Offering and planned for a goal of $55,000 for 1991, which grew to a goal of $123,000 in 1993.[18] By 1993, however, the Alliance's growth began to subside and the organization began to shrink because of the formation of the Cooperative Baptist Fellowship (CBF). The CBF formed in the wake of the moderate coalition's failure to elect Daniel Vestal as president of the Southern Baptist Convention in the summer of 1990, and its emergence showed the wide breadth of diversity among moderates. Despite trying to merge, the two organizations remained separate entities.

In 1992, the Alliance distinguished itself from the Cooperative Baptist Fellowship and other moderate Baptists when its newly elected president, Ann Quattlebaum, appointed a Task Force on Human Sexuality, a radical statement for moderate Baptists at the time. Appointed at the gathering at Providence Baptist Church in Charlotte, North Carolina, the task force took three years to draft a statement and process of implementation. It addressed the question of sexuality and, specifically, of LGBT persons participating in the life and ministry of the Alliance. At the Charlotte convocation, the membership also approved changing the organization's name to the Alliance of Baptists.[19]

The willingness of the Alliance to even consider questions of homosexuality and the formation of a more centrist organizational option for moderate Baptists, the Cooperative Baptist Fellowship, created financial pressure. By the fall of 1992, the Alliance had made plans for the possibility that its funds might fall beneath $10,000.[20] At the 1993 convocation in Daytona, Florida, the leadership proposed a Global Missions Offering that included only organizations the Cooperative Baptist Fellowship refused to support.[21]

At the following year's convocation, again at First Baptist Greenville, the board of directors received a statement from the Task Force on Human Sexuality. Instead of adopting the statement, however, the board chose to wait for a "concrete process proposal." The statement needed a process of implementation.[22] Having the report was important, but the Alliance needed a procedure to guide the organization in employing the statement, as well as to explain the policy to its roughly 123 affiliated congregations.[23] The statement and process were released to the larger organization in their entirety the following year.

At the 1994 convocation, John Roberts, pastor of Woodbrook Baptist Church in Baltimore, Maryland, was elected president for a two-year term. Roberts guided the Alliance to make a commitment to interfaith relations, specifically with the Jewish faith. During its convocation at Vienna Baptist Church in Vienna, Virginia, in 1995, the Alliance held the first Christian worship service at the Holocaust Museum in Washington, D.C.[24] The Alliance also held a joint service with the Progressive National Baptist Convention Inc. in Charlotte, North Carolina, in August of the same year.[25]

The following year, 1996, the Alliance held its annual gathering at Myers Park Baptist Church in Charlotte, North Carolina, where the membership received an invitation to pursue an international partnership with the Baptist Convention of Zimbabwe. The group also reiterated its commitment to the Fraternity of Baptists in Cuba.[26] At the meeting, Nancy Hastings Sehested was elected president. She would focus on the upcoming ten-year anniversary of the organization.

Under Sehested's leadership, the board of directors began a visioning process to examine the Alliance's purpose statement and covenant. This strategic planning continued until 1998.[27] At that year's annual meeting, held at Calvary Baptist Church in Washington, D.C., the membership approved the report of the Visioning Committee, which added a mission statement to the end of the covenant. The leadership also authorized Stan Hastey and Jeanette Holt to "initiate discussions with the National Council of the Churches of Christ in the USA concerning Alliance membership."[28] After much dialogue, the Alliance became the 36th member of this historic ecumenical organization.

In Washington, the Alliance elected Welton Gaddy to a two-year term as president. During Gaddy's presidency, convocations were held in Richmond, Virginia and Austin, Texas. While in Richmond, the organization honored the ten-year anniversary of the founding of Baptist Theological Seminary at Richmond. At the convocation in Austin, the Alliance passed statements opposing the death penalty and the United States' economic embargo on Cuba, which adversely affected the Alliance's international partnership with the Fraternity of Baptists. During Gaddy's tenure, the Alliance also began a dialogue with the United Church of Christ regarding how the two denominational bodies might partner, and it began services of clergy recognition and chaplain endorsement.[29]

At the conclusion of Gaddy's presidency in 2000, Paula Clayton Dempsey was elected president. In addition to Dempsey's election that year, all but one person nominated to serve on the board of directors had served previous terms. Alliance member Chris Copeland, recognizing the partiality to former board members, began advocating for the nomination of newer and younger voices.[30] Copeland's recommendation was well received, and the Nominations Committee began taking his suggestion into account.

At the 2001 annual convocation in Decatur, Georgia, the board of directors struggled to respond to a Cooperative Baptist Fellowship policy that prohibited the hiring of LGBT individuals. Although the organizations maintained a cordial and cooperative relationship with one another, such a statement limiting LGBT persons' leadership capabilities cut against the Alliance of Baptists' commitment to freedom. In addition, the Alliance considered opening a discussion to change the organization's name to be more accommodating to the Baptist World Alliance, but the idea failed.

In January of 2002, the Alliance board met on the West Coast for the first time. A few months later, at the annual convocation in Winston-Salem, North Carolina, the membership elected Craig Henry president. During the gathering, the leadership reported that the dialogue with the United Church of Christ had grown to include the Christian Church (Disciples of Christ), a denominational body in full communion with the UCC.[31]

During Henry's presidency, the Alliance held convocations in Virginia at Vienna Baptist Church and in Ohio at Crossroads Community Church. At Vienna Baptist Church, the organization adopted a strategic plan to support becoming "ever more an inclusive people . . . ever more a missional people . . . ever more a Spirit-led people on the move."[32] In 2004, at Crossroads Community Church, the membership adopted a statement in support of same-sex marriage, which prompted discussion regarding the nature of position statements. The declaration passed so quickly that the leadership questioned whether or not the procedure for proposing statements needed more oversight.[33] In subsequent years, the board of directors re-evaluated the practice of receiving proposed statements.

The election of Cherie Smith and Chris Copeland as president and vice president, respectively, in 2004 marked a significant transition in the life and ministry of the Alliance of Baptists. Smith and Copeland practiced a model of shared leadership, which they attempted to implement within the Alliance staff structure. In addition, they began shifting the emphasis of the work of the organization from the staff to the larger Alliance community. They recognized that as of 2004, Stan Hastey and Jeanette Holt had worked for the Alliance for fifteen years, and the time was fast approaching when the two would retire. Smith and Copeland looked to prepare the organization for Hastey's and Holt's inevitable departures.

In 2005, the Alliance held its annual meeting at Furman University in South Carolina. The board of directors continued to examine the process of proposing position statements, and the leadership also grappled with financial issues. The previous year, the organization had fallen $20,000 short of the annual missions offering, and the following year, Carole Collins, chairperson of the financial committee, noted that the Alliance's "expenditures exceed receipts by nearly $17,000."[34] At the meeting, the Alliance elected Jim Hopkins president and Kristy Pullen vice president. Both had backgrounds in the American Baptist Churches USA (ABCUSA).[35] Their elections marked the first time these two positions had not been simultaneously filled by former Southern Baptists.

The 20th anniversary convocation of the Alliance of Baptists took place in 2007 at Calvary Baptist Church in Washington, D.C. Jeanette Holt's retirement this year prompted the Alliance to move forward with its model of shared leadership. Stan Hastey became the minister of partnership and ecumenical relations, and former vice president Chris Copeland was hired to fill the position of minister of leadership and congregational life. At the board meeting prior to the annual convocation in 2008, the leadership, for the first time, attempted to make decisions via consensus rather than through Robert's Rules of Order.[36]

Brooks Wicker served as president from 2008 to 2010. During her presidency, the Alliance held the organization's first teleconference board meeting in March of 2009. During the meeting the leadership made a number of important decisions. First, the Alliance began transitioning to an organizational model centered upon the presence of "communities" that would be open to the membership, rather than committees composed solely of board members. Second, Paula Dempsey was appointed to succeed Stan Hastey as minister of partnership and ecumenical relationships, and Carole Collins stepped down as chairperson of the Finance Committee to become a part-time employee as director of finance.[37] These new staff members joined Chris Copeland and Mary Andreolli, the director of communications.

In July 2010, the Alliance held its first annual gathering on the West Coast, at the Asilomar Conference Grounds in Pacific Grove, California. While there, the Alliance implemented its community model of organizing. These communities sought to encourage members to participate in the life and work of the organization. The first communities created included the Communications Community, the Peace and Justice Community, the Women in the Church Community, and the Cuban Partnership Community. In addition, the board of directors launched an examination of the clergy recognition and chaplaincy endorsement processes.[38]

During the gathering, Carol Blythe was elected president. She served for the next four years, which included the Alliance's 2011 convocation in Louisville, Kentucky. At the meeting, the board discussed unifying its operational budget and missions offering budget. A unified budget would not only be simpler, but would also aid the leadership's fund-raising efforts.[39] After much discussion, the board adopted a unified budget in 2013.

At the Alliance's 2012 convocation in Austin, Texas, disagreements arose between the board of directors and the communities for clergy recognition and chaplaincy endorsements. The conflict centered on the relationship of these communities to the board. They were not public communities because of confidentiality restrictions, but the board was legally responsible for the actions of endorsed and recognized clergy. Resolving this internal debate was a long process.[40]

The following year's convocation was planned for Atlanta, Georgia, but after a scheduling mishap, it took place at First Baptist Church in Greenville, South Carolina. At the meeting, the Alliance attempted to unveil its new web-based, resource marketplace called Alliance*Connect*. A software malfunction delayed the launch, however, and the organization had to wait to unveil it at the 2014 convocation in Portland, Maine.[41]

During Carol Blythe's four years as president, she drastically increased the number of position statements adopted by the organization. At the same time, she tried to resolve the conflict between the board of directors and the clergy recognition and endorsement communities. At the 2014 meeting, Blythe stepped down and Mike Castle was elected her successor. Castle was ordained as both a United Church of Christ (UCC) and Baptist minister, and was the first minister to serve as the Alliance president since 2008. During the first few months of his presidency, the Alliance joined a UCC lawsuit in North Carolina against a ban on same-sex marriage.

The process of leaving the Southern Baptist Convention was a long one, but by the second decade of the 21st century, the Alliance no longer resembled a group of disillusioned Southern Baptists. In reality, the membership was now composed of American Baptists, members of the United Church of Christ, Cooperative Baptists, and more. They had left the familiar to venture into uncharted religious territory. The exodus took many years for some of the founders of the Alliance. The Southern Baptist Convention was all they had ever known, and in the course of leaving, friendships were broken and memories tarnished. This process of exodus — this process of leaving — opened the possibility for the Alliance to be a testing ground for interrogating, questioning, and even reimagining what denominational life could be.

Part II:

Reimagining Zion

Chapter 4

We Commit Ourselves To

To understand the history generally and the identity specifically of the Alliance of Baptists, one must recognize that its identity operates on two levels. The first level, addressed most extensively in Part I, functions through the lens of "exodus." Members of the Alliance of Baptists, as Walker Knight has suggested, are "an Exodus People." They were not exiled from the Southern Baptist Convention; they left. While this metaphor, more than twenty years old, may be one many individuals wish the Alliance of Baptists could move past, it will forever be a part, whether consciously or subconsciously, of the Alliance's identity.

Even into the 21st century, the Alliance of Baptists continued to provide a home for those wandering beyond the denominational affiliations of their past in search of a better denominational home — a "Promised Land." This is not to say that all individuals who have identified with the Alliance completely cut ties with their former institutional affiliations. The identity of an "Exodus People" calls individuals into a continuous process of "leaving," or moving from where they have been denominationally into the unknown of where they feel God is calling. In this way, some members of the Alliance, particularly those from American Baptist backgrounds, added the organization to their denominational commitments. Yet their presence within the Alliance of Baptists acknowledges their identity as an "Exodus People" committed to the continuous process of "leaving" and reappraising their denominational commitments to better do their work as God's people.

This element of "leaving" and "exodus" must be coupled with an additional notion of "reimagining." To understand the history and identity of the Alliance of Baptists, one must recognize that in the process of leaving there was a reciprocal process of reimagining what it looks like and means to be Baptist. The Alliance was not founded with the intention of creating simply another denominational body that looked and felt like the Southern Baptist Convention. Instead, it was formed under the influence of individuals who focused their energy on what the future held for Christians generally and Baptists specifically on a national and global scale. The founders were dedicated to reimagining what a Baptist organization might look like as the world approached the 21st century. This process of reimagining began and continued into the 21st century due in large part to the Alliance Covenant.

When the first official meeting of Southern Baptist Alliance was held in December of 1986 in Charlotte, North Carolina, four workgroups were formed to determine what the purpose and mission of the organization would be. Most importantly, they thought about the formation of an organization and, specifically, "What could be 'the glue' that could hold it together?"[1] After addressing this question, the four groups reconvened. With slightly different approaches to the prospective organization, all of the groups identified similar ideas, among them "freedom," "priesthood of the believer," "local church autonomy," "scripture," "missions and evangelism," "diversity," "women in ministry," "importance of laity," "religious liberty," and "ministry of peace and reconciliation."[2]

Nancy Hasting Sehested's workgroup called attention to the actions of the Southern Baptist Convention throughout the 1980s and listed a number of the convention's actions that they "deplored." From this list, they proposed a mission and purpose for the new organization. Alan Neely, among others, felt that these denunciations ought to be turned into affirmations to say what the organization would stand for and not what the organization would stand against.[3] As Mahan Siler recalled years later, the participants at this meeting asked each other, "to what are we saying 'no'?" Once a list was generated, the group "took [its] list and . . . responded to each 'no' with a corresponding 'yes'." In Siler's words, "The point: our Alliance Covenant was primarily a reactive document, a response to a particular moment in Southern Baptist History."[4]

All but one of the workgroups identified ideas and principles around which the organization could coalesce. The final workgroup presented a mission and purpose that centered upon responding to certain actions the Southern Baptist Convention had taken over the previous eight years. These responses took the form of supporting the Baptist Joint Committee on Public Affairs and churches no longer aided by the convention's Home Mission Board as a result of its decision to refuse funding to congregations employing female ministers. Even support for these organizations, however, related directly to many of the ideas and principles mentioned in the other workgroups. The similarity in the responses was not lost on Larry Coleman, who expressed that "there was amazement at how similar the groups were in thought."[5]

As the larger body began to think about drafting a statement, questions arose as to what it might look like or even how it would function. Walter Shurden, a Baptist historian and faculty member at Mercer University, did not believe that responses to the actions of the Southern Baptist Convention alone would generate enough passion for the new organization to get off the ground. Mahan Siler, however, thought that the passion he had experienced stemmed from not feeling at "home" within the convention. Shurden also thought that confessions were too divisive to generate support for a new movement. Some individuals were skeptical of drafting another statement altogether, fearing that it would eventually become another Baptist Faith and Message.[6] Tom Austin, a minister from Georgia, recommended that any declaration also include the previously drafted purpose statement. This statement would then be followed by a list or covenant of principles that would begin with the phrase, "We Commit Ourselves To."[7]

After the Charlotte meeting in December 1986, a committee was appointed to develop a proposed statement of "affirmations." It used the principles and ideas developed by the four workgroups.[8] On the committee were Richard Groves, Bill Treadwell, Alan Neely, Luther Brewer, and Walter Coleman. Mahan Siler served as chair.[9]

Meeting in Winston-Salem, North Carolina, at Wake Forest Baptist Church a few days after Christmas, the committee, minus Treadwell, drafted the first version of the Alliance Covenant. When the document was presented to the larger group in early February of 1987, only a few minor changes, mostly concerning semantics, were made. "The covenant was affirmed by consensus" only a couple of weeks before the official unveiling of the Southern Baptist Alliance on February 12.[10] The final draft of the document read:

The Alliance Covenant

In a time when historic Baptist principles, freedoms, and traditions need a clear voice, and in our personal and corporate response to the call of God in Jesus Christ to be disciples and servants in the world, we commit ourselves to:

1) The freedom of the individual, led by God's Spirit within the family of faith, to read and interpret the Scriptures, relying on the historical understanding by the church and on the best methods of modern biblical study;

2) The freedom of the local church under the authority of Jesus Christ to shape its own life and mission, call its own leadership, and ordain whom it perceives as gifted for ministry, male or female;

3) The larger body of Jesus Christ, expressed in various Christian traditions, and to the cooperation with believers everywhere in giving full expression to the Gospel;

4) The servant role of leadership within the church, following the model of our Servant Lord, and to full partnership of all of God's people in mission and ministry;

5) Theological education in congregations, colleges, and seminaries characterized by reverence for biblical authority and respect for open inquiry and responsible scholarship;

6) The proclamation of the Good News of Jesus Christ and the calling of God to all peoples to repentance and faith, reconciliation and hope, social and economic justice;

7) The principle of a free church in a free state and the opposition to any effort either by church or state to use the other for its own purposes.

The covenant continued to be the guiding document of the Alliance of Baptists well into the second decade of the 21st century.[11] Over the years, the statement provided form and purpose to the organization. For many individuals frustrated with the theological trajectory of the Southern Baptist Convention of the late 1980s, the Alliance Covenant proved to be a poignant document. After watching for eight years as their denominational home was slowly taken over, many "moderate" Southern Baptists found hope in the covenant. Anne Thomas Neil, a former Southern Baptist missionary, recalled her first reaction to the covenant: "I read these seven principles and then I read them again. I knew I had been waiting since my early childhood for this moment. To be honest, I never expected to see the formation of such a community of faith in my lifetime."[12] Through the covenant, Baptist women like Neil were able to see themselves as full participants in the life and ministry of the local church.

Don Garner, professor at Carson-Newman College in Tennessee, wrote, "As long as I live I will never forget the feelings when I opened the *Biblical Recorder* and read that some Baptists had announced a new group that would stand for something positive. The seven-point covenant read and felt like a cool, moist wind on my parched spirit."[13] The Southern Baptist Alliance gave an isolated and fragmented group of moderates, tired from the politicking of the Southern Baptist Convention, a community in which to hope.

Through the covenant, the Alliance founders put into words the hopes and desires they had for a new and reimagined denominational organization. The aspirations for the Alliance were innovative for multiple reasons. First, the covenant was new statement of progressivism among Anglo-Baptists in the South. By the liberal standards of the 21st century, the Alliance Covenant hardly reads like a statement of radical progressivism. At the specific moment and context in which it was drafted, however, it was a progressive document. For many Southern Baptists in the late 1980s, as Alan Neely reflected years later, the covenant "represented the essence of theological, social, and political liberalism."[14] Neely explained that many individuals within the Alliance really did not recognize the radical nature of the covenant. In his 2002 Alliance Covenant address, he explained, "What is not clear is that in the Covenant we thought we were synthesizing and reaffirming what most Baptists believed. As the years passed, however, and as I have read and reread these seven articles, I now see how far we were from the mainstream of Baptist thinking in the South."[15]

Second, the covenant articulated a distinct model of Baptist cooperation because of what it was — a covenant and not a statement or confession of faith. The Alliance attempted to covenant with individuals and congregations to support seven principles, or ideas. This differed from more traditional confessions of faith that required adherence to particular doctrinal tenets. The covenant provided a description of how the religious community looked and operated, instead of identifying doctrinal criteria to determine those within the Alliance and those outside. In some ways, this difference between a statement (or confession of faith) and a covenant may be considered semantic; in other ways, it marked a clear transition from the ways many previous Baptists organized.

Third, the Alliance Covenant set a standard for welcoming those often marginalized by Southern Baptist life. Women were represented alongside men as equally "gifted for ministry." Christians of various traditions were honored, as they helped give "full expression to the Gospel." The covenant gave voice to scholars who employed methods of critical inquiry in their study of scripture and theology. Instead of qualifying the ways in which these groups of people could participate in community, the covenant welcomed all.

It is clear that the founders of the Alliance, whether they knew it or not, had a progressive vision of what Baptist denominational life could look like.

According to Walker Knight, the covenant not only gave the founders' dream "form and substance," but it was also "a dream to which we aspire, it [was] an attempt to say who we are, it [was] a statement of identity."[16] However, Knight moved beyond the metaphor of dream to express a hope that the "Covenant . . . must also be recognized as the seedbed of confrontation."[17] Knight believed that the covenant was a challenge to be part of a greater identity that confronted the status quo of both religious and secular life. Because of this, he believed, "The process of writing and assimilating the Covenant must continue if it is to remain a living document, for any covenant reflects the historical period in which it was written."[18]

Throughout the history of the Alliance, individuals have expressed a desire to revise or expand the covenant. For example, at the first annual convocation, Charles Worthy of Florida proposed an additional affirmation that read: "We affirm the equality of the races and unity of the human race, and we wish to be a multi-racial, pluralistic body." Alan Neely recalled that the amendment was considered and referred to the board of directors for further discussion. Years later, Neely wrote that in the commotion of the Alliance's first year, the amendment was forgotten and never discussed.[19] Other proposed changes to the covenant included an explicit affirmation of LGBT persons and an amendment supporting ecological justice.

These additions were never added, for multiple reasons. First, during the early years of the organization, maintaining the Alliance's existence took precedent over amendments, changes and additions. The evolving nature of the Southern Baptist landscape meant that the Alliance was constantly responding to different actions taken by the convention, and so, for better or worse, some responses fell through the cracks. Second, there was a desire to maintain the historic value of the covenant. This did not mean that the organization wanted to remain tethered to the past, but instead, individuals wanted to remember how the Alliance came into being. Third, and probably most importantly, individuals over the years saw the covenant as implicitly supporting ideas of racial diversity, LGBT rights and ecological justice. With implicit support for such issues, the Alliance as an organization did not feel the need to explicitly refer to them in its founding document.

In 1997, the Alliance of Baptists went through a visioning process that included an examination of the covenant. After ten years of existence, the Alliance decided to investigate whether or not the covenant still served as an adequate statement of identity. Rather than making changes, the organization chose to add a mission statement.[20] Mahan Siler, chair of the committee that drafted the covenant, participated in examining how the document might be changed.

Siler expressed a desire, like that of Knight, that the Alliance would always examine whether the covenant remained relevant to the organization's mission and purpose. He wrote, "It is not as if the Covenant is imperfect and we set out to perfect it. Obviously it will always be an imperfect Covenant. But fussin' with it can help us keep working on our identity . . . identity always in process . . ."[21]

At the end of the process, the Visioning Committee reaffirmed "the role of the Covenant as a statement of identity which, for the Alliance, serves a function similar to the vision statements in other organizations." The committee also recognized that the covenant reflected "the historical and contextual situation in which it was written." Accordingly, the committee declared, "one function of a covenant is to speak with the voice of memory."[22] While retaining the covenant as it was written, the Alliance adopted a mission statement that read:

Mission

To keep faith with our covenant we will:

1) Make the worship of God primary in all our gatherings.

2) Foster relationships within the Alliance and with other people of faith.

3) Create places of refuge and renewal for those who are wounded or ignored by the church.

4) Side with those who are poor.

5) Pursue justice with and for those who are oppressed.

6) Care for the earth.

7) Work for peace.

8) Honor wisdom and lifelong learning.

9) Hold ourselves accountable for equity, collegiality, and diversity.

It is not an understatement to say that the Alliance Covenant is the single most important document pertaining to the identity of the Alliance of Baptists. Some might even suggest that the covenant is the single most important contribution the Alliance has made to progressive Baptist life. Alan Neely wrote in 1993,

> It is my hope that one of the most long-lasting contributions of the Alliance to Baptist life will be the Covenant. It is a document that bears the fingerprints of a number of people. No single individual nor any identifiable group can claim credit for having written it. . . . Several of the principles that became the core of the covenant statement were recorded in the Meredith College meeting in September 1986, and the "affirmations" approved in Charlotte the following December constituted the basic framework utilized by Mahan Siler, Walter Coleman, Luther Brewer, Richard Groves, and I when we drafted the Covenant later that same month. What was remarkable about their compositions was not so much the content of it, but the fact that when it was presented in the plenary meeting in February 1987, only three words were deleted.[23]

The Alliance Covenant has served as a guiding light of the Alliance of Baptists throughout its history. In an article published in *Baptists Today*, Stan Hastey recalled Walter Shurden describing the covenant as one of the 20th century's "most significant Baptist pronouncements."[24]

Because of its significance, the Alliance Covenant has been used to organize the following seven chapters. Each chapter will address a different tenet of the covenant. These chapters should be read with a significant degree of fluidity, as many parts of the Alliance's history inevitably touch on different tenets within the covenant. The use of the covenant does, however, concretely establish what the Alliance of Baptists has stood for throughout its history, as well as the ways in which the Alliance has ministered in the wider world.

Chapter 5

The Freedom of the Individual

1) The freedom of the individual, led by God's Spirit within the family of faith, to read and interpret the Scriptures, relying on the historical understanding by the church and on the best methods of modern biblical study.

From their beginnings, Baptists espoused an understanding of freedom of conscience, later referred to as soul freedom, soul competency, or the freedom of the individual. This concept claimed that individuals were capable of making their own decisions regarding faith and belief and were not beholden to a higher authority to instruct them on how to interpret scripture or how to believe the Christian message. For some, this concept is inherently individualistic. Some Baptists push back against this claim, arguing that the freedom of the individual stems from humanity's shared identity in the *Imago Dei* — being one with humanity made in the image of Christ.[1]

When the Alliance Covenant was drafted, however, the first tenet most directly sought to address the individual's right to interpret the scriptures. Various agencies of the Southern Baptist Convention were gradually tightening the confessional requirements of employees in an effort to ensure that all agency employees affirmed the inerrancy of scripture. This placed tremendous pressure on biblical scholars who were caught between affirming inerrancy and using modern methods of biblical criticism.

The Alliance's commitment to the freedom of the individual rose from a desire to protect and trust individuals in their faith journey. As Cecil Sherman said in the Alliance's first book, *Being Baptist Means Freedom*, "The right of the private interpretation puts an enormous confidence in the individual."[2] Sherman also claimed, "To put the Bible in the hands of ordinary people is audacious."[3] Over the years, guided by this principle of the freedom of the individual, the Alliance entered into a number of audacious conversations. Perhaps the most notable dealt with the question of how the church should respond to issues related to LGBT persons and inclusion in the body of Christ.

This chapter provides a brief history of the Alliance's journey in regard to LGBT inclusion. In addition, it addresses the ways in which individual members pushed the Alliance toward a greater focus on the environment and the role of Christians in promoting ecological justice. The chapter concludes with a brief discussion of conflicts that have occurred within the Alliance that have been shaped by various individuals who have dissented from the majority opinion. While these are not the only ways in which the Alliance has supported the freedom of the individual, these three sections exemplify some of the ways in which the Alliance has lived by its first covenant principle.

When the first covenant principle was written, the Alliance was concerned solely with the interpretation of scripture, not with issues of LGBT inclusion, ecology or conflict. The reason for highlighting these topics within this chapter, however, results from the broader implications of the first covenant principle. LGBT inclusion and ecological justice are issues that relate directly to specific scriptural passages. In a similar manner, the first covenant principle places significant trust in the individual. While not all the included conflicts are scripturally grounded, their inclusion in this chapter shows how the Alliance held and affirmed a plurality of individuals and opinions. Each of these issues could be highlighted elsewhere, as could much of the Alliance's history in the preceding chapters. Because of this, the organization of the following seven chapters must be read loosely. The covenant serves as a tool and guide for organizing the Alliance's history.

The Freedom of the Individual
on LGBT Issues

The Alliance did not begin as an organization that was welcoming and affirming of LGBT persons. But because of the climate within the Southern Baptist Convention and the nature of the then Southern Baptist Alliance, certain individuals felt the Alliance was the type of organization to wrestle with questions related to LGBT inclusion. The first Alliance executive director, Stan Hastey, wrote to Pullen Memorial Baptist Church pastor Mahan Siler after the 1990 convocation, saying, "I have encountered the issue of inclusion of gays and lesbians in two recent chapter meetings — Georgia and Texas. So we are aware that the Alliance is being looked to by gays and lesbians as a haven or, perhaps, as a potential haven, depending on our willingness to address their concerns."[4] Thus the question of how the Alliance would respond was present from early in the organization's history.

Siler, who believed that the issue of human sexuality was a topic of increasing importance for Christians, responded, "I would hope that we in the [Alliance] could provide a forum for dialogue, soul searching and theological debate about what will no doubt become an increasing justice concern in the coming years."[5] Two years later, in Charlotte, the Alliance took the first steps toward dialogue and discussion about questions of sexuality.

During the 1992 meeting, the topic of "human sexuality" became an officially recognized "issue" within the Alliance, as Siler led a breakout session on the topic and a Task Force on Human Sexuality was appointed. Siler had expressed reservations about presenting a workshop on the church and homosexuality, and "he suggested that the Alliance form a task force on the topic."[6] Prior to the gathering, a motion was raised for Siler to not hold the workshop, but it was defeated. Although it was called a "Task Force on Human Sexuality," the group predominantly focused on the subject of homosexuality.

In 1993, the task force presented a report on its progress to the board of directors and was encouraged to "develop a working statement on human sexuality, specifically regarding issues of homosexuality." Siler proposed that the task force also develop a "process for the use of the working statement."[7] The following year, the board received a working statement from the group but held off on taking further action until "recommendations on process" were provided. The board preferred to know how the Alliance should implement a working statement. A motion was made and seconded to table the action and work of the task force, but it failed.[8] The nervousness of some individuals within the leadership did not outweigh the commitment of others to support the task force's work until its end, despite repercussions.

At the following year's convocation at First Baptist Church in Greenville, South Carolina, Stan Hastey addressed the Alliance's decision to appoint the Task Force on Human Sexuality. He explained that the task force was making progress on an organizational report and implementation process. While a statement had been completed, some individuals on the board of directors remained adamant that the task force "propose a 'process' to be followed by the board as it deals with the Task Force statement." This process would help remove some of the charged points of debate among Alliance members.[9] Hastey made clear, however, that regardless of what the organization agreed upon, "that [everyone] agree to honor one another's freedom of conscience."[10]

When the Task Force on Human Sexuality presented its proposed process and statement in September 1994, the minutes described the conversation as a "fervent discussion."[11] Much debate centered upon making sure the report

from the task force reflected "Respect for one another" and "mutual acceptance."[12] After receiving the report, the Alliance moved to adopt a hiring
policy of non-discrimination with regard to sexual orientation for staff and
board members. However, a substitute motion carried by a slim margin that
called for a more general "ongoing discussion" on the "fundamental truths
affirmed in [the] report."[13]

The statement excited many within the LGBT community, but it also
excited persons within Baptist life who were not entirely comfortable with
affirming the LGBT experience. Bill Johnson, pastor of Northwest Baptist
Church in Oklahoma, had "a number of concerns about the human sexuality
statement." Johnson, however, expressed enthusiasm at the opportunity to
"have a history-making dialogue" that could "lead to a statement of openness
and acceptance of homosexual people — without violating the autonomy of
local churches or individual conscience."[14]

There were also individuals and churches opposed to discussing the
topic. Even prior to the task force's report, Providence Baptist Church in
Charlotte withdrew financial support from the Alliance after hosting the
1992 convocation. Providence "supplied 7 to 10 percent of [the] operating budget" for each of the first five years of the Alliance's existence, and
its pastor, Henry Crouch, served as the first president of the organization.
Hastey attempted to persuade the church to continue to make gifts to ministry projects rather than the organization itself, but this was a compromise
the congregation was unwilling to accept.[15] In 2014, the congregation began
giving a designated gift to support summer interns through the Alliance to
the Family Tree (formerly Hyaets), an intentional community in Charlotte,
North Carolina.[16]

The report of the Task Force on Human Sexuality created tension
between the Alliance and the Cooperative Baptist Fellowship (CBF). Many
individuals did not understand why the Alliance did not merge into the
Cooperative Baptist Fellowship. One of them, Cindy Clanton, a member of
First Baptist Greenville, changed her mind after the 1994 convocation. She
"realize[d] that the Task Force on Human Sexuality is just one small part of
the Alliance, [and] that homosexuality is an issue that churches must face."
Clanton was "alarmed at the fear and anger that mere discussions of homosexuality and the church elicit." She remained "hopeful that the Alliance
[would] help us all to realize that we cannot hide from considering matters
that have no easy answers."[17]

Homosexuality was a question the Cooperative Baptist Fellowship had no
desire to discuss. When CBF executive director Cecil Sherman "denounced

homosexuality" in an article in the Associated Baptist Press, his friend and Alliance founder Alan Neely wrote to him, stating that he was grieved by Sherman's statements. Neely claimed they "betray a lack of awareness and sensitivity that I find totally out of character with the Cecil Sherman I have known since 1948." Neely further explained, "The most distressing aspect of your reported statement, however, is the tone of it." Neely concluded his letter to Sherman by saying:

> If you and other leaders of the CBF are unable to make room for all would-be followers of Jesus Christ and for people like me who want to be inclusive of all who are trying to be Jesus' disciples, then please do not ask me to continue on the Missions Committee. I will not lend my support [to] any organization or movement that consciously and knowingly is discriminatory.[18]

The positions of Neely/Alliance and Sherman/CBF highlighted the diversity of Baptist opinions emerging within "moderate" Baptist life outside the confines of the Southern Baptist Convention. Once the Alliance entered the process of becoming inclusive to LGBT persons, many, like Neely, did so wholeheartedly. This does not mean their inclusivity was perfect, but it was something to which the Alliance remained committed.

The Alliance over the years has received a lot of backlash about its position on human sexuality, but the organization's responses have remained resolute. Lay members from various churches frequently wrote letters to the Alliance asking about the organization's position on "homosexuality." In one such letter, William Crisp asked Stan Hastey, "What is the Alliance's view of the practice of homosexual relations by Christians? . . . May practicing homosexuals hold positions of leadership in a church or other Christian organization? (I realize this last question is a matter of local church action but I'd like your opinion, please, i.e. how would you vote as a church member?)" Hastey unwaveringly responded to each letter by mailing a copy of the report from the Task Force on Human Sexuality.[19]

In 1999, the Baptist Peace Fellowship of North America, the Alliance of Baptists and the Association of Welcoming and Affirming Baptists began creating a resource for churches struggling with the subject of sexual orientation. Ken Sehested, then executive director of the Baptist Peace Fellowship, led the project, which gathered the experiences of various welcoming and affirming churches in preparation for a retreat in August of that year.[20]

The retreat took place for the purposes of producing an article and gathering information on the types of resources needed for a congregational curriculum on the topic of sexual orientation.[21] It also provided a time for congregations that had undergone the process of welcoming LGBT persons to share their experiences.[22]

The result was a book called *Rightly Dividing the Word of Truth: A Resource for Congregations in Dialogue on Sexual Orientation and Gender Identity.* In addition to Ken Sehested, Millard Eiland of Covenant Church in Houston, Texas, and LeDayne Polaski of the Baptist Peace Fellowship helped to organize additional resources and articles that were included in the curriculum. The project was largely facilitated by the Baptist Peace Fellowship and was completed in time for the 2000 convocation.[23] In 2014, the work was revised and reissued by Alliance member and Baptist Peace Fellowship board member Cody Sanders.

The Alliance's identity as an inclusive, welcoming and affirming organization took time to cultivate but was helped by its covenant commitment to the freedom of the individual. In the midst of this process, however, the Alliance never attempted to force individuals or churches to adopt a similar position. Instead, it upheld both its commitment that every individual is free to believe however she or he chooses and its commitment to the freedom of the local church, addressed in Chapter Six.

The Freedom of the Individual on Environmental Justice

When the Alliance formed in the late 1980s, environmental justice had not yet become a cutting-edge issue. By the middle of the 1990s, however, individuals in the organization began to press the board of directors to engage global warming, pollution, and other issues of environmental justice. Leading this push was Herman Greene, a legal professional from Raleigh, North Carolina and a member of Pullen Memorial Baptist Church. Elizabeth Barnes, a professor of theology and ethics at Baptist Theological Seminary at Richmond, also helped bring attention to these issues.

In the spring of 1996, the Alliance leadership invited Greene to make a presentation at the board of directors meeting on the ways in which the organization could become more informed about ecological issues. He explained, "I believe that the Alliance should not approach the ecological issue primarily from the ethical/environment approach, but instead should approach the issue first as a religious issue and second as a question of how does our religious experience inform how we are to live."[24] Greene recognized that the issue of global warming was growing in importance, and he believed there were religious implications for this ecological problem.

In his presentation, Greene proposed a workshop for the March convocation at Myers Park Baptist Church in Charlotte, North Carolina. He suggested the workshop would either "begin organizing an Alliance task force to deal with" environmental justice or would seek to educate the Alliance through a "session on the spirituality of the earth."[25] Greene hoped the Alliance would "take on" ecology and creation spirituality as an important issue.[26] At the annual gathering, a "Work Group" was appointed to study the Alliance's response to the environment. The group included both Greene and Barnes.

In 1999, the Work Group on Ecology held a concluding workshop called "Care for the Earth: An Invitation to Reflection and Action." The group argued, "Ecology is not a social issue but a theological issue that ought to be a central concern for Christians."[27] The workshop was the culmination of the three-year study that resulted in a twenty-eight-page report, which the membership "received with gratitude." The report sought to encourage individuals to view the world and environment from a human perspective but also to imagine a divine perspective and to act as participants in the ecological environment.

The subsequent publication of the congregational resource, *Care for the Earth*, however, was criticized by a few in the Alliance who did not believe it addressed the issue in its entirety. Rick Goodman, a member of Calvary Baptist Church in Washington, D.C., felt the publication lacked the prophetic voice so characteristic of the Alliance and failed to address the problem beyond "the level of personal ethics." For Goodman, the work needed to address corporations or free trade agreements that were "devastating to the environment" on a more institutionalized level.[28]

Over the years, the Alliance has consistently returned to issues of environmental justice and creation care. For instance, the 2003 convocation focused on the theme of Ecology and Faith. Dr. Jay McDaniel, a process theologian and member of the Department of Religion at Hendrix College, was the keynote speaker and led two breakout sessions, one on consumerism and the other on globalization.[29] Six years later, the Alliance adopted its first statement on climate change, and in 2011 it passed a statement responding to the British Petroleum oil spill in the Gulf of Mexico.[30]

Through the work and advocacy of individuals like Herman Greene and Elizabeth Barnes, the Alliance became an organization committed to combating global climate change and protecting the environment. The Alliance affirmed, recognized and listened to Greene, Barnes and others who interpreted scripture in such a way as to support ecological justice. Through the support of these individuals, the Alliance further demonstrated its commitment to the freedom of the individual and became more aware of environmental issues.

The Freedom of the Individual in
Times of Conflict

Throughout any organization's history, conflicts arise. Often they are hidden and buried within letters and minutes of meetings. The history of the Alliance is no different. The task of the historian is to portray these disagreements to the best of her or his ability, but invariably these conflicts remain difficult to unmask. Some of the clashes described here resulted from differences in scriptural interpretation, organizational preferences, and even spiritual discernment.

At the Alliance's fourteenth convocation at University Baptist Church in Austin, Texas, a conflict arose between the host congregation and representatives of both Baptist Women in Ministry and the Women in the Church Committee. Prior to the convocation, University Baptist Church terminated Rebecca Gurney, its associate minister and the former president of Baptist Women in Ministry. Some people believed that Gurney's termination was unfair and uncalled for.

Members of the Women in the Church Committee and Baptist Women in Ministry discussed staging an alternate event or offering recognition for Gurney, an Alliance member. At the convocation's final worship service, a group of women stood in the balcony with Gurney. For those not involved, the action appeared to be a protest, but for those standing in the balcony, "this ritual was a creative and positive attempt to honor both the Alliance and the reality of Rebecca's wounds."[31]

The action spurred much discussion. Some members believed there was too little consideration for the possibility of "voicing protest in the business meeting," which they thought might have been a better place for protest rather than a worship service. Participants in the protest/ritual explained, "The desire to acknowledge the pain while affirming the Alliance meant there was a need to express the pain during the Austin Convocation. A flyer was printed inviting folks to come to the balcony during the final worship service to demonstrate solidarity with women who had been fired unfairly."[32]

The balcony protest/ritual was "an act of conscience in the tradition of Baptist soul competence. It was not vengeance, nor a boycott." Some of those involved said that they "felt the process of decision-making about the Convocation left [them] with a forced choice between sisterhood and the Alliance." For those who participated, it was extremely meaningful to give voice to the pain of Gurney and other women who had been treated unfairly and been left "voiceless."[33] The issue was addressed at the following year's convocation at Oakhurst Baptist Church in Decatur, Georgia, through a theme centered on gender equity. Paula Dempsey, who was elected president at the convocation, called for the women to keep standing in the balcony as long as injustice of any kind continues.

In 2005, the Alliance relocated its convocation from First Baptist Church in Greenville, South Carolina, to nearby Furman University. After some members of First Baptist Greenville learned that April Baker, minister at Glendale Baptist Church in Nashville, Tennessee, was scheduled to preach at the Friday evening worship service, the church rescinded its offer to let the Alliance use its facilities because of Baker's sexual identity, although it reaffirmed its commitment to be the "host congregation."[34] The Alliance was forced to move the meeting to Furman, a few miles down the road. This change of location was ironic, because in 1989 First Baptist Greenville had hosted the Alliance's annual convocation when Furman rescinded its offer to host for fear of financial repercussions from the South Carolina Baptist Convention.

Alliance supporters at First Baptist Greenville were "angered, embarrassed, and grieved by this decision, by how it was made, and by what it [said] about [their] church."[35] Recognizing that this could become a greater source of conflict, executive director Stan Hastey, associate director Jeanette Holt, president Cherie Smith, and Alliance founder Mahan Siler all considered the best way to respond. Some suggestions included having a breakout session discussing and explaining what happened. In the end, Glendale Baptist Church responded with an open letter to the congregation of First Baptist Greenville.[36] The letter read, "Our conviction and calling is to stand in support of both you in your struggle to be faithful to your identity and mission as a congregation, and of our pastor in her efforts to bring the full scale of her vocation and gifts to bear in her work. In so doing we are attempting to walk the "sharp edge" of the Gospel, bearing the good news of Christ."[37] The letter was not vindictive or angry. The members of Glendale Baptist simply desired to show their support for their minister, April Baker, but also for their fellow Alliance congregation.

When the Alliance leadership recognized First Baptist Greenville for its effort in hosting the 2005 Convocation, congregation members were met by a standing ovation from the annual gathering. The Alliance community sought to show members of the church support, encouragement and gratitude. The larger body recognized the difficulty and conflict already present at FBC Greenville and did not want to add more stress to this large, diverse church. In the midst of this "hosting" conflict, the larger organization remained committed to the freedom of both individuals and congregations. While the Alliance as an organization unapologetically supported the inclusion of LGBT persons, individual members or congregations were not required to come to similar conclusions.

Other conflicts arose in the Alliance over the years, particularly around the adoption of position statements. The 2004 statement supporting same-sex marriage spurred enough discussion that the policy for proposing statements was revised. The revision caused a noteworthy conflict in 2006 when Alliance founding member Jim Strickland recommended a declaration decrying Exxon Mobil. His statement was rejected for not following the procedure set forth in the newly adjusted statement policy. This rejection created tension between those more sympathetic to the old policy and those in favor of the new policy.

Another conflict arose in 2005 when a conscientious objector declaration was proposed. The issue centered on "keeping language that says 'war is contrary to the will of God' while removing language about 'participation' in such violence."[38] The Alliance had to accept a revised statement that was more inclusive of the various positions of members regarding warfare.

Approving statements has always been difficult within any Baptist organization, but the documents serve a prophetic role. They represent the opinions of many people and are often subject to revisions and opposing opinions, but they give the organization a public voice. The Alliance's practice of passing statements will be addressed further in Chapter Ten.

These conflicts serve as examples of how the Alliance has struggled to support dissension and disagreement. Supporting people on both sides of the metaphorical aisle can be difficult, but the Alliance has always attempted to support the right of the individual to come to her or his own conclusions. This does not mean that the Alliance has condoned or granted authority to positions that denigrated or harmed others, but it does mean that the Alliance has granted authority to the individual to come to her or his respective position. In this way, the Alliance attempts to honor the freedom of the individual not only through differing scriptural interpretation, but also through varying organizational opinions and discernments.

✦

For individuals within the Alliance, the principle of the freedom of the individual lies at the very heart of what it means to be Baptist. As the Southern Baptist Convention began tightening the boundaries of orthodoxy in the late 1980s, the Alliance opened up those boundaries for individuals to decide questions of belief for themselves. In opening the parameters of faith, the Alliance as an organization has often sided with positions that most Christians would identify as theologically "liberal."

Reducing the Alliance of Baptists to a "liberal" Baptist organization, however, fails to recognize the organization's commitment to the freedom of the individual. Persons with more "conservative" theological perspectives had a place within the Alliance, but often they already had other denominational entities in which they happily participated. Those people with more "liberal" understandings of God and humanity often had fewer denominational opportunities, particularly within Baptist life. As an organization, the Alliance attempted to transcend rough conservative/liberal binaries, but in practice this remained difficult. American society perpetuates these binaries, and religious organizations like the Alliance strive to fight against them.

The Alliance's commitment to LGBT inclusion and environmental justice are examples of how the organization affirmed individuals to interpret scripture and set a particular course for its commitment to justice. In dealing with the conflicts identified in this chapter, the Alliance demonstrated a commitment to supporting the freedom of the individual in whatever way the individual chose to approach or understand a particular issue. This does not mean that the Alliance supported multiple positions on a particular issue, but it does mean that it respected the conscience of those who chose to dissent. In so doing, the Alliance affirmed one of the organization's central understandings for what it means to be Baptist — the freedom of the individual.

Chapter 6

The Freedom of the Local Church

2) The freedom of the local church under the authority of Jesus Christ to shape its own life and mission, call its own leadership, and ordain whom it perceives as gifted for ministry, male or female.

The freedom of the local congregation is a defining characteristic of Baptist life in America. Baptist congregations are independent entities that are not required to conform to the practices and beliefs of a larger denominational body. When the "inerrantist" movement began gaining influence within the Southern Baptist Convention, "moderates" were concerned that the freedom of local congregations might be compromised. In October of 1986, their fear was confirmed when the convention's Home Mission Board decided to stop providing financial assistance to congregations that employed female ministers.[1] For many churches, this monetary support was vital to their life and work.

Richard Groves, the third president of the Alliance of Baptists, believed the decision of the Home Mission Board did not inherently take away the freedom of the local congregation. While many felt that the decision made small congregations choose between financial assistance and their theological integrity, Groves claimed churches always had options. For Groves, "The only way [congregations] could lose [their] autonomy would be if [they] were to decide to allow the Home Mission Board to dictate to [them] the kind of person [they] could call as pastor."[2] Freedom was intrinsic to the life of the congregation, and no larger, over-arching organization could take that freedom away. According to Groves, "*Under our system of church governance, we can give away our autonomy, but it cannot be taken from us.*"[3]

At the time the Alliance formed, the primary threat to the principle of the freedom of the local congregation centered upon the question of hiring a female minister. The Alliance, however, did not initially support women in ministry; it took several years for the organization to do so. While issues of women in ministry and local congregational autonomy are separate, for the

Alliance they were intrinsically linked because of the historical context out of which it formed.

The Alliance has supported the freedom of the local congregation in many ways throughout its history, but this chapter focuses specifically on its support for women working in the local church. The question was not simply a "women's issue" for the Alliance, but an issue of church autonomy. As support grew within the Alliance for local congregational freedom, and particularly to hire female ministers, so did the need for gender-inclusive worship resources. This chapter concludes with a brief section on worship in the local church and how the Alliance supported diverse and inclusive worship practices. Both the issues of women in the local church and worship in the local church serve as examples of the ways in which the Alliance sought to support the right of local churches to operate freely.

Women in the Local Church

By the second decade of the 21st century, the Alliance of Baptists unequivocally supported women in positions of leadership and ministry within the local church. This did not mean that the Alliance, or Alliance congregations, never fell victim to incidences of misogyny or patriarchy. Particularly during the formation of the Alliance, the question regarding women in ministry remained open for debate. Over the years, the Alliance attempted to exemplify the freedom of the local congregation through an organizational commitment to support all facets of women's leadership in religious life.

Because of the climate within the Southern Baptist Convention, there were questions about women's place in ministry at the time of the Alliance's founding. Significant decisions at the group's first official meeting helped propel the organization toward supporting the "women's issue." The twenty-four individuals who attended this meeting made a pronouncement to include the voice of women in the creation of the Alliance. At that time, however, only four women were present — Edna S. Langley and Sarah Wilson of Baptist Church of the Covenant in Birmingham, Alabama, Nancy Hastings Sehested of Oakhurst Baptist Church in Decatur, Georgia, and Susan Lockwood of Cornell Baptist Church in Chicago.

Jim Strickland, a minister from Georgia, expressed a desire to offer financial assistance to churches that called female ministers. Strickland served as a member of the Home Mission Board when it decided to withhold financial assistance to churches with female pastors. Individuals present at the meeting, such as Larry Coleman, questioned whether Strickland's proposal would be an issue that the average Baptist could rally behind.[4]

Over the course of the conversation, Susan Lockwood interjected her objection to the use of the women's issue "as a means to reach larger ends." Her comments altered the course of the Alliance's history. The men in the room did not understand what Lockwood meant. As Alan Neely wrote years later, "The shock was palpable. The men were totally unprepared for such a reaction."[5] While Sehested and Lockwood were both in favor of supporting congregations who called female pastors, they felt the financing of congregations with female pastors should not be used as a tool to promote the new organization. The question should not revolve around whether or not women could serve as pastors but whether a local church should be allowed to hire a female minister. If a congregation chose to hire a female pastor, it was within its rights to do so without fear of penalties or repercussions.

After much struggle, the men slowly began to understand what Lockwood and Sehested were saying. Women should not be a prop upon which the Alliance stood. Still, the Alliance as an organization continued to struggle with the questions of women in ministry and gender equity for many years.[6]

The impulse for gender equity began the moment the organization appointed a board of directors. This first group of board members included only three women, as opposed to eighteen men. The organization worked hard over the next few years and throughout its history to include a better mix not just among men and woman, but among clergy and laity. After five years, Alan Neely reported that 107 persons had served on the board — 68 men and 39 women. Eventually, racial diversity as well as diversity in terms of sexual orientation would become priorities for the Alliance, but during the early years, supporting gender diversity was not yet a given.[7]

Motions were made at the organization's founding to seek "equality between clergy and laity, women and men" on the board of directors. There was even a suggestion to require that one of the two organizational vice presidents be female, with the recognition that the vice presidents would eventually become president. "In this way there would be a woman president at least every three years."[8] These motions did not succeed, primarily because of concerns regarding placing such prescribed standards on a new organization. The idea, however, remained a seed in many people's minds — a seed that would organically flourish in the future. As early as 1989, the board of directors formally began the ongoing process of working "toward a balance of men and women, ministers and laity in their representation."[9]

To move toward more gender-inclusive and equitable representation, the Alliance created a Task Force on Women at its first convocation and named Anne Thomas Neil its chair.[10] Her leadership became instrumental in keeping individuals like Sehested and Lockwood committed to and involved in the organization. At her first board meeting, Neil candidly asked the male leadership if they supported women in ministry. She believed that if the board did indeed support women in ministry, a major restructuring of the "normative issue" needed to take place.[11]

The Southern Baptist Convention shaped much of the normative thought on women in ministry. In a letter to the Women's Task Force on August 4, 1987, Neil explained the frustration of many women in the convention who had "no voice . . . no participation, little representation and no power."[12] According to Neil, the convention's nomination of 20 women (out of 246 positions available) to agency boards was appalling and needed to be remedied. She called on the task force to see "what can we do to see that women are included as whole and worthy persons in gospel partnership in the context of the Southern Baptist Alliance?"[13]

Recognizing the gender disparity already present, Neil advocated that the Alliance board begin to balance its representation in terms of "gender, vocation and ethnicity." She proposed other suggestions that included featuring women in the pulpit more often, writing letters to the editors of Baptist papers, aggressively presenting women's names to search committees, funding positions for young women, and promoting educational materials. She asked, "Is the [Alliance] committed to taking women seriously? If so we need to realize this entails a radical transformation in our lives — a radical reconstruction of the normative tradition."[14]

While Neil pushed the Alliance toward thinking differently, the actions of the Home Mission Board remained in the forefront of many Alliance members' minds. At a few meetings, "There was concerned discussion that the next move of the Home Mission Board might be not to hire or fund divorced persons."[15] Norman Langston became a "founding member" of the Alliance because as an employee of the Home Mission Board, he was disappointed by its decision to withhold financial support to women ministers. Other individuals, including Bob Richardson and David and Rachel Bishop, also joined the Alliance because of frustration with the Home Mission Board's resolution. These individuals often wrote Alliance president Henry Crouch, urging him to set up a fund to support congregations with women ministers.[16]

In many ways, the Alliance as an organization had to address the actions of the Home Mission Board. It did so in a letter to the HMB's trustees in which it claimed that "by withholding aid from churches with women pastors, the board has, by policy, attempted to limit the freedom of the local congregation to choose its pastor."[17] This was largely a reactive measure to give voice to the individuals upset and hurt by this decision. While reactive measures were meaningful and important, Neil and other female members continued to advocate for a more proactive approach to gender equity.

The proactive side included partnering with Southern Baptist Women in Ministry, also known as Baptist Women in Ministry (BWIM). When the Alliance formed, Baptist Women in Ministry "wrote a strong letter of affirmation" for the new group."[18] Over the years, the two organizations maintained a close connection. The Alliance's "issues committee" explained at the organization's first fall board meeting that "there may be a need for a paid position with the SBA for a woman to work on women's concerns or to help fund the Southern Baptist Women in Ministry."[19] Instead, the Alliance approved in 1988 "a minimum grant of $5000 to be made in support of the [BWiM's] publication *Folio* and the staff of the Center for Women in Ministry."[20] At this point in time, Baptist Women in Ministry struggled financially, and the Alliance's support was helpful in perpetuating its newsletter. The relationship was mutual, however, as Baptist Women in Ministry director Libby Bellinger looked to find ways in which *Folio* could expand its readership, either through *SBC Today* or the Alliance.[21] In this way, both organizations maintained an overlap in supporters for many years.

In addition to its proactive stance supporting Baptist Women in Ministry, the Task Force on Women in the Church took a stand on inclusive language in 1988. Bellinger became chairperson of a newly appointed standing committee, "Women in the Church," stemming from the task force chaired by Neil.[22] Bellinger and the committee proposed a statement on inclusive language that was reaffirmed by the board of directors, who agreed that "All who plan future SBA meetings will be given a copy of this policy."[23] The statement sought to shift language from words like "mankind" to "humankind." It also sought to shift theological language about "God" away from solely masculine imagery and language to include an expansive vocabulary that described the many facets of the divine, both masculine and feminine.

The process of employing the inclusive language policy was long and difficult. For the 1989 convocation, Bellinger wrote Hardy Clemons, the Convocation Committee chairperson, to request that he send a copy of the inclusive language statement "to all program personalities and musicians asking them to be sensitive to the power of language to include or exclude one another." She also requested that the committee "use women in prominent speaking and preaching roles and that these women be supportive of the SBA covenant and causes."[24] While the planning committee attempted to use the inclusive language statement, its attempt fell short for some Alliance members. After the gathering, Rebecca Albritton sent a letter requesting more female speakers and more inclusive language at future convocations.[25]

In 1989, the Southern Baptist Alliance made a number of strides in its pursuit of supporting women in the local church. That year, Anne Thomas Neil became the group's first female president. The Alliance also published her edited volume, *The New Has Come: The Emerging Role of Women in the Southern Baptist Convention.*[26] In addition, the board of directors encouraged Bellinger to work on an "anthology of sermons by Southern Baptist Women." Bellinger was interested in the project, but based on the poor sales from *The New Has Come*, there was a question as to whether such a work should be produced. Executive director Stan Hastey explained that because of financial constraints the board thought Bellinger might seek publication options elsewhere. The project was never finished.[27]

The first three years of the Alliance's existence were difficult for its women members. To be sure, life in the new organization was better than in Southern Baptist circles. Years later, in recalling the Alliance's founding, Neil wrote, "The Alliance . . . provided me with a place to stand, a place to renew old dreams, to dream new dreams, to envision a new reality — not alone but in a supportive, caring family."[28] Neil recalled the struggle of becoming an inclusive organization with regard to male and female leadership and representation. She remembered being "asked by several men in not so friendly a tone, 'Just what is it you women want?'"[29] Neil did not think the conversations were addressing the proper questions. Her "concern was [that the Alliance was] not addressing the larger picture — the place and role of women in the local congregation not just the role of women in professional ministry."[30]

The most painful moment Neil recalled was at an Alliance meeting in November 1987. The Southern Baptist Women in Ministry requested $15,000 for three consecutive years to publish the newsletter *Folio.* The Executive Committee agreed to send $1,000, which Neil felt was "less than acceptable." In the same meeting, Frank Gilreath moved to give $5,000 to the newly formed chapter of the American Association of University Professors at Southeastern Baptist Theological Seminary. No request for money had been made, but the motion passed. As Neil protested, someone interrupted her, saying, "Can't you see the blood of these faculty members flowing here on the floor?" Neil responded, "Yes, I can; but can you see the avalanche of blood of women that has been flowing for nearly 2000 years?" A male board member later told her "how offensive and unappreciated [her] words and sometimes [her] presence were seen by many of the men present."[31]

Neil's experience represented the struggle moderate Baptists faced. They were beginning to envision a new organization, and every faction from within the movement struggled to address their particular concerns. Some individuals focused on crafting a proper missiology. Some focused on women in the local church. Some focused on theological education. Neil was a strong, passionate, patient and prophetic woman who made space at the Alliance's table for women.

Inspired by the work of individuals like Anne Thomas Neil and Libby Bellinger, the Alliance continued developing its identity and support for women in the local congregation. During the 1990s, however, the Women in the Church Committee fought to establish an identity. Throughout this period, the leadership discussed the issue and even invited individuals to talk about sexism in the church, but the Women in the Church Committee struggled to find a voice.[32]

By 1994, the Women in the Church Committee began "sensing that not much energy [was] being directed toward issues concerning women in the church."[33] That year, Nancy Hastings Sehested chaired the committee and requested that the group "practice the art of imagining." She wrote, "Let us . . . think wildly about women serving big deal Baptist Churches like First Baptist Church Washington, D.C., and Myers Park Baptist Church . . . Let us recommend women to serve as interim pastors in churches of all sizes."[34] Over the next two years, the committee wavered back and forth on discontinuing, eventually concluding there was "plenty of work remaining for the Committee to undertake."[35]

By the late 1990s, the Women in the Church Committee turned its attention to issues of gender equity, and the 2001 convocation focused on the issue.[36] As referenced in the previous chapter, the annual gathering in 2000 experienced serious tension over the firing of Rebecca Gurney by the host congregation, University Baptist Church in Austin, Texas. Convocation planner Cherie Smith proposed ideas for the 2001 convocation that included "a Wailing Wall . . . a place for women and men to express their pain." She also wanted to bring in stories of people from other congregations who had created "'listening groups" of men and women.[37]

As the Alliance progressed into the 21st century, the organization maintained strong ties to Baptist Women in Ministry.[38] According to Baptist Women in Ministry statistics, in 2010 28.2 percent of Alliance-affiliated congregations had women pastors or co-pastors. In terms of the Alliance's 142 endorsed chaplains and counselors, eighty, or 56.3 percent, were women.[39]

Throughout the first decade of the 21st century, the Alliance went through considerable change, which in turn led to changes in the role of the Women in the Church Committee. In 2005, board member Rick Mixon proposed changing to a Committee on Inclusiveness that would incorporate race, gender and sexual orientation. The idea was considered but not acted upon.[40] Two years later, the Women in the Church Committee acknowledged that "every year there seems to be some question as to whether this committee is still needed given the Alliance's diligence in maintaining its overall commitment to the roles of women in the church." The group, however, went ahead and planned a workshop for women new to the ministry at the upcoming convocation. In addition, the committee pledged to work more directly with staff member Chris Copeland to examine questions of discernment "as specifically related to women."[41]

When the Alliance shifted from being an organization led by committees to one of open-membership communities, the "Equity for Women in the Church Community" quickly became one of the most active groups. According to the Alliance's website, the community was founded with the intention of "advocating and networking for clergywomen across denominations and cultures, connecting them to clergy positions for the transformation of church and society . . . "[42]

Worship in the Local Church

Largely spurred by the Women in the Church Committee and its proposed statement on inclusive language, a need arose for worship resources that adhered to the Alliance's gender-inclusive initiative. In 1995, the Alliance published *For the Living of These Days*, a hymnal supplement whose title became the theme of that year's convocation at Vienna Baptist Church in Virginia. In conjunction with the release of this resource, its editor, Michael Hawn, former professor of church music at Southeastern Theological Seminary, conducted a hymn festival on the Friday evening of the gathering. Hawn embodied the Alliance's commitment to diversity in worship and inclusive language.

Although 1995 marked the Alliance's release of the hymnal supplement, the emphasis on worship in the local church began years earlier. In 1991, the Church-Ministry Relations Committee recommended "the formation of a Worship Resources Committee as a standing committee." This new group sought to create worship resources for Alliance churches.[43] Co-chaired by Steven Shoemaker and Paula Dempsey, the team, with Hawn's help, began compiling a hymnal supplement.[44] The project was something that Alan Neely had suggested to Hawn two years earlier.[45] Working on a shoestring budget, the Alliance allotted $750 to produce the work.[46]

The following year, the hymnal supplement was poised to become a 50- to 60-page worship aid that would include sixty hymns to complement those already included in the 1991 *Baptist Hymnal.* The worship liturgies and hymns were "ecumenical and inclusive in [the] fullest sense." Prior to publication, the committee explained, "attempts will be made to include resources from various cultures, i.e. global ways of addressing God . . . resources for occasions not covered in other material will be included, i.e. Earth Day."[47]

The Worship Committee sought "to develop greater inclusiveness in worship" and "assist in the revitalization of all elements of worship," as well as "increase ecumenical awareness."[48] The committee sponsored workshops on worship and provided resources to churches, but its primary purpose remained to produce a hymnal supplement.[49] Once *For the Living of These Days* was released in 1995, the committee disbanded.

Michael Hawn remained an active and oft-sought voice in Alliance circles regarding new and innovative hymnody and worship practices. Over the years, Hawn advocated for "worshippers in the United States . . . to experience the drama of salvation from different cultural perspectives — taking different seats in the theater — in order to more fully appreciate the sacrifice and salvation of the incarnation."[50] He suggested, "If the liturgy of the church in the United States is to continue to have vitality, then we must listen to new voices and incorporate them in our worship experience. Among these voices are those from places that we considered in the past to be our mission field" — Latin America, Asia, and Africa."[51] Hawn's emphasis on multiculturalism, inclusivity and an expansive view of God's love aided congregations in their attempts to make their worship services more meaningful and more congruent with the Alliance's overall missiology and commitment to diversity and inclusivity. In this way, the Alliance supported the freedom of the local congregation — the freedom to worship in imaginative, expansive and diverse ways.

✦

The Alliance formed with a desire to keep the local congregation free from any overarching and imposing authority. Congregations that affiliated with the Alliance were not required to meet any doctrinal standards — these decisions were left to the people in the pews. From its beginning, the Alliance supported the local church, and most specifically women in ministry. While the Alliance never set out to become an organization that supported women in ministry, over the years this support matured. In a similar and related way, the Alliance supported the right of local congregations to worship as they chose. The publication *For the Living of These Days* and the expertise and thought of Michael Hawn encouraged congregations to think about expanding their worship experiences beyond more traditional hymnody.

One often-neglected area of the Alliance's support for the local congregation was that of youth and children. The Alliance struggled throughout its history to find meaningful ways to incorporate youth and children within the organization. From the early 1990s, the Alliance financially supported Baptist Youth Camp, a summer camp attended primarily by youth groups of Alliance congregations, and this partnership remained into the second decade of the 21st century. The partnership was long-lasting but connected youth to other congregations more than the larger Alliance body.

Chris Copeland, who eventually became an Alliance staff member, helped plan a "Gathering for Ministers of Youth and Children September 23-25, 2004." The following year, the Alliance board recommended a youth convocation to be held in conjunction with the 2005 annual gathering.[52] An "electronic discussion group" advocated planning a "second retreat" and commitment to the inclusion of youth and children as "a part of the 2005 convocation." As a result, four workshops on children and youth were held at the meeting.[53] But aside from Baptist Youth Camp and the energy produced by Copeland in the mid-2000s, the Alliance had difficulty finding ways to support the local church's ministry toward youth and children. Other individuals and events attempted to make the Alliance's commitment to youth and children a priority, but these ministries often eluded the Alliance.

Even so, the Alliance maintained support for local congregations and the freedoms of these institutions that served as the backbone of its ministry in the world. In many respects, the work of the organization took place in local congregations. The Alliance desired for these bodies to be free from hierarchical strictures so that they could develop imaginative and innovative ministries. The Alliance supported this freedom in a number of ways, perhaps none as exemplary as its support for women in ministry and for diverse and inclusive worship.

Chapter 7

The Larger Body of Jesus Christ

3) The larger body of Jesus Christ, expressed in various Christian traditions, and to the cooperation with believers everywhere in giving full expression to the Gospel.

The Southern Baptist Alliance was founded with a commitment to the "larger body of Jesus Christ," but this pledge ran counter to most of the history of the Southern Baptist Convention. Perhaps the most ecumenical endeavor of the convention in its more than 150-year history was its participation in the Baptist World Alliance, from which it withdrew in 2004. Southern Baptists never fully participated in broader ecumenical associations like the National Council of Churches or the World Council of Churches. These coalitions were seen "as more theologically and socially liberal."[1] For the Alliance to embody a spirit of ecumenism meant that the membership needed to reject the traditions of regionalism and Landmarkism that did not always dictate but always influenced the direction of the Southern Baptist Convention. The Alliance had to rethink the ways in which Anglo-Baptists in the South understood their place within the larger Christian church.

The Alliance's proclamation of ecumenism excited many moderates within the Southern Baptist fold, as well as individuals within non-Baptist traditions. People from various denominational backgrounds praised the Alliance's commitment to the wider Christian community. According to Alan Neely, Roman Catholics, Methodists, Presbyterians, Episcopalians and Jews, among others, provided words of affirmation at the founding of the organization.[2] So pervasive was the membership's commitment to ecumenism that a 1999 newspaper article described the Alliance as an organization dedicated to "building bridges to other Baptist Bodies and the larger Christian community."[3]

This commitment manifested itself in many ways. Throughout the organization's history, the leadership was intentional about providing space for members to meet and make connections with denominational leaders from the American Baptist Churches USA, the Progressive National Baptists and the United Church of Christ, among others. Other examples of partnership emerged with Canadian Baptist groups such as the Atlantic Baptist Fellowship and The Gathering of Baptists, the Cooperative Baptist Fellowship, the National Council of Churches and the Disciples of Christ. The Alliance's formal ecumenical relationships were supplemented by more personal and informal relationships that reached across Christian traditions in ways impossible to fully trace.

When Rachel Richardson Smith spoke about the third tenet of the Alliance Covenant at the first convocation in 1987, she exclaimed, "We seek unity amidst diversity, a oneness of purpose and spirit, recognizing common bonds in witness to the gospel message. In so doing, we have the opportunity to assist in the birthing of new ideas [and] to become midwives to greater understanding and cooperation."[4] Through this covenant principle, the Alliance reimagined what it meant to be Baptist in the wider Christian context. Through crossing racial and geographic boundaries among Baptists and other denominations, the Alliance offered a new way of being for Baptists that was built upon mutuality and respect for difference and diversity within the body of Christ.

The Atlantic Baptist Fellowship
and The Gathering of Baptists

Over the course of its history, the Alliance of Baptists crossed national boundaries through partnerships with organizations like The Atlantic Baptist Fellowship and The Gathering of Baptists. The Atlantic Baptist Fellowship, later known as the Canadian Association for Baptist Freedoms, was founded in 1971 by Baptists in the maritime provinces of Canada who "wanted to witness to historical Baptist principles and to be involved with non-Baptist communions in joint worship, social action and ecumenical discussions of the nature of the Church."[5] The Gathering of Baptists, which emerged as a similar group in 1994, was founded by individuals within the Baptist Convention of Ontario and Quebec.[6]

After the Alliance's founding in 1987, Morris R.B. Lovesey quickly contacted Alliance president Henry Crouch to inform him about the Atlantic Baptist Fellowship (ABF). Lovesey explained that the "Atlantic Baptist Fellowship bears the same kind of relationship to the Atlantic United Baptist Convention (of Canada) as your Alliance does to the SBC."[7] Four years later, representatives from the Alliance and the ABF connected in person when Alliance executive director Stan Hastey traveled to the 20th anniversary gathering of the ABF. Hastey admitted at this gathering that the partnership between the two organizations had been "amorphous," but the Alliance leadership was excited about the opportunity to "flesh out more specific ways and means of regularizing interaction should this notion be appealing to ABF people."[8]

By 1993, the ABF and the Alliance of Baptists entered into a formal partnership. According to the Alliance leadership, "the extent of the proposed relationship would involve visits and a presence at annual meetings. Other possibilities in relationship include sharing of information and resources for ministry and witness."[9] The following year, the first representatives from the Atlantic Baptist Fellowship attended the Alliance convocation in Greenville, South Carolina. In his State of the Alliance address that year, Hastey described the Atlantic Baptist Fellowship as "an Alliance kind of people . . . Or, more appropriately, given the fact that we are but seven years old and the ABF is 22, we are an ABF kind of people."[10]

The partnership between the Alliance and the ABF was primarily one of mutuality and encouragement. In 1998, when the Alliance became aware of The Gathering of Baptists in Ontario and Quebec, Hastey claimed, "These good Baptist people say they need us, and I submit we need them too."[11] While the relationship between the Alliance and The Gathering of Baptists developed in much less prescribed ways than the relationship with the ABF, the Alliance held both organizations as spiritual kin. In 2004, Hastey attended a meeting of The Gathering in Canada.[12]

Over the years, the Alliance's relationship with the ABF and The Gathering became less formal and less consistent. The leadership discovered through attending ABF meetings that "there is simply no substitute for . . . [a] face-to-face encounter."[13] In 2005, Hastey sent greetings to the ABF, saying, "We celebrate the relationship we have enjoyed with you . . . knowing we have much to learn from you and your experience as faithful Baptist Christians in another setting. We seek a continued and expanded interaction with one another as this relationship solidifies."[14]

The relationship was perpetuated and aided in many ways by the support of John Boyd, pastor of First Baptist Church in Halifax, Nova Scotia. Boyd had strong connections to the ABF, having served as the organization's president, and from 2008 to 2012 he served as a board member for the Alliance.[15] In like manner, First Baptist Halifax was one of the only congregations outside the United States to affiliate with the Alliance. By 2011, Boyd encouraged the Alliance to think about the ways in which it and Canadian churches could become better partners. The following year, board member Mandy England Cole visited the annual meeting of the newly named Canadian Association for Baptist Freedoms, re-establishing a connection between the two organizations.[16]

The Cooperative Baptist Fellowship

The relationship between the Cooperative Baptist Fellowship and the Alliance of Baptists was probably the most contentious of all the relationships the Alliance fostered in its history. The Cooperative Baptist Fellowship (CBF) formed out of the Southern Baptist Convention when the "moderates" failed to elect Daniel Vestal president in 1990. Moderate organizations such as Baptists Committed and Baptists Concerned, who chose to continue the political struggle within the convention rather than join the Alliance in the late 1980s, came together after the 1990 defeat to form "The Fellowship." By the 21st century, the CBF described itself as "a fellowship of Baptist Christians and churches who share a passion for the Great Commission of Jesus Christ and a commitment to Baptist principles of faith and practice."[17]

Although the Cooperative Baptist Fellowship was comprised mostly of individuals who continued within the convention, in many ways the CBF was also a product of the Alliance of Baptists. Because the Alliance remained in the convention during its earliest years, most Alliance members were well connected to the moderate political movement. When the larger moderate movement decided to form a new organization, discussions regarding unifying the new "Fellowship" and the Alliance were common among individuals who had connections to both organizations.

While many within the moderate political movement refused to join the Alliance, others, like Cecil Sherman and John Hewitt, participated within both the political movement and the Alliance. Both men also became leaders in the CBF. Sherman had close relationships to Alliance leaders, like Henry Crouch and Alan Neely, and was a champion among "moderates" who opposed inerrant views of scripture. When Sherman was invited to speak at the first Alliance convocation in Raleigh, North Carolina, he felt it "was an honor to be associated with so fine a group of real Baptists." He wrote to Henry Crouch afterwards to offer numerous suggestions for the organization. Sherman, at the time a minister in Texas, thought the next convocation should be held farther west to appeal to Texans.[18]

Sherman wrote often to Crouch in the early days of the organization to offer suggestions regarding positions he thought the Alliance should take on certain issues. Despite the Alliance's desire to remain out of convention politics, Sherman was politically motivated. He believed the "woman's issue" should never order the agenda for the Alliance, and leadership should make decisions to choose "temperate people to speak . . . forceful but not strident."[19] Sherman supposed that if the Alliance went "public with a strong agenda 'for women' or anti-inerrancy, [they were] asking for rejection."[20] The Alliance, however, was never in the business of calculating the effects of its particular stances on organizational membership.

Another individual like Sherman was John Hewitt, then pastor of First Baptist Church in Asheville, North Carolina. Hewitt was a keynote speaker at the 1990 Alliance convocation in St. Louis, Missouri, and went on to become the first moderator of the CBF less than a year later.[21] At the first Alliance convocation after the formation of the Fellowship, executive director Stan Hastey celebrated the new organization. He was particularly pleased to report that 24 of the 70 members of the CBF steering committee were Alliance members. Hastey claimed, "It is the Alliance that has modeled much of that which The Baptist Fellowship is beginning to develop."[22] With a steering committee composed of more than one-third Alliance members, the Fellowship indelibly took on characteristics and traces of the Alliance. There was discussion and even agreement about merging the two organizations, but both were maneuvering in new space outside the bounds of the Southern Baptist Convention. The emergence of the Fellowship highlighted the vast diversity among "moderate" Southern Baptists jockeying for positions within a new organization — or, in reality, organizations.

As an Alliance member and the first moderator of the CBF, Hewitt helped lead the first discussions about the possibility of merging in the summer of 1991. Hastey recalled this meeting two years later, saying, "Agreement was reached on a number of questions, including the prospect of dissolving both groups in order to create a true merger, adoption of the Alliance Covenant for the hoped-for merged body, and retention of Alliance personnel in the merged body, among others."[23] Individuals present at this meeting took this mutual agreement back to their respective organizations for further discussion. By September of 1991, the Alliance Board of Directors affirmed the following statement and dialogue process:

> "In light of a very candid and harmonious dialogue, we agree unanimously that there is a possibility we can accomplish our goals and mission more effectively together than separately, and that we will work toward that goal with the expectation of making a definitive decision about the future of the SBA and CBF by the spring of 1993."[24]

By the time the Alliance board met again in the spring of 1992, the leadership had received no contact from the CBF.[25] Six months later, the board noted that there was an "uneasy relationship and perceived rivalry between the Cooperative Baptist Fellowship and the Alliance."[26]

The Alliance board was concerned about the direction the Fellowship was taking with regard to missions, intra-Baptist dialogue, personnel policy, and general "inclusiveness issues," among other things.[27] From the perspective of the Cooperative Baptist Fellowship, there were reservations "that the Alliance agenda was too liberal."[28]

At the 1992 convocation, Hastey addressed at length the difficulties of merging the Alliance and the Fellowship. He admitted that he was distressed by the Fellowship's lack of concern for reaching out to other Baptist bodies like the American Baptists. Hastey claimed, "I am utterly convinced that it would be wrong — indeed sinful — for a new body of Baptists to form that would proceed to operate in the kind of self-sufficient isolationism and arrogant exclusivity that came to characterize the Southern Baptist Convention."[29]

By September, both groups passed a joint statement agreeing on "the continued existence of each group." The statement also encouraged working toward "common sites and dates" for annual meetings and for cooperation in "mission endeavors."[30] The Alliance proposed that the first step toward a beneficial and mutual relationship might be the Fellowship's financial adoption of the Alliance's mission projects. Alliance founder Alan Neely, however, still believed that the Alliance needed to exist to "support people and causes that [were] too controversial or risky for the Fellowship . . . to address."[31]

The Alliance membership decreased during this period because of the quick growth of and the overlapping constituency with the Cooperative Baptist Fellowship. Discussion between the two organizations continued, and a non-competing relationship took form by early 1993, when the two bodies agreed

> that those projects previously funded by both groups hereafter will receive funding from CBF only. These include the Baptist Joint Committee on Public Affairs, Associated Baptist Press, Baptist Center for Ethics, Baptist Theological Seminary at Richmond, and the Baptist studies programs at Chandler School of Theology and Duke Divinity School. Similarly CBF will dispense all theological education scholarships.[32]

The Alliance supported all of these organizations and causes, but to maintain a non-competing relationship with the CBF, it surrendered its financial support.

In 1994, Hastey announced, "This year's Alliance Global Missions Offering causes are those CBF declined to support. They truly represent causes that others consider too risky or too controversial." Among the line items in the Global Mission Offering were the Baptist Peace Fellowship of North America and Southern Baptist Women in Ministry.[33]

The agreement between the Alliance and CBF remained loose for many years, and in some ways remnants of this decision persisted into the second decade of the 21st century. Eventually, the Alliance continued to fund the Baptist Joint Committee while providing mostly ceremonial financial support to different seminaries and divinity schools. The Alliance never, however, looked to provide scholarships for theological education — most likely because of a combination of this agreement and a general lack of financial resources. For the Cooperative Baptist Fellowship, the arrangement held true until the organization became comfortable with funding Baptist Women in Ministry (formerly Southern Baptist Women in Ministry) in the mid-1990s.

The relationship between the two bodies pushed the Alliance to the fringes of Baptist life. In 1993, Mark Buckner, a pastor who identified with the Alliance, said, "The Fellowship has taken over much of what we used to do. People who still see us in that role think of us as stubborn egos who won't let go."[34] As the Alliance became more and more of a fringe organization, a large number of people began to identify more with the CBF for practical and financial reasons. Individuals like Molly Marshall, former professor of theology at Southern Baptist Theological Seminary, participated more in CBF but claimed to feel "much more at home theologically and socially" with the Alliance.[35] Julie Pennington-Russell, a well-known CBF pastor by the 21st century, acknowledged upon the formation of the CBF that she continued to "support and believe in the existence and purpose of the Alliance!"[36] These two individuals were typical of a much larger group who supported the Alliance in spirit but believed the CBF had the institutional infrastructure to support their ministry.

Some, like Sharyn Dowd, chose not to renew their Alliance membership in the wake of the formation of CBF. Dowd claimed,

> I think the Fellowship has a much broader base and is more in touch with the values of Baptist people. Your romantic, unrealistic attachment to . . . reunion with ABCUSA, and of union with

the Progressive Baptists (who do not recognize the ordination of women) have contributed to my decision.[37]

Hastey found Dowd's accusations "puzzling."[38] The Alliance did not look to a union with these other Baptist groups, but instead sought to form partnerships of mutuality and respect for the diversity within Baptist life. Her comments were also "puzzling" because the CBF at that time refused to support Baptist Women in Ministry, while Progressive National Baptists generally supported women's ordination. These allegations and other misunderstandings about the Alliance were not uncommon during this period.

Mark Olson, then pastor of First Baptist Church in South Boston, Virginia, informed the Alliance that his congregation could not support an organization that supported churches like Binkley Memorial and Pullen Memorial, both of which affirmed LGBT persons. According to Olson, "the homosexual issue in Charlotte [at the 1992 convocation] made it easier for us to choose the CBF over the Alliance."[39] As the Alliance sought to protect and fund projects on the margins of Baptist life, churches like First Baptist South Boston began to transition from supporting the Alliance to supporting the CBF.

While some individuals and churches saw the choice of supporting the Alliance and the Fellowship as an either/or decision, others within the two organizations were far more supportive and cordial with one another. Cecil Sherman, the first executive director of the CBF, wrote in 1996 of the Alliance:

> I want to thank you for standing for the truth and for the Baptist way. I wish it had been possible for the Alliance and CBF to find ways to come together. That did not happen. But I have noted and been very aware all the while that we are working off the same page. We understand our history the same way, and we understand Baptist polity in the same way.[40]

The friendliness in the above message characterized many exchanges between leaders of the two organizations throughout the 1990s. When Sherman retired, Hastey nominated former Alliance president Richard Groves to become the CBF's second executive director.[41] Ultimately, Daniel Vestal was chosen for the position, and he continued a tradition of thanking the Alliance for its ministry.[42] In 1997, Vestal even went so far as to thank the Alliance for helping "birth the Cooperative Baptist Fellowship."[43]

Over the years, Hastey remained openly critical of the CBF's "lone ranger" mentality. For him, it seemed "almost unthinkable . . . that . . . a new group of Baptists in the South would be spending millions of dollars annually sending out new missionaries without any consultation with other Baptist mission agencies." Hastey thought this was "one of the worst features of the old convention."[44] The Alliance as an organization was also critical of the 2001 CBF "Statement of an Organizational Value," which was described by the Associated Baptist Press as a statement of being "'Welcoming but not affirming' of homosexuals."[45] The policy sought to prohibit the hiring of LGBT persons and to make sure that financial allocations were not being used in ways that supported or affirmed "homosexuality." Because of the statement, the Alliance almost decided to "have no official presence" at the CBF's General Assembly in Atlanta in June 2001.[46] Instead, the Alliance maintained a booth at the meeting to serve as a witness to its position on LGBT inclusion.

Despite the Alliance's criticisms of the CBF, both organizations remained amiable until 2002, when Sherman made some disparaging comments about the Alliance. According to Hastey, Sherman described the membership of the Alliance as a bunch of "nuts" and "fruitcakes" to a group of moderate Baptists in Texas.[47] These comments eventually developed into a semi-public conflict regarding the founding of the Cooperative Baptist Fellowship and the reasons the two organizations did not merge.

Hastey responded to Sherman's comments in a *Baptists Today* article, explaining that Sherman could not fully comment on the proposed merger because he was not present at the first meeting between representatives of the Alliance and CBF, when the two organizations created an agreement to merge.[48] In a series of letters between Sherman and Hastey, Sherman blamed the fourth president of the Alliance, Ann Quattlebaum, and the Alliance's acceptance of gay and lesbian individuals as the two reasons the groups didn't merge.[49] Sherman claimed that during the period of dialogue between the two bodies, Quattlebaum "was ready to compromise Baptist polity for the sake of the Women's issue."[50] This was something, Sherman claimed, CBF was unwilling to do.

These comments drastically damaged friendships within the two organizations. Sherman's statements particularly pained his longtime friend, Alliance founder Alan Neely, who wrote to Sherman asking for an explanation of his comments in Texas. Neely was hurt by being labeled a "fundamentalist of the left." Neely wished Sherman had more diligently attempted to "build bridges between the organizations . . . instead of walls of suspicion, resentment, fear, and distrust."[51] Sherman never responded to his longtime friend, who died a year later.[52]

In many ways, this disagreement persisted into the second decade of the 21st century, as a tone of skepticism remained present between both organizations. Despite the suspicion, many individuals still believed that there was a need for both groups to continue their respective ministries. Perhaps one of the most gracious ways of describing the role of the two organizations came from Walker Knight in his 1992 Covenant Address. Knight suggested that the CBF was best characterized as a Martin Luther King Jr. type figure, while the Alliance was best characterized as Malcolm X. According to Knight, "in the course of history each serves a needed purpose, and the future may give us a synthesis of the two."[53] The point being, both organizations were looking to accomplish similar things in different ways. Since a large number of churches continued to be dually aligned with the CBF and the Alliance, it seemed many moderates agreed with Knight.

The relationship between these two bodies was contentious, to say the least. Both organizations represented different ways moderate Baptists responded to leaving the Southern Baptist Convention. Ideas of merging and cooperation remained present throughout their histories, but the CBF and the Alliance were amalgamations of different variants of moderate Baptists. Both groups struggled to make sense of their faith outside the Southern Baptist fold. The CBF might best represent those Southern Baptists who fought for their convention to the bitter end, while the Alliance might best represent those who were a little quicker to give up their former denomination. The history of the relationship highlights the gradation and variety of the former Southern Baptists who found themselves to be more progressive theologically than the inerrantists of the Southern Baptist Convention.

The American Baptist Churches USA

When the Alliance hired Stan Hastey as executive director two years after forming, cultivating a relationship with the American Baptists Churches USA became an immediate priority. The American Baptists were officially constituted as the Northern Baptist Convention in 1907. The organization traced its roots back, however, to the Triennial Convention, Tract Society and Home Mission Society of the early 19th century — the societies that southern Baptists broke away from to form the Southern Baptist Convention in 1845. When the Alliance was founded, one of the goals embedded in the covenant principle of ecumenism was to attempt to repair a relationship between these two geographically estranged groups. With the hiring of an executive director, this intention became a reality.

In the 1980s, the leaders of the American Baptist Churches (ABCUSA) were so concerned about how the controversy within the SBC might affect their organization that they formed a task force to study the issue. At the time, many moderate southern churches within the convention were beginning to make contact with the ABCUSA about the possibility of joining the American Baptist Churches of the South (ABCOTS), a regional body within the larger denomination. The inquiries were so prevalent that by 1990, Daniel E. Weiss, general secretary of the organization, had a sample letter drafted to send to Southern Baptist churches seeking further information about the American Baptist Churches USA.[54]

In the early days of the Southern Baptist Alliance, no organization was more helpful and supportive than the American Baptists. Malcolm Shotwell, a regional minister from Illinois, wrote to Hastey in 1991 to say his regional convention had passed a resolution stating, "We hurt with our sister churches in the Southern Baptist Convention, and stand ready to be supportive in any way we can for the benefit of Christ's Kingdom."[55] In the same year, another representative of the American Baptists, Eugene Ton, wrote that "we feel that the Southern Baptist Alliance represents positions and interests most compatible with the ABC."[56] For the Alliance, having fellow Baptists stand in solidarity with them was encouraging.

In September of 1990, the Alliance board of directors passed a statement affirming the "process toward cooperative ventures in ministry and mission with the American Baptist Churches and recommend[ed] to the Spring Convocation that affirmation and support be given to the ongoing process."[57] When the leadership met in 1991 in Richmond, Virginia, the group voted to strike Southern Baptist from its statement of purpose and approved moving forward in formal dialogue with the American Baptist Churches.[58] The prospect of formal dialogue had been problematic a year earlier, as the Alliance was concerned with how other moderate Southern Baptists would perceive such discussions. The wording surrounding partnership with the ABC needed to be handled delicately so as not to distance the Alliance from fellow moderates who were continuing the political struggle within the Southern Baptist Convention.

In its early years, the Alliance always invited American Baptist representatives to its convocations. For the third annual gathering in St. Louis, the planning committee invited John Sundquist, executive director of the Board of International Ministries of the American Baptist Churches, to be one of the keynote speakers.[59] Two years later, in 1992, American Baptist representative Daniel Weiss was invited "to be one of the major presenters" at the convocation in Charlotte, North Carolina.[60] Along with Weiss, Walter Parrish was invited as executive minister of the American Baptist Churches of the South to lead a workshop on churches interested in affiliating with ABCOTS.[61] In a reciprocal way, the Alliance was represented at multiple American Baptist biennial conventions in the early 1990s.[62]

By the middle of the 1990s, the American Baptist Churches USA were undergoing significant organizational transition. According to the minutes of the Alliance board in August of 1995, "Dialogue with American Baptist Churches [was] over, due in part to their deep division over the homosexuality issue."[63] While the divisiveness over this topic stifled cooperation at the organizational level, the abrupt conclusion to dialogue did not end partnership altogether.

Through the years, a recognized caucus within the ABCUSA known as the Roger Williams Fellowship often partnered and worked closely with the Alliance. The Roger Williams Fellowship sought to protect the Baptist distinctives of individual and local church autonomy, among other things. Hastey participated in this group's 1991 conference focusing on Williams, an early proponent of religious freedom and the separation of church and state. Hastey's presence at the conference laid the initial groundwork for a relationship between the Alliance and the Roger Williams Fellowship.[64]

In 1994, the Roger Williams Fellowship and the Northeast and Virginia chapters of the Alliance sponsored a joint conference called *Together . . . For Freedom's Sake!* The conference took place at Calvary Baptist Church in Washington, D.C., and provided workshops on issues from militarism to racism, family systems, and environmental concerns.[65] Ken Sehested, executive director of the Baptist Peace Fellowship of North America, thought "the gathering was deeply significant . . . because of the historical breakthrough of Northern and Southern Baptists coming together."[66]

In 1995, both organizations took this historical breakthrough even further by holding a joint conference commemorating the 150-year anniversary of the split between the southern and northern Baptists.[67] The conference took place at The First Baptist Church in America and was called "Division, Diversity, Dialogue: A Baptist Journey."[68] Another joint gathering the following year, in conjunction with the Cooperative Baptist Fellowship and the American Baptist Churches, focused on Baptist distinctives.[69]

These joint meetings were particularly meaningful for the attendees generally as well as for the Alliance at large. In the wake of the American

Baptists' withdrawal from dialogue because of the Alliance's position on issues of human sexuality, the Alliance leadership recognized that progress had "stalled between American Baptists and the Alliance." In response, the Ecumenical Outreach Committee suggested having more "joint events with the Roger Williams Fellowship."[70] While these events did not become a regular occurrence, more joint events did take place, including a fellowship gathering in 2001 at the biennial meeting of the American Baptists in Providence, Rhode Island, sponsored by the Alliance, the Roger Williams Fellowship and the Coalition for Baptist Principles.[71]

In 1998, two regional bodies within the American Baptist Convention, Rochester-Genesee and Connecticut, began to consider affiliating with the Alliance of Baptists.[72] Their interest was spurred by prominent voices within the ABCUSA leadership advocating against LGBT inclusion. In his State of the Alliance Address that year, Hastey said, "What is most amazing about these new expressions of interest in the Alliance is that they come against the backdrop of our initiative six years ago to explore the explosive subject of sexuality and particularly homosexuality and the church."[73]

The following year, the American Baptist national body upheld the expulsion of four churches from their respective regional associations for being welcoming and affirming. All of these churches expressed interest in joining the Alliance, as did other regional American Baptist bodies that were more sympathetic to welcoming and affirming churches. The Alliance leadership had found that many churches experienced a "feeling of disloyalty to the ABC if they" thought about affiliating with the Alliance, but these feelings dissipated for some.[74] The Alliance began to serve as a shelter for American Baptist churches that chose to affiliate, just as the American Baptists had been a shelter for many moderate Southern Baptist churches a decade earlier.

The Alliance board of directors noticed another increase in inquiries from American Baptist congregations in 2006 after "an open letter to American Baptists from General Secretary Roy Medley . . . caused considerable upset among those advocating for [LGBT] inclusiveness."[75] Despite statements like this, some American Baptists stayed within the ABCUSA largely through the work of the Association of Welcoming and Affirming Baptists, founded in 1993, and the Evergreen Association, founded ten years later to support welcoming and affirming congregations on the West Coast. Some churches affiliated with the Alliance for the benefits of having a national denominational body willing to endorse and recognize LGBT chaplains and clergy.

A large number of American Baptist congregations joined the Alliance of Baptists over the years. In 2006, the Alliance celebrated its shift from an organization predominantly located in the southeastern United States to a more national organization. In this year, Jim Hopkins and Kristy Pullen, both American Baptists, were nominated to serve as Alliance officers. According to Stan Hastey, "Their nominations as president and vice president, respectively, speak to the evolution of the Alliance from a predominantly regional movement across the Bible belt into a truly national body of Baptists."[76] The leadership of Hopkins, Pullen and other American Baptist leaders and churches kept the Alliance in an informal and personal relationship with the work and ministry of the ABCUSA into the second decade of the 21st century.

The connection between the Alliance and the American Baptist Churches changed over the years. American Baptists initially served as a supportive denominational body, excited by the possibility of partnership. Eventually, support would stem from a group within the American Baptist Churches USA — the Roger Williams Fellowship. By the twenty-first century, the Alliance began to serve as a supportive denominational body ready and eager to partner with congregations that were committed to LGBT inclusion and struggled with the policies and attitudes of those in American Baptist leadership.

The United Church of Christ and
The Christian Church (Disciples of Christ)

The Alliance of Baptist's partnership with the United Church of Christ and The Christian Church (Disciples of Christ) represented its movement beyond Baptist ecumenism to wider Christian ecumenism. The relationship was more defined with the United Church of Christ (UCC), although that is not to suggest the Alliance and The Christian Church (Disciples of Christ) had a less cooperative relationship with one another.

The United Church of Christ was founded in 1957 through the unification of the Evangelical and Reformed Church and the Congregational Christian Churches. In many ways, the UCC is a religious experiment in Christian ecumenism. The Disciples of Christ was a denominational body of the Second Great Awakening known for its desire to restore the church to New Testament Christianity. After much discussion, these two denominations — the UCC and Disciples of Christ — entered into full communion in 1989, mutually recognizing each other's sacraments and ordained ministers.[77] The Alliance entered into dialogue with both denominations in the late 1990s and remained open to the idea of striving toward full communion into the second decade of the 21st century.

The idea of partnership began in 1996 when the Alliance learned of a large projected turnover of clergy within the UCC by 2000. This prediction caused the Alliance's Ecumenical Relations Committee to recommend "exploring issues of partnering, educational credentialing and endorsements with [the] UCC."[78] Executive director Stan Hastey affirmed the recommendation by explaining that affiliation with the UCC would provide a venue for congregational affiliation, ministerial standing and endorsement of chaplains.[79] When the Disciples of Christ learned that the Alliance sought to partner with the UCC, its general minister and president, Richard Hamm, wrote to Hastey asking if the Alliance was interested in a similar relationship with his denomination.[80]

At the 1997 Alliance convocation, Hastey announced "new conversations with leaders of the United Church of Christ (UCC)."[81] Rollin Russell, the conference minister for the Southern Conference of the UCC, was present. In the same year, the UCC invited Hastey to be a part of its General Synod as an ecumenical guest.[82] In 1998, the United Church of Christ and the Alliance met again, with two representatives from the UCC, Rev. John Deckenback and Kwame Osei Reed, attending the Alliance convocation.[83] By 1999, the Alliance and UCC had voted to proceed into a "formal dialogue with . . . conversations to take place over the next two years."[84]

These conversations concluded in 2003 with the Alliance's ongoing resolution to "continuing dialogue, and joint public witness . . . with the United Church of Christ and the Christian Church." The commitment included working with the Global Ministries Board of the UCC and Disciples of Christ, as well as encouraging "progressive Baptist seminaries and theological schools to offer courses on the history and polity of the United Church of Christ and the Christian Church." In addition, the Alliance proposed to "extend a seat (voice without vote) on the Board of Directors of the Alliance of Baptists to a representative of the United Church of Christ and a representative of the Christian Church (Disciples of Christ) as an expression of Christian hospitality and ecumenical partnership."[85] Reflecting on the dialogue, Hastey reported that "in this partnership we seek, first and foremost, to give witness to the essential oneness of the whole church of Jesus Christ and to be living witnesses to the efficacy of Jesus' prayer, 'that they may all be one'."[86]

The two organizations continued their dialogue beyond 2003. By the second decade of the 21st century, churches such as Harmony Creek in

Dayton, Ohio, and Circle of Mercy in Asheville, North Carolina, established a dual Alliance/UCC identity. In 2010, the Alliance began a partnership with the UCC to sponsor a summer ministry placement program for students. By 2014, Harmony Creek Church pastor Mike Castle, a UCC and Baptist minister, became president of the Alliance of Baptists.

Progressive National Baptist Convention Inc.

The relationship between the Progressive National Baptist Convention Inc. (PNBC) and the Alliance of Baptists in many ways began as an attempt by the Alliance to be a more racially inclusive body. The PNBC was founded in 1961 in the wake of the civil rights movement as a religious body "which reflected the religious, social and political climate of its time."[87] This was the denomination of Martin Luther King Jr., and it serviced one of the more progressive wings of the African American religious experience in the United States.

Contact between the two organizations happened at the third annual Alliance convocation when Charles G. Adams, president of the Progressive National Baptist Convention and a pastor in Detroit, Michigan, was invited to preach. This was the same meeting that the Alliance adopted its statement, "A Call to Repentance: A Statement on Racism and Repentance." Through this declaration, the Alliance made the first apology of any group of Anglo-Baptists in the South for the role the Southern Baptist Convention played in the perpetuation of slavery. After the gathering, Adams suggested to Stan Hastey that the Alliance "pursue contacts with Progressive Baptist pastors and congregations about some form of mutual affiliation."[88] Hastey relayed Adams' suggestion to the Alliance board, which quickly began to examine the possibility.

Representatives of both organizations met on January 21, 1992, and agreed to meet again to discuss position papers surrounding ideas of freedom from a multiplicity of perspectives.[89] The second meeting took place two months later in Charlotte, North Carolina. Those present brought a number of position papers on a wide array of topics, from theoretical ideas of freedom to questions of race and gender identity.[90]

In conjunction with the second meeting, Tyron Pitts, general secretary of the PNBC, attended the 1992 Alliance gathering at Providence Baptist Church in Charlotte, North Carolina, and brought greetings on behalf of his organization.[91] Over the years, Pitts, a friend of Hastey, led a number of workshops on race and the PNBC at Alliance gatherings.

By 1994, both organizations began planning a joint meeting for the following year in Charlotte, where they planned to release a collaborative curriculum about racism for children, youth and adults.[92] The meeting took place in August of 1995. Program participants included the respective presidents of each organization, John Roberts of the Alliance and Bennett Smith of the Progressive National Baptists, as well as Thomas Kilgore (chair of the Joint Committee on Alliance/PNBC Dialogue), Richard Groves, and Charles Adams.[93] The keynote speaker was President Bill Clinton, who delivered a speech about the importance for groups within the United States to "fight for common ground."[94]

Unfortunately, the curriculum on racism was not released, and by 1997 it seemed that the curriculum was "not going to happen."[95] Individuals from the Alliance of Baptists felt that their desire and interest in the material was greater than the desire of the writers from the PNBC.

As the relationship waned in the following years, the Alliance continually brought up the possibility of reconnecting with the PNBC. In 2003, the Ecumenical and Interfaith Relations Committee reported that the joint curriculum was "shelved due to seeming lack of interest on the part of the PNBC." The committee, following the initiative and leadership of Willard Bass and Jim Hopkins, decided to look into pursuing other "areas of mutual concern."[96] Despite the lack of formal partnership between the two organizations after the first ten years, the Alliance continued to consider the PNBC as spiritual kin.

National Council of Churches of Christ

The National Council of Churches (NCC) formed in 1950 out of the Federal Council of Churches and other ecumenical bodies. Over the course of its history, the NCC focused on different issues, but by 2014 it claimed to still be "committed to proclaiming God's word and expressing the love of Christ for all persons at every level of society."[97] The Alliance's membership in the NCC stemmed from a desire to work in the wider ecumenical community in ways the Southern Baptist Convention declined to pursue. While the convention did participate in certain NCC programs, such as the Faith and Order Commission, Southern Baptists never fully committed to the NCC.

In 1991, the Alliance invited Joan Brown Campbell, general secretary of the National Council of the Churches of Christ in the USA, to be a major presenter at the organization's annual gathering.[98] It was not until 1994, however, that the Alliance had its first "official observer," William Johnson, sit in on the General Board meeting of the NCC.[99] Johnson reported back to the leadership, "No other organization exists with the purpose and resources available in the NCC. Even all the insider tension betrays a break with the past and a desire to look afresh to the future."[100]

By 1998, the Alliance applied to the National Council of Churches, but the timing of the application in conjunction with the NCC's "criteria for eligibility" forced the Alliance to wait until the following year.[101] When officially voted into the National Council of Churches in November 2001, the Alliance became the 36th member body.[102] Soon thereafter, David Waugh recommended that the Alliance board begin appointing representatives to the various units of the NCC.[103]

While the Alliance considered joining the Baptist World Alliance (BWA) in 2005, the Committee on Ecumenical Partnership recommended investing more into the National Council of Churches. Board member Jim Hopkins believed the BWA would not accept the Alliance because of its stance on sexual orientation.[104] Since then, the Alliance has maintained strong ties with the National Council of Churches. In 2006, Stan Hastey acknowledged the Alliance's far-reaching representation within the NCC. Alliance members served on the NCC's governing board (David Waugh), Justice and Advocacy Committee (Sylvia Campbell), Interfaith Relations Committee (Willard Bass), Communications Committee (Sue Harper Poss) and Church World Service board (Jeanette Holt). The Alliance also had connections with the associate general secretary for interfaith relations (Shanta Premawardhana) and the associate general secretary for communication (Pat Pattillo). Into the second decade of the 21st century, the Alliance remained an active participant with the National Council of Churches and continued to appoint representatives to its various entities and committees.

✦

While many of the ecumenical partnerships the Alliance of Baptists formed over the years were with other Baptist bodies, these collaborative efforts represented a new way of associating. Various coalitions of Baptist organizations have been formed in the past, much like the Baptist World Alliance, but rarely have such groups sought to have individual relationships with other Baptist denominational groups. The Alliance felt called to change this culture within Baptist life both by reaching out to other Baptist groups and by enthusiastically accepting help from others.

Unfortunately, as the history of the Alliance progressed, some of these partnerships waned and even faded away. In some respects this was due, in part, to theological differences between the Alliance and the groups with which it partnered. Perhaps another reason might have been the difficulty in sustaining such a radically new approach to denominationalism. These relationships were fluid and were formed between organizations that might traditionally be understood as competitors, with varying levels of power, affluence and constituency. Striving for mutuality and equity was difficult.

Despite the evolving nature of these partnerships, the Alliance continued to seek new ways to partner with other Christian bodies. Whereas some relationships with other Baptist groups may be strained or simply no longer desired, the Alliance formed friendships with the United Church of Christ, the Christian Church (Disciples of Christ) and the National Council of Churches. For Baptists who grew up in the Southern Baptist Convention, conceiving of these collaborative efforts was a near impossibility when the Alliance was formed. As the Alliance grew and matured, however, these partnerships became integrally important to its identity as an ecumenical organization. In the process of breaking away from the historic regionalism and exclusivism of the Southern Baptist Convention, the Alliance attempted to rethink what it meant for Baptists to claim their voice within the diverse chorus of the wider Christian church.

Chapter 8

The Servant Role of Leadership

4) The servant role of leadership within the church, following the model of our Servant Lord, and to full partnership of all of God's people in mission and ministry.

As with all of the covenant principles of the Alliance of Baptists, the "Servant Role of Leadership" attempted to address a particular aspect of the inerrantist-moderate controversy within the Southern Baptist Convention in the 1980s. A 1988 convention resolution that qualified the priesthood of all believers clearly illustrates the debate to which this principle applied. Through the declaration, the convention affirmed "the truth that elders, or pastors, are called of God to lead the local church." In addition, the resolution cited Hebrews 13:17, stating, "Obey your leaders, submit to them; for they keep watch over your souls, as those who will give an account."[1] This pronouncement sought to justify the actions of charismatic, inerrantist leaders who made little room to share authority with the laity in their congregations or in the convention.

The Alliance responded to the idea that the pastor was the sole authority in the church by emphasizing a servant role of leadership. William Turner, pastor of South Main Baptist Church in Houston, wrote about the Alliance's understanding of servant leadership by saying that pastors "are graced, worthy, gifted, called persons who choose servanthood as the shape and style" of leadership.[2] Turner and others within the organization were not interested in a model of leadership that placed clergy over and above the members of the congregation.

He wrote that "full partnership in mission and ministry for clergy and laity" was the desired model. This meant that ministers needed to identify their own "gifts for ministry," exemplify being "inclusive in understanding and language," be "good listeners," have patience with church processes, share power, and encourage the "gifts of the laity."[3] The Alliance saw leadership in the local congregation, as did Turner, through the lens of "equipper and catalyst."[4] Leaders in local congregations did not have more power than those who were mere members; theirs was an authority to encourage and to develop more leaders.

This chapter addresses some of the ways in which the Alliance attempted to apply its commitment to servant leadership. The three sections deal with the history of the Alliance's organizational structure, important leaders who embodied the principle of servant leadership, and the Alliance's policies on clergy recognition and endorsement. Each section pays particular attention to the ways in which the Alliance endeavored to facilitate the creation and perpetuation of servant leaders at both the national organizational level and the local congregational level.

Alliance of Baptists Organizational Structure

Over the course of the Alliance's history, the organization underwent significant changes to its leadership structure. Coming out of the largest Protestant denomination in America with much uncertainty surrounding the ultimate size and scope of the group, such change should be expected. While the organizational structure did change with regard to the Alliance's size, the leadership also intentionally transformed the structure over time to better reflect a servant model of leadership. The process of transformation included changes to the board of directors, staff structure and annual meetings. By the second decade of the 21st century, the transformation remained a work in progress.

From the beginning, the Alliance's leaders desired to create a strong board of directors from across the United States. The steering committee that met in Charlotte, North Carolina, in January 1987 suggested that the board would be composed of eight "at large" individuals as well as persons representing twelve regions — mostly states. Representatives for the board were initially chosen as follows: two from individual state "conventions," eight at large, and two from clustered state conventions, including the Northeast, the Capital States, the Great Lake States, the Plain States, the Mountain States, the Western States and the Southwest States.[5] The executive committee included five officers — president, first vice president, second vice president, secretary and treasurer.

Within this model, members of the board were subsequently appointed to serve on committees that oversaw various aspects of the Alliance. Some documents cite different committees as being the inaugural committees. Among those referenced are the Literature Committee, Membership and Finance Committee, Missions Committee, Placement Committee,

Theological Education Committee, and Women in the Church Committee.[6] Other sources suggest that the first committees included a Convocation Committee, Membership Development Committee, Missions Committee, Public Relations Committee, and Organization Review Committee.[7] The discrepancy between documents merely shows the amount of fluctuation within the Alliance during the early years of its existence.

Through the proposed model, the leadership saw the organization becoming a large institution. As early as 1988, questions arose regarding hiring state ministers or even agency heads — positions the Alliance never staffed.[8] In that year, the Alliance also approved a leadership model that required the number of board members from a particular state or region to reflect the size of that regional association. For instance, a board member would be appointed once a region had sixty Alliance members, a second board member for 500, and a third for 2000, up to eight members. The total number of board members under this model would not exceed forty.[9]

The problem with this model, however, became finding board members. Of the forty-two people nominated for positions in January 1987, only fourteen agreed to serve. As Alan Neely wrote, the Alliance encountered "resistance to the idea of a nonpolitical alternative organization."[10] Individuals were unsure about leading a new organization with such a unique purpose. When the Alliance managed to find committed leaders to serve on the board, employment changes created problems. David Holladay, for instance, was a board member and pastor in Louisiana, but he moved to Florida during his term.[11] Finding replacements for individuals like Holladay was difficult. The Alliance consisted of individuals accustomed to the enormity of Southern Baptist infrastructure, so adjusting to a drastically smaller organization with a smaller pool of potential board members took time.

Early on, the Alliance pondered many questions and ideas about structure. It eventually settled on having one set of officers for the whole organization, rather than having one set for the organization and one for the board.[12] The Alliance also adopted a policy for a short time to return ten percent of its revenue to state or regional groups that would make requests "as they need money."[13] These groups fizzled so quickly, however, that the policy became unnecessary.

Of the ideas that stuck, the Alliance chose to be more inclusive in the nominations of organizational officers and to abandon the use of titles. In September 1987, a motion was made to require two of the five officers of the Alliance to be women and two to be laypersons. While the motion failed, the sentiment remained in the minds of both the leadership and general membership. The Nominations Committee often made officer selections with a desire to achieve diverse representation.[14] Additionally, the Structure Committee "recommended that in all mailings and listings of members no titles . . . be used" because "the use of titles [had] been confusing, plus some members [were] offended by such use."[15] In an attempt to value all persons as equal participants in the life and work of the Alliance, titles such as "Dr.," "Mr." and "Rev." were abandoned whenever possible.

When the Alliance hired Stan Hastey as executive director in November 1988, the board "recommended that the SBA office be moved to Washington, D.C., to be housed at First Baptist Church there."[16] The transition meant leaving offices at Myers Park Baptist Church in Charlotte, North Carolina, and moving to space with a more national perspective. After Hastey was hired, the organization hired Jeanette Holt as associate director. The presence of Hastey and Holt as employed staff, as well as a functioning board of directors, provided the Alliance strong leadership.

With the formation of the Cooperative Baptist Fellowship in 1991, the Alliance's organizational model began to break down, and the organization questioned whether or not its existence was even necessary. A year later, Hastey issued a memo to significant leaders and founders of the Alliance, calling for its dissolution. Hastey explained that the growth of the Cooperative Baptist Fellowship put too many financial pressures on the Alliance and that "from the beginning, the Alliance . . . told the world we would not perpetuate our structures for the sake of the structure." Hastey proposed that the Alliance help the Baptist Peace Fellowship of North America move its offices to the Washington, D.C., area and merge with that organization, while at the same time seeking office space from the Progressive National Baptist Convention. Hastey believed this would be a "significant statement to the Baptist world about the seriousness of our commitment to build bridges across the old racial and regional divides." He admitted that he had made inquiries about finding a new place of employment, and that if he found one, "the Spirit would open the way for me to have a significant ministry elsewhere."[17]

Hastey's proposal was rejected, and the Alliance began to forge a new, more streamlined structure. In 1995, the organization clarified policies for electing board members to include having two nominations from each state or regional chapter, while at-large directors would be chosen with consideration for geographic diversity.[18] That same year, the leadership chose to disband the Worship Committee and Public Affairs Committee. The work of the Public Affairs Committee was to be completed through Alliance representatives of partner organizations like the Baptist Peace Fellowship of North America and the Baptist Joint Committee on Public Affairs.[19]

In September 1996, Nancy Hastings Sehested "led the Board [of Directors] in a process of 'visioning for the future of the Alliance.'"[20] As the group began approaching its ten-year anniversary, Sehested wanted to re-evaluate its structure and overall mission. The following year, the leadership agreed to discontinue having state or regional board members, since the only active remaining state chapters were in Virginia, North Carolina and Georgia. The visioning process produced a mission statement that was added to the end of the Alliance Covenant. Aside from producing these tangible products, the visioning process also served to help members think about the organization's structure and the way the Alliance now functioned institutionally.

Again in 2000, a committee was appointed to examine the organization's structure.[21] At this time, tensions were rising within the American Baptist Churches USA, and "there was a need to bring West coast churches into the Alliance by providing them with information about how a church can affiliate."[22] The group was no longer composed of Baptists looking *for* help; the Alliance was looking *to* help.

Much was changing. In this year, the organization altered its bylaws to allow board members to serve one four-year term with a one-year break before returning for another four years, instead of two consecutive three-year terms.[23] The leadership also evaluated the standing committees, which now included the Congregational and Clergy Services Committee; Convocation Committee; Ecumenical and Interfaith Relations Committee; Budget and Development Committee; Missions Committee; Peace and Justice Committee; and Women in the Church Committee.[24] The following year, the Alliance held its first board meeting in Oakland, California, which offered the leadership a different perspective.[25]

During this period of transformation, president Welton Gaddy explained, "form follows function." He suggested that the Alliance needed to decide what its purpose was and how it could fulfill that purpose.[26] In response, Cherie Smith, an endorsed chaplain within the Alliance, and Chris Copeland, an associate minister at Oakhurst Baptist Church, sought to show that "members of groups beyond the SBC" were deeply involved in the organization. According to Smith and Copeland — two second-generation Alliance leaders — the group needed to better accommodate individuals coming from areas outside the Southern Baptist Convention. They saw the Alliance's identity as "no longer coming from who we aren't."[27] The Alliance was beginning to more fully understand its purpose beyond being simply a breakaway group from the SBC — and to reimagine what it could look like.

Smith and Copland became president and vice president respectively in 2004. Although the titles were a slight formality as they began to model a shared form of leadership that sought to reshape and guide the future leadership identity within the Alliance. The organization started a significant shift, which began with "changing titles for Alliance staff and . . . appointing a task force to explore how Alliance staffing might be restructured to model collegiality, mutuality and equity."[28] As a justification for these changes, Smith argued that the Alliance had "grown in ways our founders might not have imagined . . . we will need to learn together how to move ahead of this time of growth and discernment."[29]

Two years later, the Task Force on Staff Structure and Titles proposed a model that included "three full-time positions, with actual job responsibilities yet to be spelled out. Tentative titles [were] Minister of Stewardship; Minister of Leadership and Congregational Life; and Minister of Ecumenical and Missional Life."[30] Supporting this model was a risk, because the Alliance had never had more than two full-time employees. As the board of directors continued to review this model, executive director Stan Hastey expressed his belief that he could fit into the role of minister of ecumenical relationships and mission partnerships. Hastey's support was an important piece in the Alliance's attempt to make this change.

The transition to the new model of leadership affected the organization in multiple ways. First, it would shift the Alliance away from a hierarchical model of leadership. For years, Hastey served as executive director while Jeanette Holt served as associate director. The new model sought to remedy the disparity in recognition and compensation that came with those jobs.

Second, the board of directors attempted to shift the focus of the Alliance from Hastey and Holt to the membership. For years, Hastey and Holt served as the face of the Alliance. Smith and Copeland attempted to envision life after Hastey's and Holt's inevitable retirements, and the new leadership model placed a greater emphasis on enabling the congregations and members of the Alliance to take responsibility for the organization. Through the transition, Smith and Copeland shifted the work of the Alliance to the broader community.

Hastey, Holt and other leaders agreed with the move. Once the organization implemented the three-employee staff structure, Smith proposed that the board look to fill the tentatively titled position of minister of leadership and congregational life."[31] In 2007, the Alliance hired Copeland, its former vice president, to fill the position. To aid the transition to shared leadership, Alliance founder Mahan Siler agreed to facilitate monthly meetings between Copeland and Hastey.[32] Upon hiring Copeland, the Alliance also moved to employ a minister of stewardship.[33]

Holt retired in 2007 and expressed enthusiasm about the changes to staffing, but she wondered how administrative tasks would be covered.[34] In response to her concern, a part-time office manager was hired to help run the office in Washington. Recognizing the difficulty of this change, the board of directors agreed in September that the monthly sessions with Copeland, Hastey and Siler were beneficial and should be continued.[35] In the second decade of the 21st century, the Alliance staff continued to work through the shared model of leadership, acknowledging that the prospect of sharing power is an ongoing process that requires constant and open communication.

On the heels of implementing the shared model of leadership, the board in 2007 began to transition to making organizational decisions based on consensus voting.[36] The process was difficult for members who were accustomed to making decisions using Robert's Rules of Order, which was often used in church business meetings as well as Southern Baptist Convention meetings. Consensus voting rubbed against the historic Baptist principle of dissent. The decision-making process attempted to draw everyone to common understanding and agreement. Dissenting within this framework sometimes required long, drawn-out conversations and dialogues to come to a mutual understanding — something at which Baptists have historically not been very good.

In addition, the Alliance began a restructuring of the organization to incorporate more of the membership. In 2008, the board accepted "the recommendation to create 'communities' to do the ministry work of the Alliance and to expand the involvement of Alliance of Baptists people in its life and mission."[37] Rather than task forces or committees, the Alliance created "communities" around different topics and initiatives. Certain "closed" committees, including the Convocation or Gatherings Committee and the Finance Committee, remained active because of their importance, but the majority of the Alliance's work shifted to "open" communities.

Although proposed in 2008, the "communities" idea remained ambiguous and theoretical until 2011, when it became more concrete. According to the minutes from the 2011 fall board meeting,

> Communities shall serve as collaborative bodies of Alliance of Baptists persons who organize themselves for ministry and action.

Communities shall provide a place of belonging for Alliance of Baptists people within the Alliance but shall also seek a wider engagement with the Church and the world.[38]

This new, community-based structure sought to incorporate a wide range of individuals who were passionate about particular topics. The board of directors required each community to have a coordinator as well as a liaison from the Alliance staff.[39] Communities were able to submit budget requests and plan events as independent groups under the larger umbrella of the organization, and were "expected to reflect the values represented by the Alliance of Baptists Covenant and Mission."[40]

As the Alliance made these major changes, challenges and unforeseen issues emerged. The restructuring of the organization necessitated that the board of directors shrink from forty members to twenty.[41] The shared model of leadership compelled the Alliance staff to advocate for salary equality — "to share the responsibility of leadership equally among the leadership team."[42] Discussion regarding the need for a unified budget as opposed to both an operational budget and the Bridges of Hope "missions" offering initially failed to reach consensus, which raised questions about consensus voting.[43] By 2013, the unified budget became a reality, and 20 percent of undesignated giving went to the Alliance's ministry partners.

Many of the leadership's changes affected the organization in fruitful ways. By April of 2011, there were 19 active communities, and the board of directors continued to think of ways "to facilitate and aid the communities in remaining viable."[44] As of November 2012, the Equity for Women in the Church Community, the Justice for Palestine & Israel Community, and the Racial Justice and Multiculturalism Community were active in planning their own independent gatherings. The shared model of leadership continued to require attention as the organization transitioned through the retirement of Stan Hastey and the departure of Chris Copeland. By 2010, the Alliance leadership team of Paula Dempsey, Mary Andreolli and Carole Collins persisted in promoting shared leadership. In like manner, consensus voting remained new and difficult for members so accustomed to Robert's Rules of Order. The Alliance, however, strove to pursue these organizational changes to remain faithful to its covenant principles of servant leadership and "full partnership of all God's people."

Personalities in the Alliance of Baptists

Any treatment of servant leadership within a history of the Alliance of Baptists ought to address some of the individuals and personalities who embodied the concept and contributed to the formation and development of the organization. Anecdotally, Jeanette Holt claimed that the history of the Alliance is a history of the people who formed it. The relationship between the organization and its organizers, according to Holt, was inseparable. Throughout its history, the Alliance took on the personalities and interests of particular leaders. This section will address the contributions of a number of those leaders.

Alliance founder Alan Neely noted the importance of the organization's early leaders and identified specifically Henry Crouch, the first president. Prior to and during his tenure as president, Crouch served as pastor of Providence Baptist Church in Charlotte, North Carolina. Crouch took on much of the responsibility for helping the Alliance weather the first two years of its existence. Frank Gilreath and Dawn O'Neil helped him by working out of office space provided by Myers Park Baptist Church in Charlotte.[45] According to Neely, Crouch was one of the only founders with a significant reputation in the Southern Baptist Convention at the time.

As a servant leader and well-known pastor in Southern Baptist life, Crouch paid a price to lead the Alliance. Providence was one of the largest Southern Baptist churches in the state, and his father had been a longtime pastor of First Baptist Church in Asheville, North Carolina. Crouch had more to lose than any of the other Alliance founders.[46] He remained committed to the Alliance despite being slightly more conservative than much of the other leadership. In 1989, after mounting criticism within his congregation over his leadership in the new organization, Crouch offered to resign from the church. Despite the criticism, the congregation asked him to reconsider and offered him a vote of confidence. Crouch remained at Providence but never again had the same level of support. Many of the founders admitted anecdotally that without a figure like Crouch involved in the organization's formation, the Alliance would never have survived.

Mahan Siler, Jim Strickland, and Richard Groves were also influential figures in the founding of the Alliance. Siler was nominated to serve as the first president but declined, citing his potentially problematic role as pastor of Pullen Memorial Baptist Church, a congregation dually affiliated with the American Baptists and Southern Baptists. The Alliance leadership often called upon Siler to be a voice of wisdom and clarity because of his personality and his training as a pastor and counselor.

Strickland, a pastor from Georgia, received a nomination to be the first executive director but, like Siler, turned down the position to help ensure the early financial stability of the organization. Strickland also advocated for greater representation of women and became well known in the Alliance by bringing forward position statements at convocations.[47]

Groves served as pastor of Wake Forest Baptist Church and was the Alliance's first secretary and third president. During his presidency, Groves, along with Strickland, helped push the Alliance to be proactive with regard to racial reconciliation, particularly through partnership with the Progressive National Baptist Convention.

Susan Lockwood, Nancy Hastings Sehested and Ann Quattlebaum embodied servant leadership as well. Lockwood guided the Alliance as the first vice president. She pushed for inclusion of women and expanded the Alliance's early geographic outlook to include her congregation in Chicago — Cornell Baptist Church, later known as Ellis Avenue Church.

As president from 1996 to 1998, Sehested helped the organization move through a visioning process during its ten-year anniversary. Sehested, along with Lockwood, also advocated for greater inclusion of women within the group.

Quattlebaum, who served as the fourth president from 1992 to 1994, invaluably steered the Alliance through perhaps the most difficult part of the organization's existence. She navigated both the discussions about merging with the Cooperative Baptist Fellowship and the formation of the controversial Task Force on Human Sexuality.

In terms of Alliance employees, Stan Hastey and Jeanette Holt were instrumental in stabilizing the organization. Both Hastey and Holt came to the Alliance as former employees of the Baptist Joint Committee on Public Affairs. Hastey accepted the position as executive director in 1988, and Holt agreed to be associate director shortly thereafter.[48] Both tirelessly kept the Alliance afloat on a day-in and day-out basis for nearly twenty years. They sacrificed other employment opportunities and their own time and energy because, as Hastey explained, both believed they "were where [they] ought to be."[49]

At the ten-year anniversary of the Alliance of Baptists, humorous "Athletics Awards" were given to various members. Bill Puckett was recognized for leaving "his pastorate and his career" for the sake of the organization. The Alliance recognized Max Hill for making the "most 'illegal' mission trips" to Cuba. The award for "Most Offensive to Alliance Opponents" went to Priscilla Asbury for her "outstanding leadership on the Task Force for Human Sexuality."[50]

Other leading Alliance members were John Roberts, Walker Knight and Brooks Wicker. Roberts served as president from 1994 to 1996 and pushed for greater interfaith dialogue, particularly with members of the Jewish faith. Knight was an Alliance founder and founding editor of *Southern Baptists Today* (also known as *Baptists Today*). Wicker served in various financial and administrative capacities and filled the role of president from 2008 to 2010 during a significant staffing transition.

As the Alliance turned over leadership to another generation, new leaders emerged. After the relationship with *Baptists Today* ended, Sue Harper Poss produced the organization's newsletters for many years.[51] Todd Heifner worked as "fund development consultant" for a few years starting in 2004, helping the organization find some financial stability.[52]

Chris Copeland and Cherie Smith, as mentioned previously, led the Alliance through major organizational changes. Smith pushed the Alliance to embody a shared model of leadership as well as to encourage individual members to take ownership in the organization. Copeland shared this vision but also served as a staff member, contributing significant time and energy to developing the clergy recognition and endorsement processes.[53]

Alliance presidents Jim Hopkins and Carol Blythe contributed in meaningful ways as the organization adjusted to the 21st century. As president, Hopkins continued the work of Smith and Copeland and helped to include the voices of American Baptists. Blythe served as president from 2010 to 2014. As a Washington D.C. Metro area resident, she pushed the Alliance to become more involved in social justice and advocacy.

Paula Clayton Dempsey, Carole Collins and Mary Andreolli were also influential servant leaders in the second generation of Alliance staffing. Dempsey served as president from 2000 to 2002, and through her role as director of partnership relations became the face of the Alliance in the second decade of the 21st century. Collins guided the Alliance through financial difficulties in the mid-2000s and in 2009 became director of operations and finance. Andreolli worked for a number of years as a communications specialist and full-time employee, greatly aiding in the formation of the online marketplace known as Alliance*Connect*.[54]

While the founding of the Alliance of Baptists cannot be reduced to two people, if any two could be considered the respective mother and father of the organization, they would be Ann Thomas Neil and Alan Neely. Their work was so influential that in 2006 the Alliance approved the creation of the

"Anne Thomas Neil/Alan Preston Neely *Sustaining the Vision* Endowment Fund."[55]

Neil chaired the initial task force on women in the church, which became a standing committee that fought for the inclusion of female ministers and the use of inclusive language. She also served as the organization's third president in 1989. As a former missionary in Ghana and Nigeria, she greatly influenced the Alliance's approach to partnership missions, which in turn affected the overall understanding of its work and ministry.

As the first interim executive director, Neely volunteered countless hours and resources for the sake of the Alliance of Baptists. Neely, like Neil a former missionary, also influenced the Alliance's approach to partnership missions. He edited the first Alliance publication, *Being Baptist Means Freedom*; wrote "The History of the Alliance of Baptists" in Walter Shurden's edited volume *The Struggle for the Soul of the SBC*; and planned to write the first book-length history of the Alliance before his death.

Both Neil and Neely continued to serve the Alliance until their respective deaths in 2014 to 2003. Their work was surpassed by none, but accompanied by a great many. One should note that the individuals named and discussed here do not comprise an exhaustive list of everyone who embodied servant leadership for the sake of the Alliance. In reality, anyone who has served in any leadership capacity has risked much to lead this small band of progressive Baptists.

Clergy Placement, Recognition, and Endorsement

Since the founding of the Alliance, the organization has developed support services for servant leaders in positions of ministry, as well as for those looking for positions of ministry. To foster servant leadership within individual members and specifically among ministers, the Alliance recognized that it needed to provide help and support. Some of the services the organization provided included clergy placement, clergy recognition and chaplaincy endorsement.

From the Alliance's founding, the Ministry Placement Committee began channeling the résumés of individuals looking for jobs to churches that might be interested. Donald Retzer chaired this committee and matched prospective ministers with progressive congregations.[56] By 1988, the Alliance had received thirty-five applications, had placed one person, and had been in contact with twelve churches.[57] The Southern Baptist Convention never offered services like this, and for moderate or progressive Baptist ministers, placement aides were greatly needed because they struggled to find congregations receptive to their theological orientation.

By the late 1990s, the leadership began exploring the possibility of offering official recognition for Alliance clergy. A major question revolved around such recognition and the "appropriateness of providing assistance to churches in the ordination of clergy." Since Baptists held a strong belief in individual church autonomy, the Alliance solicited opinions from a number of Baptist historians as to whether offering assistance in the ordination process overstepped the bounds of church autonomy. Most scholars agreed that aiding the local church in the ordination process was a valid role for the denominational body.[58] In 1999, the Alliance board of directors affirmed a policy that stated, "Consistent with the historic role of associations in our Baptist heritage, the Alliance of Baptists will offer its services to congregations upon request in their processes of ordaining Alliance members to the ministry."[59]

Concurrent with the approval of ordination assistance and clergy recognition, the Alliance also sought to become "an endorsing body for counselors, chaplains, and ministers in specialized settings."[60] To become an endorsing body, the Alliance needed to "receive recognition [. . . from] the Association of Professional Chaplains; the American Association of Pastoral Counselors; and the Association for Clinical Pastoral Education, Inc."[61] The ability to endorse chaplains allowed the Alliance to become the supporting body for officially recognized hospital and military chaplains. The possibility of offering this service for military chaplains raised questions for some of the membership with more pacifistic sentiments, but the larger body affirmed the endorsement of military chaplains after much discussion and a workshop at the 2000 Convocation.[62]

In 2003, the Alliance developed a strategic plan focusing significant attention on clergy services that included placement, recognition and endorsement. In the plan, the Alliance made commitments to "increase pastoral placement of women in ministry and the awareness and participation of women in the church." In addition, the leadership sought to "increase the quality of ministry to those chaplains and pastoral counselors endorsed by the Alliance."[63] By 2003, the organization had endorsed ninety-five "chaplains and pastoral counselors" and begun looking for ways to support these ministers beyond mere endorsement. In the same year, the board of directors began discussing the creation of a minister registry to include personal information of ministers looking for placements as well as an "Affirmation of Ethical Behavior."[64]

When Chris Copeland became an employee of the Alliance, he spent a significant portion of his time refining the placement, recognition and endorsement processes. The clergy registry had grown out of control because of a lack of guidelines and oversight, which led to its termination. Copeland also recognized that the Endorsement Committee was receiving inquiries "from people currently endorsed by other groups, including SBC, CBF, ABCUSA and Quakers."[65] These were often people with no personal connection to the Alliance. Copeland developed a more in-depth process for evaluating candidates and guiding them through the process of recognition and endorsement. By 2010, the Alliance had endorsed more than 140 clergy.[66]

As the Alliance shifted to a system of "communities" rather than committees, the status of the Clergy Recognition and Clergy Endorsement Committees became muddled. Initially, the committees were recognized as independent "communities," but because of confidentiality issues, they were not open to the larger membership. Since the two committees operated on behalf of the larger body of the Alliance of Baptists, they were designated councils in 2011.[67]

Amid the creation and development of the processes of recognition and endorsement, the board had concerns regarding the "liability the Alliance might face concerning actions of endorsed persons."[68] The process of developing clergy services in legally responsible ways, which began in 2002, was long and difficult. By 2011, Carol Blythe began working with David Massengill, an Alliance board member and retired lawyer from Manhattan, to create committees or councils for endorsement, clergy recognition, and search and call. They sought to make sure that the board of directors was legally prepared to handle complaints about misconduct or other issues among recognized clergy and chaplains.[69] Discussion surrounding the Alliance's legal liability continued into the second decade of the 21st century. Although all parties desired to provide professional services to recognize and endorse clergy, reaching consensus on how best to do so proved difficult.

These programs of clergy support served a wide array of leaders within the Alliance network. The organization strove to maintain contact with its chaplains and recognized clergy throughout each calendar year, or at the very least at spring and fall convocations. Through its processes of placement, recognition and endorsement, the Alliance fostered a form of servant leadership in the lives of these individual Alliance members.

✦

In his 2002 Covenant Address, Alan Neely mentioned that few Baptists, if any, ever said anything negative about the fourth article of the covenant and servant leadership. Most Baptists agreed about the term but might disagree about what it meant. According to Neely, "A 'servant leader' is a contradiction in terms. Servants don't lead. They do what they are told." He claimed that for the Alliance,

> The historical background for our accentuating and underscoring servant leadership in the church was that in the 1970s and 1980s pastors were being told by the leaders of the 'super churches' that if you wanted to have a growing church, if you really wanted to have a big church, you had to have the fortitude to exercise your God-given authority.[70]

Neely contended that "the idea of an authoritarian or autocratic pastor appeared to be a polar opposite of the example of Jesus."[71]

For Neely and for the Alliance, the idea of servant leadership encompassed the totality of what it meant to lead as Christ led — to bring attention to such issues as the gap between the rich and poor, homelessness, adequate health care, a living wage, and mass incarceration.[72] This meant that authority should be shared rather than filtered down a chain of command. Servant leaders took responsibility, followed their passions and instincts, and gave their time and energy to support something greater than themselves. Mahan Siler once anecdotally claimed that one of the most remarkable aspects of the Alliance's history was how few egos there were. The Alliance fostered a commitment to service and leadership that stayed focused on the larger picture of serving Jesus and the "least of these."[73]

Certainly, conflicts arose and egos were present. Much like any organization, the Alliance at times failed to live up to its envisioned ideal. The model of shared leadership continued to cause difficulties into the second decade of the 21st century. There were differing opinions as to how the process of clergy recognition and endorsement should be instituted. As with any organization, disagreements arose regarding how the organization should look and function. Despite these difficulties, the Alliance attempted to sustain the larger vision outlined in its covenant and grounded in a commitment to servant leadership — leadership that strove for "full partnership of all of God's people."

Chapter 9

Theological Education

5) Theological education in congregations, colleges, and seminaries characterized by reverence for biblical authority and respect for open inquiry and responsible scholarship.

All of the Alliance's covenant commitments stemmed from the political struggle within the Southern Baptist Convention, but its dedication to theological education was perhaps the covenant principle that responded most directly to the controversy. As the inerrantists appointed trustees to all major institutions of the convention, the effects of the slow takeover of the Southern Baptist seminaries were most painful for moderate Baptists. As with any institution of higher learning, the seminaries formed and shaped their graduates through three years of theological training. In the late 1980s, Southwestern Baptist Theological Seminary was the largest seminary in the world, and the other Southern Baptist seminaries were by no means small. As trustees were appointed, faculty harassed and academic policies changed, many Southern Baptists saw their beloved institutions altered in drastic and unrecognizable ways. These events created the backdrop for this covenant principle.

As Baptist historian Walter Shurden explained in 1988, this tenet expressed a purpose, place and process — "Theological Education *in* congregations, colleges, and seminaries characterized *by* reverence for biblical authority and respect *for* open inquiry and responsible scholarship" (emphasis added). Shurden clarified the principle as a desire to cultivate within future ministers tender hearts, tough minds and trained hands.[1]

The controversy in the Southern Baptist Convention might have prompted the Alliance to focus solely on theological education in the context of seminaries, but the founders desired to include a commitment to theological education in local congregations as well. Over the years, the organization balanced its commitment to both seminary training and education in the local congregation.

In an attempt to show how the fifth Alliance Covenant principle evolved, this chapter is divided into two sections. The first addresses the Alliance's quest for a new seminary (particularly the founding of Baptist Theological Seminary at Richmond) and its involvement in seminary education more generally throughout its history. The second section discusses the pursuit of theological education in the local congregation, particularly with respect to resources and curriculum.

The Quest for a New Seminary

The quest for a new seminary was an important agenda item for the Southern Baptist Alliance in its first year (1987), but it was not a priority. Later that year, however, the first of the Southern Baptist seminaries "fell" (as moderate Baptists would anecdotally say), altering the Alliance's priorities.

In the fall of 1987, the board of trustees at Southeastern Baptist Theological Seminary in Wake Forest, North Carolina, reached an appointed majority of inerrantists. Conflict between the board and the administration soon led to an exodus of many faculty and administration, prompted by the resignations of president Randall Lolley and academic dean Morris Ashcraft. Many individuals within the Alliance were connected to the seminary, and many moderate congregations relied on students from Southeastern to fill positions in their churches. In the wake of these events, the Alliance began to explore more diligently how to respond to the need for moderate Baptist theological education.

The Alliance leadership was initially unsure how to handle the inerrantist "takeover" of Southeastern. In a letter to the Alliance Executive Committee, president Henry Crouch asked whether or not the organization should help the faculty and students or look to start a new seminary. He acknowledged that already Wake Forest University, Mercer University and even First Baptist Church in Greenville, South Carolina, the church where Southern Baptist Theological Seminary was founded, were considering beginning a new seminary.[2]

In September of 1987, the Issues Committee recommended the formation of a Task Force on Theological Education to "consider the current situation in denominational seminaries and to consider and recommend alternative forms."[3] By the time the Alliance appointed the task force, some Baptist universities were already beginning to contemplate establishing divinity schools. The task force agreed to "dialogue with universities" and "give creative thought as to how theological education can be done in non-traditional ways."[4] By March of 1988, the Task Force on Theological Education contacted moderate Baptists in Virginia and at Wake Forest and

Mercer universities. In Virginia, the task force discovered that "there [was] no interest in establishing a divinity school." With regard to Wake Forest, Richard Groves commented, "Wake Forest is proceeding seriously but cautiously." Tom Conley, a minister from Georgia, reported that Mercer would make a decision by December of the same year.[5]

By September 1988, the leadership was enthusiastic about a number of possibilities that had emerged from the conversations of the newly formed Theological Education Committee. Support developed within the board of directors for the creation of a Duke Divinity School Baptist House of Studies, as well as the "active conversation" regarding the potential of a divinity school at Wake Forest University.

Besides the Theological Education Committee, another response to the events at Southeastern emerged through meetings with the American Baptists. The Alliance and American Baptists appointed a committee to examine the state of theological education. The committee included ABCUSA representatives Larry Greenfield, Harold Germer and John Kinney, and Alliance representatives Morris Ashcraft and Alan Neely. This group considered the possibility of using the resources of Andover-Newton Theological Seminary, Colgate-Rochester Theological Seminary, Eastern Theological Seminary and Virginia Union School of Theology to create a "proposal based on the model of Oxford University and Regents Park."[6] (Regents Park is a Baptist college within the larger Oxford University system that trains Baptist ministers all across Europe.)

The joint committee greatly influenced the work of the Alliance's Theological Education Committee. In November of 1988, the Alliance board continued to affirm the opportunities at Wake Forest and Duke, but also began to examine the possibility of starting a seminary in Richmond with the help of pre-existing theological schools in the area, such as Virginia Union College and Union Theological Seminary. The proposed seminary sought to draw on the work of the joint American Baptist and Alliance committee proposal. The Alliance board approved the hiring of a development person "to develop the resources of the fund for theological education for the amount of $250,000 ($49,000 is already on hand)," but this decision proved to be premature, as no individual was hired.[7]

At the same time it was examining alternative avenues of seminary training, the leadership created a task force with the intention of establishing "procedures for responding to persons who have lost their positions with denominational agencies." While the structure of this task force remained undefined, the Alliance recognized the need to help individuals affected by the inerrantist "takeover" — specifically the faculty of Southeastern Seminary.[8] The loss of a moderate presence at Southeastern was a jarring change to Baptist life in North Carolina and Virginia. Even the Theological Education Committee announced the need for an Alliance "fund for theological education" to pledge support for current faculty and students.[9]

While the Alliance was examining alternative avenues for seminary training, it invested a significant amount of resources to aid individuals affected by the events at Southeastern and elsewhere. In 1987, the board gave $5,000 to Southeastern, and in 1988 another $1,000. In June of 1988, the board approved $4,271.50 to cover legal fees of the faculty.[10] In 1990, the Alliance gave a token $100 to acknowledge and support the struggle of Southern Seminary faculty members, as well as $1,441 for the International Seminary in Ruschlikon, Switzerland. In addition to the monetary contributions, the Alliance board spent time and energy crafting a statement to express "support for all faculty, staff and students in SBC seminaries who are seeking to pursue the truth of God with integrity during these difficult days for Southern Baptists."[11]

This was a busy time in the Alliance's history. The organization was attempting to rescue and save people and institutions affected by the inerrantist movement while at the same time envisioning an alternative avenue for theological education. In 1989, the Theological Education Committee reached an agreement to suggest the "establishment of a school in Richmond for the preparation of ministers, in hopes that it [would] be a cooperative venture between the Southern Baptist Alliance and the theological institutions in Richmond and elsewhere." The school was to be "distinctly Baptist in terms of the Baptist heritage . . . racially and gender inclusive . . . [and] would include . . . opportunities for hands on practice in ministry . . . while seeking excellence in scholarship." The faculty eventually determined the school's curriculum, but the proposal offered several suggestions that included educational opportunities surrounding "globalization studies" and "praxis on personal, ecclesial and social/public levels."[12]

The committee's proposal, however, did not pass unanimously, as not all members favored the recommendation.[13] When the committee presented the proposal at the annual gathering of the Alliance in 1989 in Greenville, South Carolina, considerable discussion took place. Some members of the Alliance thought the idea of a new seminary was premature, while others, like Southeastern faculty member Elizabeth Barnes, felt the need was urgent, particularly for the sake of supporting and training female ministers. The debate ran over the allotted time, and the gathering ended the business session and began to worship. In worship, Catherine Allen of the Women's Missionary Union delivered a message advocating that the Alliance strive to be a middle-of-the-road organization, which rubbed a number of individuals the wrong way. After worship, seemingly in response to Allen's message, the membership voted overwhelmingly to move forward with the creation of Baptist Theological Seminary at Richmond (BTSR).

According to Stan Hastey, the debate surrounding BTSR was contentious because of the dynamics between the graduates and faculty of Southern Baptist Theological Seminary (Southern) and those of Southeastern Baptist Theological Seminary (Southeastern). He wrote,

> there has been tension between [Southern] and [Southeastern] since 1959 and the influx of fired faculty members onto the [Southeastern] faculty. Some of those people and many of their students are still around and have the memories of pachyderms! Beyond that, an understandable institutional jealousy also has colored relations between the two schools, with [Southeastern] in the role of younger sibling trying to outdo the first-born . . .(Larry McSwain [Dean of Southern] . . . resigned his Alliance membership in anger over the tone of the debate and subsequent action to proceed with the new school.)[14]

The rivalry between Southern and Southeastern exemplified the divisions among "moderate" Baptists in the late 1980s. Those loyal to Southern believed it would always be a bastion of "moderate" theological education. Persons connected to Southeastern, on the other hand, already had witnessed the inerrantist takeover of their institution, and they did not believe or trust that Southern would be able to avoid the same fate.

Some individuals like Mahan Siler, pastor of Pullen Memorial Baptist Church, were surprised by the final vote to create BTSR.. Their surprise stemmed from the drastic change of attitude before and after worship. Siler believed that transforming "that kind of emotional response to a more substantial response [would] be quite a challenge."[15]

Once Baptist Theological Seminary at Richmond was founded, the school became its own entity, separate from the Alliance. The leadership was leery of creating another system like the Southern Baptist Convention, which oversaw and controlled its seminaries. Morris Ashcraft, former dean of Southeastern, became the acting president until the school opened in 1991. Tom Graves, an Alliance member and pastor of St. John's Baptist Church in

Charlotte, North Carolina, became the first official president. That year, the Alliance board commended "the Baptist Theological Seminary at Richmond in its election of Dr. Thomas Graves as its President."[16] Although the Alliance maintained a substantive role in founding the institution, it could not by itself sustain the school financially.

In 1992, Alan Neely suggested that the seminary might be the Alliance's "most obvious legacy." This physical institution was a direct response to a need that the Alliance saw and filled. Reflecting on the formation of BTSR a few years after the school's founding, Hastey remarked, "at the heart of the vision of BTSR is the Alliance Covenant principle that theological education cannot and must not be divorced from the local church, that the best theological training is rooted in the congregation."[17] Admittedly, however, BTSR would have never been established without the help of the Baptist General Association of Virginia and the Cooperative Baptist Fellowship. The Alliance never had the funds to support its own freestanding institution of theological education.[18]

While some individuals might contend that BTSR was the Alliance's most obvious legacy, the organization did not stop exploring other possibilities for supporting seminary training. In November of 1989, the Alliance moved to continue discussions with Wake Forest, Duke, Emory and Vanderbilt for alternative forms of theological education.[19] Another possibility emerged from Pullen Memorial Baptist Church, which began to examine the feasibility of a two-year congregational residency program as an addendum to a seminary degree. This type of program exemplified some of the creative ways members of the Alliance were looking to supplement the standard three-year seminary education.[20]

While the freestanding Baptist Theological Seminary at Richmond served as a considerable achievement for the Alliance, the organization also helped found many Baptist houses of study. In 1999, Stan Hastey acknowledged the Alliance's role in founding the Baptist houses of study at Duke Divinity School, Chandler School of Theology at Emory University, Brite Divinity School at Texas Christian University, and Wesley Theological Seminary. These programs better exemplified the Alliance's ministry model. Rather than a freestanding, independent institution, these houses of study relied on partnerships with schools from both Methodist and Christian Church (Disciples of Christ) traditions. As with BTSR, however, the Alliance did not have the resources to sustain these programs financially.

When Baptist Theological Seminary at Richmond first opened its doors in September of 1991, the Theological Education Committee recommended giving it five percent of the Alliance's budget. The committee also recommended giving $1,200 for Baptist houses of study at Candler School of Theology and Duke Divinity School.[21] BTSR was often identified as the first Baptist seminary to emerge in the wake of the inerrantist controversy, which is true; however, the houses of study at Candler and Duke were also operational in 1991. While not freestanding institutions, they represented initial responses to the need for seminary education among moderate Baptists in the late 1980s and early 1990s.

The formation of the Cooperative Baptist Fellowship in the early 1990s undoubtedly helped the Alliance pursue alternative forms of seminary education in the context of formal higher education. After the Alliance and the Cooperative Baptist Fellowship decided not to merge, CBF agreed to assume much of the financial responsibility for BTSR, Duke's Baptist House of Studies, Candler's Baptist House of Studies, and all scholarships for divinity and seminary students. Starting in 1993, BTSR no longer appeared "as either a line item in the operating budget or as part of [the Alliance's] mission offering."[22] The agreement took financial stress off the Alliance, but in some ways it hindered and limited the organization's role in supporting seminary education. Without a financial investment, making an impression on future ministers and leaders had to take place more organically.

According to Jeanette Holt, part of the arrangement between the Alliance and the CBF stipulated that they would "not duplicate funding appeals for the same ministries and institutions." Holt spoke at Candler's Baptist House of Studies program in 1993, where many students had the "temptation . . . to write off the whole enterprise" of the CBF. Holt, however, suggested a "kind of critical involvement with the Fellowship." She encouraged the students to use the CBF to find "their support networks" while sharing "a vision of ministry with those in the Alliance."[23] Holt expressed hope that students could benefit "in a variety of ways" from both the Alliance and the CBF.[24]

Students occasionally wrote to the Alliance for scholarship money. In March of 1993, Stan Hastey responded to one student by explaining the agreement between the CBF and the Alliance as well as the new method for distributing scholarship money. According to Hastey, "all such [student] scholarships will be issued by the CBF." Hastey explained that the CBF further stipulated, "all such scholarships will be granted only to students attending non-Southern Baptist Convention institutions."[25]

By 1995, despite relinquishing much of its financial support for students and schools to the Cooperative Baptist Fellowship, the Alliance continued to try and serve students in seminary and divinity school degree programs.

The Theological Education Committee reached out through "invitations for student attendance and seminary exhibits at the 1995 national Convocation . . . [and] Expressions of the willingness . . . to assist with church placements after graduation."[26] Students welcomed the hospitality, encouragement and support of the Alliance. In 1998, one student from BTSR wrote to thank the Alliance for choosing to host the following year's convocation in Richmond as well as to say, "I have never felt more comfortable as I did at the Convocation. You have given me a place to be."[27] This repeated outreach to students continued within the Alliance over the years. Hastey noted in 2004 "a renewed interest in the Alliance on seminary campuses, a trend we must nurture continuously."[28]

By the start of the 21st century, the Alliance's relationship with BTSR had slowly waned to the point that it had little connection with the school. Jeanette Holt wrote in 2004 to Kathy Gore Chappell, the school's vice president for advancement and community life, with the intent of re-establishing the connection. Holt wrote, "At least once a year I try to come to the campus and meet with students who are interested in using our placement service or who simply want to learn more about the Alliance. Can I use you and your office to help with arrangements for such a visit?"[29] The relationship, at this point, was largely ceremonial because of the Alliance's inability to be a significant financial contributor to the school's budget. From time to time, the Alliance was even forgotten as the school's founding organization. At the 10th Anniversary Convocation of BTSR, the *Religious Herald* (a Virginia Baptist newspaper) published an article that failed to acknowledge the Alliance's contribution to the school's birth.[30] Examples like this further strained the relationship between the school and the Alliance.

In 1999, Holt proposed the creation of a Founders Day fund that would "support an annual 'Founders Day' event each year to highlight and celebrate the partnership and principles that produced BTSR originally."[31] A Founders Day event continued over the years, allowing the Alliance to celebrate the achievements of BTSR as well as allowing BTSR to honor its founding organization without financially burdening either entity.

By the second decade of the 21st century, the Alliance of Baptists recognized only three seminaries in the United States as partner schools — Brite School of Divinity, Wake Forest School of Divinity and Andover-Newton Theological Seminary. The Alliance did not offer any financial assistance to these institutions but did support them from an ideological perspective.

The Alliance found ways to support theological education financially through its international ministry partners. Beginning in 1999, Stan Hastey explained, "Internationally, we are seeing the beginning of a new trend in theological education as the [Southern Baptist Convention's] International Mission Board gets out of theological education. This gives us an opportunity to step in and fill some gaps."[32] That year, a surplus of missions money led to the organization giving $2,500 "to the seminary in Liberia through the Baptist Missionary and Educational Convention of Liberia for students doing home missions work during their holiday breaks."[33] The Alliance also provided financial support for seminary training and education through its ministry partners in Zimbabwe, the Republic of Georgia and Cuba — an interesting phenomenon that highlighted the Alliance's commitment to international ministry as well as theological education.

The Pursuit of Theological Education in the Local Congregation

When the Southern Baptist Alliance formed in 1987, its commitment to theological education in the context of the local congregation centered upon a reactive desire to have theologically sound Sunday school material. As inerrantists began gaining influence in various institutions, many moderate Baptists feared the Southern Baptist Convention's Sunday School Board would stop producing material for a more progressive audience. Eventually, however, the Alliance transitioned to an innovative and proactive approach to theological education principally through a web-based marketplace of resources and curriculum known as Alliance*Connect*.

The idea of producing alternative Bible study material emerged from the first meeting in December 1986 in Charlotte, North Carolina.[34] Those in attendance were disappointed with the ideological trajectory of the material being produced by the convention's Sunday School Board. As the possibility of producing an alternative curriculum became more of a reality, some leaders grew concerned that "producing our own literature be the first step toward becoming a new convention." They asked, "Would publishing tend to compromise our position as 'loyal opposition'?"[35] They feared producing alternative Sunday school literature might be too political an action for the Alliance.

Despite the differing opinions, the Alliance slowly moved forward in its production of an alternative Bible study curriculum. As early as 1987, Everett Gill proposed that the already-raised $5,000 for educational materials be used to fund a survey through *Southern Baptists Today*. Founded in 1983, *SBC Today* was a publication edited by well-known Southern Baptist journalist Walker Knight to serve a more moderate audience within the convention. Since the Alliance partnered with this publication for printing its newsletter, using it for market research was a natural suggestion. The money was used to survey the newspaper's readership with regard to interest in alternative educational resources, as well as to provide Gill a stipend to collect and categorize the responses.[36]

Despite the desire for a more theologically sound curriculum, complications arose that kept the appointed Task Force on Literature from meeting during the first year of the Alliance's existence. For the new organization, coordinating people's schedules between Alliance board meetings and Southern Baptist Convention annual meetings was difficult. In addition, the Alliance did not have the budget necessary to pay travel expenses for board meetings or for the meetings of multiple task forces.[37]

As the leadership became more organized and intent on producing alternative resources, members of the Southern Baptist Sunday School Board, including Lloyd Householder and Lloyd Elder, became "distressed."[38] The Sunday School Board supplied educational material to nearly every Southern Baptist congregation, and the possibility of alternative literature threatened its fixed market. Both Householder and Elder believed they could work with inerrantist members on their board of trustees to produce more moderate material, but Stan Hastey was skeptical of their ability to do so. Hastey, however, forwarded this information to the Literature Committee to let the committee make its own decision.[39] The group agreed with Hastey that there was a need for educational materials free from any inerrantist influence.

Producing curriculum, however, was no easy task. The Alliance did not have the infrastructure or resources necessary to publish. Robert Fulbright, a minister of education from Third Baptist Church in St. Louis, Missouri, devoted himself tirelessly to developing a curriculum, both in terms of content and of financial feasibility.[40]

Fulbright was convinced that Kerygma, a non-denominational Christian publishing house, could effectively produce educational materials for the Alliance. The decision to begin a new seminary, however, strained financial resources and put pressure on the Literature Committee to find an economical approach to producing Sunday school material. Fulbright attempted in June of 1989 to partner with Kerygma to produce a product for market research among Alliance congregations.[41] Initially, Kerygma was interested in producing an eight-week study that would serve as field-testing and market research. The estimated budget was $50,000.[42] Despite interest among churches, the Alliance could not feasibly expend financial resources of this magnitude on an eight-week market study.[43] By November of 1989, Welton Seal, chair of the Literature Committee, reported "a stalemate [had] developed with Kerygma over the cost of developing new adult Sunday School Material."[44]

Once the Alliance leadership realized that cooperating with Kerygma was not an economic possibility, the Literature Committee decided to move forward independently with a market study. The committee met in February 1990 to devise a plan for a study that would be financially feasible for the young organization.[45] A number of options presented themselves, from the Kerygma proposal, to working with Judson Press, the American Baptist Publishing House, to a low-cost and high-cost Alliance-produced study.[46] The board of directors agreed that the most fiscally responsible approach would be a low-cost, six-month study that would follow the lectionary texts.[47]

When Fulbright brought a motion to the board to test a Bible study curriculum from Advent 1991 to Easter 1992, the motion passed "without objection."[48] Slowly, the venture became not only a project of the Alliance, but also of the Cooperative Baptist Fellowship. In December of 2000, Fulbright began contacting writers and drafting a handout with their biographies and photos to be used at both Alliance and Fellowship meetings.[49]

Despite Fulbright's hard work, the project was turned over to Smyth and Helwys, a publishing house that emerged concurrently with the formation of the Cooperative Baptist Fellowship. Smyth and Helwys, in turn, published a curriculum that would serve a wide swath of moderate Baptist life, from the Alliance to the Cooperative Baptist Fellowship.[50]

In addition to Fulbright's six-month study, Welton Seal, chair of the Literature Committee, pushed the idea of producing alternative Sunday school materials in *SBC Today*.[51] A curriculum partnership with the newspaper began in 1989 with the intention of publishing supplemental commentaries to the Southern Baptist Sunday school literature. The use of the newspaper in this way benefited both the Alliance and *SBC Today*. Most of the feedback regarding the commentaries was positive, and some congregations began ordering enough subscriptions to supply their Sunday morning classes.[52]

By March of 1991, however, the Alliance had transitioned entirely from creating its own publications and literature to this "joint venture with Smyth and Helwys."[53] Materials from both the partnership with *SBC Today* and the six-month test curriculum were turned over to the new publishing house. Additionally, Fulbright and Seal had previously been in talks with the educational ministries of the American Baptist Churches USA about producing a joint curriculum. Although the Alliance intended for Smyth and Helwys and Judson Bible Series to jointly produce the material, Smyth and Helwys wound up producing the curriculum independently. Smyth and Helwys began with a larger prospective market, so there was less need to partner with another publishing outfit.[54]

In addition to producing Sunday school material, the Alliance published three books in its early years of existence — *Being Baptist Means Freedom, The New Has Come,* and *For the Living of these Days. Being Baptist Means Freedom* included chapters on each Alliance Covenant commitment, and the content was drawn from speeches initially delivered at the first convocation in Raleigh, North Carolina. The work, edited by Alan Neely, also included study questions for use as an educational resource. In 1988, the Alliance approved using the profits from *Being Baptist Means Freedom* to publish a book on women in ministry (*The New Has Come*), to be edited by Anne Thomas Neil and Virginia Neely.[55] Sales from this book were low, result- ing in the Alliance withholding further publication ideas. *For the Living of these Days,* produced in the mid-1990s, served as a hymnal supplement for churches desiring to have more inclusive and diverse hymns and liturgical resources.

Through its earliest years, the Alliance's commitment to theologi- cal education within the local congregation remained largely reactive. A more proactive approach did not begin to form until 1996. At the request of Ken Meyers, a minister of Christian education in Jacksonville, Florida, the Alliance began "inviting Christian educators to develop congregational resources and models which enhance theological education in churches." The leadership also encouraged "the creation of a regular Christian educa- tion feature in Alliance publications."[56]

That same year, the Theological Education Committee reiterated a commitment to theological education in the congregation by recommending that Jean Kim of the American Baptist Churches USA be invited to pres- ent a workshop on her organization's education materials at the upcoming Alliance convocation. Another recommendation included having Meyers and Bill Rogers, former dean of the School of Christian Education at Southern Seminary, lead a workshop in March for Christian educators. In 1999, the committee recommended that the organization's convocation theme center upon theological education and the tenth anniversary of Baptist Theological Seminary at Richmond.[57]

During the mid to late 1990s, the Alliance extended its emphasis on theological education in the local congregation. The Theological Education Task Force pushed Christian educators to attend the 1997 convocation with "two workshops of special interest to them."[58] Through workshops and various materials, including *Rightly Dividing the Word of Truth, Pursuing Justice* and *Care For the Earth*, the Alliance sought to provide resources for churches to educate their congregations on issues of sexual orientation, social justice, and environmental justice.

The next significant effort in the Alliance's proactive commitment to theological education in the local congregation began in 2009 when work began on an "online Resource Market Place." The organization planned on "having a soft launch in the spring and full launch by the 2010 convocation."[59] The process took significantly longer, but the Alliance remained committed to the idea of a web-based platform where ministers could share ideas and resources, individuals could purchase materials, and communities within the Alliance could meet online. This web-based platform became known as Alliance*Connect.*

Bringing the idea into reality was not easy, as the organization did not have unlimited resources. In 2011, the Alliance looked for help and began "writing a grant proposal to the Carpenter Foundation . . . to assist with our Resource Market Place initiative."[60] By the following year, the Alliance moved forward with developing Alliance*Connect* while knowing that the decision would likely result in a $25,000 deficit for 2012.[61] The vision of a web-based hub for resources and virtual meeting space remained a priority.

In November of 2012, Alliance staff member Mary Andreolli gave an update on Alliance*Connect,* pointing out that the platform would "be introduced to the broader membership at the annual gathering."[62] At the meeting in 2013, Andreolli and the rest of the staff unveiled Alliance*Connect.* Unfortunately, the platform malfunctioned and had to be shut down. One of the programmers on the design team quit over issues pertaining to the Alliance's "stand on sexual equality," resulting in a loss of vital software.[63] After a year of retooling, the Alliance unveiled the platform at the 2014 annual gathering in Portland, Maine. Alliance*Connect* marked a transition for the Alliance from an organization trying to produce Sunday school literature in reaction to the Southern Baptist Convention to an organization attempting to create an innovative, web-based resource marketplace.

✦

The history of the Alliance's commitment to theological education was a long and winding path from conventional and reactive to imaginative and proactive. When the Alliance formed in 1987, the threat of losing institutions like the Southern Baptist seminaries and the Sunday School Board meant that the organization needed to create alternative systems and structures that supplied theological training and produced curriculum. As the Alliance developed this reactionary identity, it was unable to sustain or support the structures it created. Eventually, Baptist Theological Seminary at Richmond, the Baptist House of Studies at Duke, the Baptist House of Studies at Candler, and the effort to create educational curriculum passed from the Alliance to the Cooperative Baptist Fellowship.

In time, the Alliance began to take a more proactive attitude toward theological education, even though it was rife with growing pains. Instead of supporting big institutions of theological education, the Alliance by the second decade of the 21st century had partnerships with Andover-Newton Theological Seminary, Brite Divinity School and Wake Forest University School of Divinity. These partnerships were more relational than financial. Paula Dempsey, minister of partnership relations, greatly aided the Alliance's relationship with students at these schools.

The creation of Alliance*Connect* also served as a significant step forward in the Alliance's proactive approach to theological education, particularly at the congregational level. The platform attempted to provide congregations and individuals a database of resources and venue for connecting with people of like minds and similar interests. Aside from the challenges of creating this system, its launch generated the need for marketing the platform and teaching individuals how to use it. To help market the new resource, the Alliance hired Ken Meyers in the winter of 2014.

The Alliance remained committed to theological education on a variety of levels, although one area it struggled with was its commitment to theological education on college campuses. Groups like the Cooperative Baptist Fellowship, or state Baptist associations and conventions like the Baptist General Association of Virginia, fulfilled the need for official campus ministries among moderate Baptists on some campuses. Any Alliance connection to these institutions, however, was left to individual involvement. Despite the Alliance's lack of official presence on university grounds, the organization realized a firm devotion to theological education at both the congregational and seminary level.

Chapter 10

The Proclamation of the Good News

*6) The proclamation of the Good News of Jesus Christ and the
calling of God to all peoples to repentance and faith, reconciliation
and hope, social and economic justice.*

The proclamation of the Good News of Jesus Christ was a practice that
resonated with the early members of the Southern Baptist Alliance.
Spreading the gospel through both national and international missions was
one of the primary reasons for the formation of the Southern Baptist Convention in 1845. At the Alliance's first convocation, Anne Thomas Neil praised
the convention of her childhood for instilling in her the idea that "Proclamation was not about scaring children or adults into Heaven. Proclamation
was calling us into an empowering relationship to be Christ's persons in the
world."[1] Neil was a missionary to Nigeria for nearly twenty-seven years, and
while she praised Southern Baptists for their commitment to proclaiming the
good news, she grieved about the lack of attention they placed on corporate
sin. She explained that the word "oppression" did not appear in her "childhood vocabulary."[2]

Neil believed the Alliance needed to speak against forces of oppression
like racism, classism, sexism and militarism. She argued that the mission
and ministry of the Alliance must resist the tendency of Southern Baptists
to "set [their] own agenda without listening first to the voice of other world
Christians."[3] Instead, she advocated that the Alliance "must come together
in a spirit of mutuality and partnership with other Christians from around
the world and write the agenda together."[4] The Alliance needed to relinquish
the perceived elitism of American Christianity to more faithfully proclaim
the gospel.

Alan Neely, a former missionary in South America, also advocated
for the Alliance to adopt a partnership model of missions. Inspired by the
thoughts and experiences of these two individuals, the organization developed its particular method of missions and ministry. So influential were Neil
and Neely that in 1994 some of the leadership proposed changing the Global
Mission Offering's name to the Alan Neely/Anne Thomas Neil Global

Mission Offering "contingent upon the approval of Anne Thomas Neil and Alan Neely." Neil expressed the wish that such action not be taken in 1994, and the offering's name became "Bridges of Hope" instead.[5]

In 1999, at the request of Woodbrook Baptist Church pastor John Roberts, Neely produced a study titled *A New Call to Missions: Help for Perplexed Churches*. Its purpose was to differentiate the various missiological perspectives and approaches of the Southern Baptist Convention, Cooperative Baptist Fellowship and Alliance of Baptists. Even twelve years after the formation of the Alliance, many churches struggled to understand which organizations to fund and the differences between each.

Through his study, Neely found that the Alliance's understanding of missions did not fully form until after the formation of the Cooperative Baptist Fellowship. Neely contended that unlike the Cooperative Baptist Fellowship, the Alliance did not begin "as a missionary sending body or a 'missions'" agency."[6] By the time the Alliance formally named a Missions Committee and began taking up a Global Missions Offering, the Cooperative Baptist Fellowship was beginning to form. Despite attempts at a merger, both organizations mutually agreed to remain separate entities, leaving the question of missions up for debate. The Alliance agreed to relinquish all of its "mission projects" to the CBF, but the CBF refused to accept all of the projects. Among the organizations not accepted were the Fraternity of Baptists in Cuba, the STRIVE after-school program in inner-city Chicago, the Baptist Peace Fellowship of North America, and Baptist Women Ministry.[7]

Because of the CBF's refusal to fund all of the Alliance's partner organizations, the Alliance "faced an unfortunate dilemma." As Neely wrote, "Either [the] partnerships with the Fraternity of Baptist Churches [in] Cuba and others had to be abandoned, or the Alliance had to continue its own modest mission program. The Alliance decided to continue to do missions."[8]

As the Alliance continued to establish itself as an organization that supported missions, it remained committed to a partnership model of ministry. While this included funding other organizations and projects, "the purpose of the financial aid [was] to enable, not to control."[9] The Alliance attempted to find not just ministries aligned with its spirit and covenant, but partnerships that represented geographic diversity and "visionary risk-taking."[10] Because of this, the Alliance joined with organizations often marginalized and "denied assistance by the SBC and CBF."[11]

One of the weaknesses of the Alliance's partnership model, however, became publicizing and promoting the ministry work of the organization. According to Neely, "the Alliance . . . failed to generate the necessary awareness, excitement, and support."[12] One of the reasons for the failure stemmed from the Alliance's commitment to partnership. Individuals and congregations were accustomed to seeing the "tangible fruits" of their denominational body. Within the Alliance, however, these "tangible fruits" were produced by partner organizations, which were subsequently shared and celebrated within the Alliance. Promoting and publicizing these "shared fruits" was a continual process within the Alliance into the 21st century.

For the purposes of sharing the Alliance's commitment to the proclamation of the good news, the rest of this chapter will be divided into three loose sections — "Proclaiming the Good News in the United States," "Proclaiming the Good News Internationally," and "Proclaiming the Good News through Justice and Advocacy." One note on semantics: The word "mission" has historically been used as an umbrella term, but as the Alliance evolved, "ministry" or "partnership" became a substitute. The word "mission" continues to bear colonial implications. Throughout this chapter, "ministry" will be used most frequently, and "mission" will be used where historically relevant.

Proclaiming the Good News in the United States

Origins of the Alliance Missions Committee

The Missions Committee of the Southern Baptist Alliance was formed in 1988 to "find and promote ways of participating in world evangelism with integrity" and to "find ways of magnifying the signs of the Kingdom in reconciliation and hope, peace and justice, hunger relief, and systemic reform of oppressive structures."[13] As Alan Neely explained, the Alliance did not begin as a missions-oriented organization in part because it remained loosely connected to the Southern Baptist Convention for its first four years. During this period, projects and partner organizations were included within the Alliance's overall budget. The Missions Committee required these "SBA Projects" to submit a "request form" for review, and upon approval, a member of the committee visited the project and made recommendations to the larger committee and subsequently the board of directors.[14]

The first project supported by the Alliance was a pastoral salary supplement for Shalom Baptist Church in Louisville, Kentucky.[15] A few months later, in November 1988, the organization approved three additional ministries that included Covenant Baptist Church in Georgia, Missionary Counseling and Support Services in North Carolina, and an ad hoc committee with a budget of $20,000 to support individuals dismissed from their jobs.[16] This committee represented an extremely important component of the Alliance's early history of ministry. As "inerrantists" began holding more and more positions of power within the Southern Baptist Convention, more and more "moderates" lost their jobs. At the time, $20,000 was a large sum of money for the Alliance, but the leaders found this ministry particularly important as they watched friends and colleagues lose their jobs and, in some cases, even their health.

Michael Willett of the Foreign Mission Board lost his job because of his "moderate" beliefs. Because of the prominence of Willett's position, the Alliance adopted a resolution that expressed "support for Dr. Willet as he [sought] new opportunities for service."[17] Moderate Baptists like Willett were plentiful, and the Alliance chose to view aiding them in both financial and non-financial ways as one of its earliest ministries.

Alliance members and congregations first participated in a "Global Missions Offering" in 1990. The organization set an ambitious goal. In November of the previous year, the leadership suggested "a special missions offering be promoted among our members and churches in February of each year. That the goal . . . be $100,000."[18] The organization initially decided to divide the Global Missions Offering into four equal parts — Foreign, Domestic, Partnership and Theological Education. The distribution percentages were altered, however, to reflect "30% for foreign projects, 30% domestic projects, 30% partnership projects, 10% theological education projects other than BTSR." The motion passed, but the 16-14 vote revealed considerable opposition.[19] These percentages never became formulaic or rigid criteria for ministry funding, but are helpful to show how some persons within the Alliance approached the issue and how divided the leadership was about funding ministry opportunities.

While the board of directors struggled to come up with equitable ways to allocate the mission dollars, by March 1990 it recognized that the final tally for the Global Missions Offering amounted to only $25,000 — a quarter of the goal.[20] For the next year, "the board approved . . . a 1991 Global Mission Offering goal of $55,000 with a challenge goal of $60,000 to place two missionaries outside the USA through the American Baptist Churches."[21] Again the Alliance fell short of its goal. The idea of supporting missionaries failed to represent the ministry identity the organization was beginning to develop. Supporting missionaries, however, was the identity with which the leadership was familiar. Relearning what it meant to proclaim the gospel in an organization significantly smaller than the Southern Baptist Convention was a long process for the Alliance.

The following year, the leadership guided and urged one another to "rediscover who we are, break out of old ways of thinking, stand with the oppressed as reconcilers supporting causes that others may consider too risky."[22] Such a call went out from the board of directors because the Alliance's membership and budget were slowly decreasing in the wake of the founding of the Cooperative Baptist Fellowship. By 1995, the Alliance began to figure out how to continue its partnership ministries effectively, but the organization struggled to get churches to participate in the missions offering. That year, the board reported "no more than a third of Alliance churches [were] promoting the offering . . . It doesn't compete with the CBF's global missions offering nor does it duplicate any other sources of funding in the Baptist world for the recipients."[23]

In response to the report, the Alliance changed the name of its Global Missions Offering to "Frontiers of Hope — Alliance of Baptists Mission Offering" to ensure that its name did not overlap with the Cooperative Baptist Fellowship's.[24] The Alliance hoped the change might clear up any confusion that churches had regarding where their mission dollars went. While funding different ministry partners helped define the organizations' respective mission offerings, there was eventually some overlap in supported ministries as the two bodies developed their identities. Talks between the two organizations regarding where they might be able to work together took place over the years, although formal organizational arrangements never coalesced.[25]

Also in 1995, the Alliance reiterated its commitment to an ever-expansive ministry presence in the world. That year, the Missions Committee expressed a wish to see mission partners of "like mind and spirit" with the Alliance, but also advocated finding ministries with "geographic diversity" and organizations that dreamed "new dreams and imagine[d] new and sometimes risky ministries."[26] By always advocating for diversity and creativity in its ministry partners, the Alliance established a large footprint in the world (with respect to the organization's small size) through the numerous ministries offered by its partners.

Despite its influence, however, the Alliance struggled to create an impact through planting churches. Within a few years of the organization's founding, a discussion took place within the leadership about beginning to plant churches. In 1990, individuals like pastor Bob Balance of Youngsville Baptist Church in North Carolina thought it was important to start Alliance churches that were not dually affiliated with other Baptist groups. As executive director, Stan Hastey acknowledged such desires, but believed that church planting was problematic because the organizational mission statement claimed that the Alliance would work within the SBC. Hastey further qualified his remark by explaining that a revision of the mission statement was in progress and a church in Gainesville, Florida, was beginning to imagine what it might look like to form a solely Alliance-affiliated congregation.[27]

Most of the church planting supported by the Alliance was not traditional. The Alliance partnered predominantly with existing church plants in need of funding. As mentioned earlier, the first project approved by the Missions Committee was financial support for Shalom Baptist Church in Louisville, Kentucky, "requesting $75 per week to fund an Associate Pastor."[28] In the late '80s and early '90s, the Alliance provided salary support for a number of either "welcoming and affirming" congregations or churches employing a female minister. The model of supporting existing churches supported the Alliance's identity as an organization that partnered rather than independently started congregations.

Interfaith Relations

Over the years, the Alliance attempted to proclaim the gospel and calling of God through fostering positive interfaith relationships. Brought to the attention of the Alliance most prevalently during the presidency of John Roberts, these efforts formally addressed the relationship of Alliance members with people of the Jewish and Islamic traditions.

At the 1995 convocation in Vienna, Virginia, the Alliance held the first Christian service at the Holocaust Museum in Washington, D.C. Members of the Jewish community were invited to participate in and help lead in the service. Rabbi David Kline found the service particularly meaningful and remarked in a letter afterward, "I feel honored, as though selected to represent the Jewish people at a historical moment for Christianity . . . Reading Torah as part of your service challenged me with a fresh sense of religious interaction . . . What is going on here, I am convinced, is a millennial turning point."[29] A letter from Kline's wife Barbara read, "David and I could not stop talking to anyone who would listen about the historic declarations made by your Alliance that Sunday."[30]

At the gathering, the membership adopted "A Statement on Jewish-Christian Relations." It acknowledged the participation of Baptist Christians in perpetuating a theological understanding that historically made enemies out of the Jewish people. The statement also included a confession of sins of "Complicity . . . silence . . . indifference and inaction to the horrors of the Holocaust." In addition, the Alliance, member congregations, and individuals renounced ways of interpreting scripture that fostered "religious stereotyping and prejudice against the Jewish people." The statement also called for seeking genuine dialogue between the two faiths as well as education about the history of Jewish-Christian relations.[31]

Following the 1995 convocation, the Alliance appointed its first Committee on Interfaith Relations.[32] Three years later, the committee recommended that the board of directors endorse a trip to Israel arranged by Roberts, and to send the statement on Jewish-Christian relations to all member congregations. Recalling the Alliance's support of the Interfaith Alliance in its first years of existence in 1994 and 1995, the committee also recommended continuing to support the work and ministry of the organization.[33] Support for the Interfaith Alliance continued into the 21st century, not only because of the organization's mission to promote religious diversity and combat religious and political extremism, but because Alliance member and future president Welton Gaddy began serving as the president of the Interfaith Alliance in 1998.[34]

The Committee on Interfaith Relations helped the Alliance understand the Islamic faith in the wake of the events of September 11, 2001. But even before the tragic events of 9/11, in April of 2001, the committee had begun a "preparation of study materials on relations between Muslims and Christians and a position statement on that relationship."[35] After a time of discernment and thought, the Alliance in 2003 passed "A Statement on Muslim-Christian Relations," similar to the statement on Jewish-Christian relations. The statement acknowledged the role of Baptist Christians in perpetuating a theological perspective that failed to recognize the history and diversity within the Islamic faith. Like the statement on Jewish-Christian relations, the statement on Muslim-Christian relations confessed sins of complicity and silence with regard to "defusing hatred . . . between Christians and Muslims." Admitting that "Islam has always presented a theological challenge to Christians," the statement further called for an affirmation of shared historical roots with the Islamic faith. The Alliance membership was urged to promote dialogue, education, and religious freedom, "including the right to practice the faith of one's choice . . . whether in the US or elsewhere."[36] These interfaith initiatives were two of many ways the Alliance attempted to apply the proclamation of God's calling to all people.

Other U.S. Partners and Funding Procedures

The Alliance also partnered with other ministries over the years, including programs for homeless individuals like the Emmaus House in Raleigh, North Carolina, and the Oakhurst Recovery Program in Decatur, Georgia, and programs for children and youth like Baptist Youth Camp, Rauschenbusch Metro Ministries in New York City, and STRIVE, an educational program in Chicago for students in grades 1 through 12. Other ministry partners that emerged in the 21st century included the Edna Martin Community Center in Indianapolis, Indiana, the Samaritan Neighborhood Ministry in Oakland, California, and the Hyaets Community (The Family Tree), an intentional community in Charlotte, North Carolina.[37]

When the Alliance began talks with the United Church of Christ in 2009 to facilitate a summer missions learning experience for students beginning in 2010, it chose existing ministry partners to place students.[38] The Hyaets Community, Rauschenbusch Metro Ministries and STRIVE all became partner locations. The Alliance and UCC placed ministry interns or summer staff at multiple locations, providing students an opportunity to learn and serve. The program also provided partner ministries with additional summer help.

The Alliance retained some of its partnerships for years, while others received funding for only a few years. The diversity, variety and turnover of partners were due in part to the funding process. The Alliance underwent many procedural changes in regard to funding organizations through the Bridges of Hope Global Missions Offering. Despite these alterations, the process always required organizations to reapply for funding on a yearly basis.

In 1999, the Alliance laid out application guidelines that required all partners to turn in grant requests "by August 1 each year."[39] The deadline often frustrated and complicated certain organizational relationships with the Alliance. By 2003, the primary reasons projects failed to receive funding were "1) the application was incomplete or 2) the connection with the Alliance was unclear."[40] The process of reapplication was tedious for some organizations, but it allowed the Alliance leadership to better attend to the needs of different partner ministries on a year-to-year basis. The procedure remained in constant flux. In 2011, the Alliance looked "to revise the Mission Partner application so that this application [reflected] more of [the] relational, partnership philosophy of doing mission."[41] Two years later, the adoption of a unified budget again altered the funding of partner ministries.

The development of the Bridges of Hope Global Missions Offering continued into the second decade of the 21st century. As partner ministries ran their course and new ministries emerged, the Alliance continued to alter its process for funding partner ministries in the United States.

Proclaiming the Good News Internationally

Foreign missions had been a significant component of Baptist life in America since the early 19th century. At the founding of the Southern Baptist Alliance, many Southern Baptist missionaries worried about the ramifications of the political struggle between inerrantists and moderates within the Southern Baptist Convention. Their worries revolved around whether their positions would be affected if and when the "inerrantist" party took control of the Foreign Mission Board (now known as the International Mission Board) in Richmond, Virginia. Because of limited financial resources, the Alliance never seriously considered addressing the possibility of adopting or sponsoring full-time missionaries of its own. The Alliance also questioned whether "missionaries" were the most cost-effective method for spreading the gospel. Nevertheless, the Alliance remained concerned about the state of international missions within Southern Baptist life.

Through contacts with members at Pullen Memorial Church, including Roger and Mary Ruth Crook and Alan Neely, the Alliance developed an understanding of "global mission" through its relationship with the Fraternity of Baptists in Cuba. So influential was the Cuba partnership that it served as the litmus test for all other international ministry partners the Alliance cultivated. Ministries were founded in places such as Zimbabwe, Morocco, Sri Lanka, the Republic of Georgia and Brazil, among others. Each of these international partners evolved from a unique story that intersected with various individual members of the Alliance.

Cuba — The Fraternidad de Iglesias Bautistas de Cuba

In 1991, the Alliance invited Rev. Francisco "Paco" Rodés and a delegation from the Fraternity of Baptists in Cuba to attend its annual gathering in Richmond, Virginia. All expenses were covered.[42] The Fraternity of Baptists had separated from Cuba's larger Western Baptist Convention in 1989 because of theological differences.[43] Stan Hastey introduced and welcomed the Rev. Rodés and the other members of the group in his State of the Alliance Address, saying, "We rejoice in our new partnership with our new friends from the *Fraternidad de Iglesias Bautistas de Cuba*, whose own experience as disinherited, dispossessed people so closely parallels our own, and whose presence among us these days in Richmond so enriches our gathering."[44]

The relationship between the Alliance and the Fraternity of Baptists greatly energized Hastey. As a child of former missionaries in Mexico, he recalled the Spanish from his childhood on his first trip to Cuba in 1993. He returned from this trip in September, "determined to work for strengthening this very special relationship, primarily by encouraging partner-church relationships between Alliance churches and the . . . more than two dozen congregations in the Fraternity."[45] Through personal conversations, Hastey acknowledged that the Fraternity was a driving force behind his twenty-year tenure as executive director of the Alliance.

Max Hill, another member of the Alliance, made numerous trips to Cuba. He reported in 2003 that there were twenty-four churches in formation in the Fraternity. "Hill affirmed the Alliance partnership with the Cuban Baptists citing the values as contact that breaks isolation, expressions of concern, exchanges of resources, affirmations of worth, and a constructive outlet for missions impulse."[46] Eventually, most of the Fraternity congregations in Cuba developed partner Alliance congregations in the United States.

Over the years, the Fraternity sent many members to the United States on visits, while many Alliance churches likewise took individuals on trips to Cuba. These were not mission trips but multicultural immersion experiences for mutual edification and fellowship. For Hastey, the Alliance's relationship with the Fraternity included the primary objective of fostering "people-to-people and church-to-church contacts." If any element of "mission" existed within the Alliance's relationship with the Fraternity, Hastey explained that "for our part in the Alliance we also have engaged in one of the most precious of our rights as citizens by redressing our collective sense of grievance to our own government over the tragic and ongoing breach in relations between the United States and Cuba."[47]

Beginning in 2001, the Alliance adopted a statement on Cuba at every annual meeting except two (2005 and 2008). These resolutions evolved to address different issues over the years. The earliest addressed the economic embargo imposed by the United States from the early 1960s into the 21st century. In 2006, the resolutions began to address increased travel restrictions to Cuba that often made partnership difficult, although not impossible. In 2005, the Alliance and "numerous other national religious bodies [were] denied new [travel] licenses upon the expiration of those previously in effect."[48] In 2012, the Alliance began to encourage the release of the

"Cuban 5" — Cuban intelligence officers who were arrested in 1998 and convicted on "suspicious charges."[49]

The Alliance annually provided financial support for the Fraternity. Aside from a yearly lump sum generally given for the Fraternity's operating expenses through "Bridges of Hope," the Alliance helped raise support for the Fraternity in more directed and substantial ways. In 1997 and 1998, the Alliance applied for grants from the Myrtle Arnall Mann Missions and Scholarship Committee of Central Baptist Church of Newnan, Georgia. The Alliance received $20,000 the first year and $60,000 the next.[50] The money from these grants helped fund larger projects, such as securing a car and helping to find office space for the Fraternity of Baptists. Less than ten years later, in 2006, Jerry Kerns of Greenville, South Carolina, began working on establishing, with help from the Cooperative Baptist Fellowship, a Baptist House of Studies, to be named in honor of Alan and Virginia Neely, on the campus of the Evangelical Seminary of Cuba in Mantanzas.[51] The Baptist House was planned to help train ministers for the growing Fraternity.

Zimbabwe —
The Theological Seminary of Zimbabwe

In April 1997, Stan Hastey, David Waugh, Bonnie Dixon and Rachael Tanner visited Zimbabwe and Henry Mugabe, then principal of the Baptist Theological Seminary of Zimbabwe. The Alliance had begun providing financial support for the seminary prior to the visit, and Mugabe explained that without the gifts the seminary would have closed. "Its virtual abandonment by the [national] convention out of which most of us came had left Baptist Seminary of Zimbabwe in that precarious of a position."[52] The Alliance sponsored the trip with the intention of creating "a stronger partnership with Alliance congregations patterned after that of the Alliance and the Fraternity of Baptists."[53] A formal partnership with Zimbabwe began a few months later, in September.[54]

The partnership was in many ways the result of the relationship between Mugabe and Tom Graves, president of Baptist Theological Seminary at Richmond. Mugabe attended Southern Baptist Theological Seminary for his Master of Divinity and Ph.D. degrees, and during his time in the United States in the 1980s and early '90s, he met Graves. When Mugabe began looking for financial support for the Baptist Theological Seminary of Zimbabwe, Graves directed him to the Alliance.[55]

The Alliance held partnerships with both the seminary and the Baptist Convention of Zimbabwe for many years. According to Hastey, Zimbabwe had an "economic situation so grim it defie[d] description."[56] When the "inerrantists" took control of the Southern Baptist Convention in the early 1990s, Southern Baptists withdrew significant funding from organizations that did not directly engage in converting new Christians. For Baptists in Zimbabwe already experiencing economic difficulty, this loss of funding considerably hurt their operations — particularly the seminary. The Alliance stepped in to help individuals like Mugabe continue their ministry.

In 2007, the Alliance had concerns with how its money was being spent within the Zimbabwe Baptist Convention.[57] These concerns remained for a number of years. Since the Zimbabwe Baptist Convention was still a Southern Baptist entity, eventually the "inerrantist" political agenda became a reality abroad. The convention in Zimbabwe remained in a theological conflict into the year 2011. That year, the Alliance waited to send money until it could discern "the most appropriate way to disperse funds."[58]

In 2011, the Baptist Theological Seminary in Zimbabwe fired Mugabe for refusing to sign the Baptist Faith and Message 2000. Mugabe, having witnessed the political fight between "moderates" and "inerrantists" during his time at Southern Theological Seminary, left along with all but one of his faculty. The following year, the faculty founded the Zimbabwe Theological Seminary, and the Alliance began directing its funding there.[59] In 2014, Mugabe reported that a group of Baptist churches in Zimbabwe had broken away from the Baptist Convention of Zimbabwe to form their own organization, known as the African Baptist Churches in Zimbabwe, which adopted the Alliance Covenant as its guiding document.[60]

Morocco — Karen and Kevin Smith

In 1997, Karen Thomas Smith, an early Alliance member, expressed hope that the organization could become "connected with" her ministry in Morocco. A few years earlier, she and her husband Kevin had moved to Morocco, where he taught at the Al Akhawayn University while she led "an ecumenical Christian community of 20 some-odd folks . . . on campus." She believed her ministry in Morocco was "true to the Alliance spirit in all [its] work."[61] After initial discussions, the Alliance served as a conduit for funding the Smiths' ministry in 1998, and by 2000, the ministry received funding through the Alliance's Bridges of Hope Ministry Offering.[62]

Most of Karen Thomas Smith's work at the university involved facilitating interfaith dialogue. She often spoke at local churches and provided a valuable educational opportunity as a Christian representative on the university's campus. Many of the students who studied at Al Akhawayn had never known a Christian or were "unfamiliar with Christianity."[63]

In 1994, prior to connecting the Alliance with their work in Morocco, the Smiths were turned down for money by the Cooperative Baptist Fellowship. According to the rejection letter, the CBF claimed to "only send missionaries. We do not send medical missionaries, technological missionaries, or anything else." The letter also said, "The Global Missions Office will not stand in judgment upon those who do not make converts, but sooner or later we will stand in judgment upon those who do not try."[64] Since the nature of Karen Thomas Smith's work was ecumenical, she did not qualify to be a missionary through the Cooperative Baptist Fellowship. The Alliance, sympathetic to unwanted projects, intervened to support this ministry in its earliest years. By the second decade of the 21st century, CBF joined the Alliance in supporting the Smiths' ministries in Morocco.

Sri Lanka — Sri Lankan Baptist Sangamaya

In 2002, Shanta Premawardhana, an Alliance board member and pastor of Ellis Avenue Baptist Church in Chicago, presented information to the leadership regarding Baptists in his home country of Sri Lanka. He reported that a "working Committee of the Sri Lanka Baptist Sangamaya [was looking to] decide about inviting a partnership with the Alliance."[65]

A year later, through Premawardhana, the Alliance began a partnership with the Sri Lankan Baptist Sangamaya. As Stan Hastey explained in his 2004 State of the Alliance Address, Sri Lankan Christians "struggle in the face of repressive anti-conversion laws and sometimes outright violence."[66] As a group committed to religious liberty, the Alliance was quick to support Baptists experiencing oppression from their national government. That year, Rev. Kingsley B. Perera of the Sri Lankan Baptist Sangamaya was invited to attend the Alliance convocation, with the option of also visiting Chicago and Ellis Avenue Baptist Church.

Three years into the partnership, the Alliance heard rumors from those within the Sri Lankan Baptist Sangamaya that some of its leaders were against partnering with the Alliance. In 2007, the Alliance board approved a trip to Sri Lanka to speak with representatives of the Sangamaya. Conversations took place "about that partnership and its future, especially in light of some expressed disagreement with the Alliance's stated positions on sexual orienta-tion."[67] Representatives of the Sangamaya were unsure as to whether they should continue to partner with the Alliance. After the talks, the partnership ended over differences in theological outlook, particularly in regard to issues of sexuality.

The Republic of Georgia — Evangelical Baptist Union of Georgia

Roger and Mary Ruth Crook were longtime aids to the Alliance in making connections with Baptists in Cuba, but they also helped the orga-nization connect with the Evangelical Baptist Union in the Republic of Georgia. At times, Stan Hastey relayed his questions through the Crooks regarding the status of the Georgia partnership. In 2002, "Mary Ruth and Roger Crook from North Carolina introduced [to the board of directors] their guest, Malkhaz Songulashvili, an ordained Baptist minister and presid-ing bishop of the Baptist Union of the Republic of Georgia, which was formerly part of the Soviet Union."[68] Two years later, the board discussed the expansion of international partners to include the Baptist Union of the Republic of Georgia.[69] After becoming partners, Bishop Songulashvili, pastor of the Cathedral of Tbilisi, served as the primary contact. Eventually, Bishop Rusadon Gotsiridze also served as a contact.[70]

Over the course of the partnership with the Republic of Georgia, the Alliance helped fund the School of Elijah, a ministry of the Evangelical Baptist Church of Georgia. This school worked to bring together representa-tives from eastern and western Christian traditions for "dialogue, education, training, contemplative prayer, iconography, and liturgy."[71] In the summer of 2014, Paula Dempsey, director of partnership relations, and a group from Pullen Memorial Baptist Church took a trip to Georgia to further foster this partnership.

Brazil — *Aliança de Batistas do Brasil*

In 2004, the Alliance held a breakout session on "A New Call to Mission . . . in Brazil." The session description read,

> In recent years, changes within the SBC's mission philosophy have focused almost entirely on evangelism and church planting while abandoning Christian medical and educational ministries. Yet, a progressive movement among small pockets of Brazilian Baptist

pastors and intellectuals is forming at this very moment. To make religion relevant to the poverty of so many in their country, these Baptists are incorporating the spirit of Latin American liberation theology into the Baptist churches for the first time.[72]

Contacts with this new Brazilian group were made through Devaka Premawardhana, the son of Alliance board member Shanta Premawardhana. Through this breakout session and other discussions within the leadership, the groundwork was laid to meet with the Brazilian Baptists with the hope of forming a new international partnership. By 2006, the Alliance included Brazil in its Bridges of Hope Global Missions Offering.[73] Stan Hastey explained two years later that this "group of Brazilian Baptists . . . have so identified with us as to adopt our mission and vision statements."[74] Much like the Alliance and the Fraternity of Baptists in Cuba, the *Alianca de Batistas do Brazil* formed within the Baptist Convention of Brazil as a group disillusioned with the direction of its larger national convention. The partnership continued to thrive into the second decade of the 21st century.

✦

The international partnerships described in this chapter remained the more formal and successful collaborations, but over the years the Alliance also attempted and considered a number of other partnerships that never fully coalesced. For instance, in 1997 the Alliance received contact from the *Seminario Evangelico de Puerto Rico*, a Baptist-related ecumenical seminary in Puerto Rico. Hastey exchanged letters with the school administration, but little became of the relationship.[75] In 2006, the Alliance began thinking about a partnership with the Evangelical Baptist Union of Italy. Contacts through Baptist Theological Seminary at Richmond and Palmer Theological Seminary in Philadelphia were not enough, however, to overcome the lack of financial resources available to form a sustainable working relationship.[76] As an organization focused on partnerships, however, the Alliance also celebrated the international relationships of various partner congregations that had relationships with ministries in Nicaragua, Ecuador, and El Salvador.

It is also worth noting that the Alliance in its early years was sympathetic to the idea of sending missionaries. In 1990, the organization examined the possibility of appointing missionaries through the American Baptist Churches, but the estimated cost was "$28,000 for a single person/$56,000 for a couple per year."[77] Financial limitations made such missionary appointments unfeasible. Even when the Alliance began developing a ministry of partnership, the organization considered, as late as 1997, how it might support two missionaries from College Park Baptist Church in Greensboro, North Carolina. These missionaries, a husband and wife, were rejected for mission work by the Cooperative Baptist Fellowship because the wife was "non-U.S. born and not re-baptized as an Adult." The Alliance was energized to write and object to the decision of the CBF as well as "reinstate conversations with . . . American Baptist Churches, about this case."[78] The leadership discussed the situation at length at that year's spring and fall board meetings.[79] Rejected and unwanted causes always generated passionate and considerable discussion within the Alliance, even if those causes cut against the organization's mission model.

As the Alliance matured as an organization, its partnerships became less and less organizational and more and more personal and congregational. Facilitating this transition was a 2004 ministry project called *Face to Face*, which allocated monies to bring individuals from the international partners to the United States for annual Alliance meetings.[80] By the second decade of the 21st century, Alliance members in the United States were appointed to serve as contact persons for the various international partnerships. This helped take pressure off Paula Dempsey, director of partnership relations.[81] In addition to allowing Dempsey to focus on other ministry opportunities, these liaisons allowed the Alliance to shift the work of the organization from solely the responsibility of the employees to include the membership of the Alliance.

Proclaiming the Good News through Justice and Advocacy

The idea of Proclaiming the Good News through Justice and Advocacy was never prominent within the life and ministry of the Southern Baptist Convention. When the Southern Baptist Alliance formed, the founders were intentional about becoming an organization committed to social and economic justice; however, developing this identity was a learning process. In the first years of the organization's existence, the Baptist Joint Committee for Religious Liberty and the Baptist Peace Fellowship of North America served as the group's justice and advocacy partners. By the 21st century, the Alliance's pursuit of justice and advocacy functioned more significantly through the routine adoption of resolutions and through partnerships with other advocacy organizations, including the National Farm Worker Ministry and Churches for Middle East Peace.

Since the Baptist Joint Committee for Religious Liberty will be addressed in the following chapter, this section will discuss the Alliance's relationship with the Baptist Peace Fellowship of North America and its evolving commitment to justice and advocacy.

Baptist Peace Fellowship of North America

Since the Alliance's founding, the organization has maintained close ties with the Baptist Peace Fellowship of North America (BPFNA). Stan Hastey once claimed BPFNA's "sense of mission and purpose most parallels" that of the Alliance.[82] The Peace Fellowship was part of the first Global Mission Offering in 1990, and according to Ken Sehested, then executive director of the Peace Fellowship, the Alliance's contribution was greatly appreciated, as his organization at the time had "more bills than money." With an increased budget allocation the following year, the Peace Fellowship became a regular recipient of the Global Missions Offering.[83] When the Cooperative Baptist Fellowship cut funding to BPFNA because of the organization's position on LGBT inclusion in 1995, the Alliance saw an opportunity to continue its support as a "ground-breaking, seed-planting, risk-taking movement of freedom-loving Baptists."[84]

The Baptist Peace Fellowship of North America was founded in the mid-1980s as a venture of Baptists in Mexico, Puerto Rico, the United States and Canada. The organization, however, traced its purpose and history back to those Baptists who became conscientious objectors during the First and Second World Wars. By the second decade of the 21st century, BPFNA described itself as an organization that "gathers, equips and mobilizes Baptists to build a culture of peace rooted in justice. We labour with a wonderful array of peacemakers to change the world."[85]

Because the Peace Fellowship was an international organization, it often helped connect or keep the Alliance connected to different international partners. From time to time, the Peace Fellowship requested funds to support trips in conjunction with Baptist happenings outside the United States. In 1993, Ken Sehested requested money to help send Rev. Isabel Docampo, a Southern Baptist-ordained Cuban American, to Nicaragua for the first ordination of a woman by Nicaraguan Baptists.[86] Other opportunities arose over the years, as in 1999 when the Alliance partnered with BPFNA to sponsor a "Friendship Tour to Puerto Rico."[87]

The Alliance also worked with the BPFNA staff and organization to produce congregational curricula. In 1999, Cathy Tamsburg, an Alliance

board member, released a curriculum called *Pursuing Justice.*[88] The following year, the two organizations worked together on a curriculum on LGBT
issues in the church titled *Rightly Dividing the Word of Truth* (addressed in
Chapter Five.)

In 2005, largely prompted by members of BPFNA, the Alliance decided
to "create a file of conscientious objectors" and to endorse a statement that
acknowledged the witness of conscientious objectors.[89] Into the second
decade of the 21st century, both organizations continued to send representatives to each other's annual gatherings and sustained a significant overlap in
membership.

Statements and Advocacy

In many ways, the history of organizational statements and advocacy
began at the 1990 convocation in St. Louis, Missouri. Prior to that meeting, Alliance founder Jim Strickland informed the board of his intention to
bring "A Call to Repentance."[90] The declaration called the Alliance to declare
that "as members of the Southern Baptist family, [we] publicly repent and
apologize to all African-Americans for condoning and perpetuating the sin
of slavery."[91] The following year, Alliance president Richard Groves delivered
the statement at the Progressive National Baptist Convention's annual meeting. It was received with a standing ovation.[92] While the statement was a
significant milestone in the history of the organization, it did not prompt or
cause the Alliance to become a racially diverse and inclusive group.

The issue of racial inclusivity returned to the organization's agenda in
2002 after a few years of stagnant relations with the Progressive National
Baptist Convention. Prompted by the presence of new board member Willard
Bass, an African American divinity student at Wake Forest School of Divinity, Stan Hastey spoke of a desire for the Alliance to become more racially
inclusive. He said, "We have done better on paper in including [minori-
ties] in our governance, but we have a long way to go."[93] In his State of the
Alliance Address that year, he exclaimed,

> As long as we remain an overwhelmingly Caucasian body, we have
> work to do. As long as women remain limited in fulfilling their
> vocations, we have much work to do. As long as gay men and lesbi-
> ans 'are wounded or ignored by the church,' to cite a phrase from
> our Mission statement, we still have much work to do. As long as
> we remain content with a lifestyle that exploits the Earth to our
> own selfish desires, that tolerates cruelty to animals and the rape of

natural resources, we have work to do . . . And as long as we acqui-
esce in systemic evil that dooms any of God's children to protracted
poverty and entrenched injustice, the Lord knows we still have
much work to do.[94]

In the years following Hastey's address, the Alliance tried to become
more inclusive and more socially conscious. It looked to become more aware
of how it could better proclaim the good news of repentance and faith,
reconciliation and hope, social and economic justice.

To increase social awareness, in 2004 the Peace and Justice Committee
recommended that the Alliance "participate in a one-day diversity training to
be led by Crossroads," an organization that specialized in antiracism training
and organizing. Jim Hopkins and members of the committee wanted "the
Alliance to be one of the religious groups leading in dismantling racism."[95]
Two years later, the Alliance adopted a revised "Statement on Racism and
Repentance," in which it claimed its commitment

> to discerning the ways in which racism is present in the Alliance of
> Baptists. We commit ourselves anew to an intentional process of
> becoming an anti-racist organization. We commit ourselves anew to
> the establishment of meaningful relationships with communities of
> color. We commit ourselves anew to the full inclusion of persons of
> color in the paid staff and volunteer leadership of the Alliance. We
> commit ourselves anew to address issues of importance to commu-
> nities of color at each meeting of the Alliance of Baptists.[96]

Through this training and other events in subsequent years, the Alliance
made great strides toward racial inclusivity, although it still had much work
to do to become a multicultural organization.

Since the organization's founding, the Alliance had always been socially
conscious, but it took some time before the group found an effective way
of making its voice public. For instance, in 2001 the Peace and Justice
Committee endorsed the "Day of National Concern about Young People
and Gun Violence."[97] That same year, the Alliance held a breakout session
titled "When Violence Comes to Church, Part I: the Produce of Inequity and
the Church's Response." The session description read, "Focusing on violence
toward children, panelists will lead participants in understanding this societal violence and engage us in developing concrete ways in which our faith
might address it."[98] Breakout sessions, however, only raised the awareness

of individuals within the Alliance and did not strengthen the organization's public voice.

At the ten-year convocation, Stan Hastey called for the Alliance to consider how 1 percent of America's population owns 40 percent of the nation's wealth — more than is owned by the bottom 90 percent. He explained that 800 million people are chronically hungry, and 358 billionaires in the world hold greater wealth than the combined annual income of half the global population.[99] The following year (2008), the Alliance approved supporting legislation to increase the minimum wage by $1 over the next two years.[100] While this approval began moving the Alliance toward a more public voice, that voice remained fragmented and certainly did not comprehensively address justice issues.

In 1999, the board of directors expressed support for the Farm Labor Organizing Committee's boycott against the Mount Olive Pickle Company in North Carolina.[101] A year later, the Alliance approved financially supporting the National Farm Worker Ministry.[102] Three years later, Cathy Tamsberg expressed "the need for an Alliance representative to attend a May meeting of the National Farm Work Movement."[103] Thanks to the persistence of Tamsberg and others, this partnership grew and remained a continuing relationship into the second decade of the 21st century.

Prior to 2009, the statements and resolutions of the Alliance were dedicated primarily to standing in solidarity with international partners on ecumenical and interfaith issues. In addition, resolutions opposing the death penalty, calling for peace in the Middle East, and supporting same-sex marriage were adopted in 2000, 2002 and 2004, respectively.[104] None of this is to say that the Alliance did not have a public voice or that it was not effective, but public declarations remained random and sporadic during the organization's first twenty years of existence.

With the election of Carole Blythe as president in 2010, however, the group's advocacy work and public platform drastically increased and became significantly more unified. Blythe, the daughter of an American Baptist minister and resident of the greater Washington, D.C., area, served as president from 2010 to 2014. The year prior to her presidency, Blythe presented two statements. The first, on climate change, was based on information she received from roundtable meetings of the National Council of Churches, USA, and Church World Service. The other statement addressed economic justice and included "two parts, one supporting raising the minimum wage to $10 by 2010, and one supporting current legislation before the US Congress strengthening union rights, [—] the Employee Free Choice Act."[105]

During her presidency, she proposed numerous resolutions and brought attention to the National Council of Churches' ecumenical advocacy days in the D.C. area. She encouraged Alliance members to come individually or bring a young adult group to participate in these programs.[106] In 2012, the Alliance presented statements on Cuba, gun violence, torture, violence against transgender persons, sexual education, and priorities for a faithful budget. Initially, a statement was raised about the "Unjust Killing of Trayvon Martin" (an unarmed black teenager in Florida) but the Alliance eventually amended the statement to speak against gun violence more generally.[107] Through Blythe's leadership, Alliance resolutions began to reflect a more complete moral agenda.

By adopting more statements, the Alliance strengthened and increased its advocacy work in the United States Capitol. While these statements created internal organizational conflict from time to time, they were crucial to the Alliance's ministry and presence in the world. By the 21st century, other moderate organizations, such as the Cooperative Baptist Fellowship and the American Baptist Churches USA, began moving away from adopting statements because of their divisive nature. The Alliance, however, recognized that if progressive Baptists did not pass statements or resolutions on controversial issues, the only Baptist voices individuals and politicians would hear would come from a significantly more conservative social and theological perspective.

During Blythe's presidency, the Alliance also became more decentralized in its advocacy work. Much as it had done with its international ministry partners, the Alliance appointed individual members to represent the organization at various justice and advocacy group meetings. In 2009, Robert Tiller represented the Alliance with Churches for Middle East Peace. Stan Hastey, in his retirement, represented the Alliance before the Baptist Joint Committee, and Ana Karim represented the Alliance with the Latin American Working Group (Cuba).[108] Prior to appointing individuals to represent the organization, staff members had represented the Alliance at these meetings. These appointments were another method of transitioning the leadership of the organization from the paid staff to the broader membership.

✦

Through its many partnerships, initiatives and resolutions, the Alliance attempted to proclaim the good news. The idea of "mission" or "ministry" had been engrained in both former Southern Baptists and American Baptists.

While the understanding about the meaning of "missions" or "ministry" changed, the Alliance's commitment to proclaiming the good news remained steadfast. The organization needed to grow into its partnership model of ministry, and by the second decade of the 21st century, it was proficient in performing and supporting ministry in partnership with other organizations and entities. As Alan Neely wrote in 1999, however, financial resources always constrained the extent to which the Alliance could partner. Despite this difficulty, the Alliance managed to support all of its partnership ministries on an annual ministry offering that never eclipsed $140,000 — a remarkable achievement considering the totality of the Alliance's history in regard to developing its sixth covenant principle.

Chapter 11

The Principle of a Free Church

7) The principle of a free church in a free state and the opposition to any effort either by church or state to use the other for its own purposes.

Support for religious liberty and the separation of church and state have been central marks of identity for Baptists since their founding in the early seventeenth century. As discussed in Part I, Baptist figures like Thomas Helwys, Roger Williams and John Leland all stood up to political authorities, challenging the ideas of the religious establishment. In the late 1980s, according to Baptist lay leader Norman Cavender, so important was religious liberty for some members in the Southern Baptist Alliance that without it, he claimed, "we become, quite simply, non-Baptist."[1] The long history of Baptist pronouncements in support of religious liberty for all people was a driving force that motivated the formation of the Alliance.

In 1936, the Southern Baptist Convention created a Committee on Public Relations, and ten years later the convention entered into a partnership with the American Baptist Churches and the National Baptist Churches Inc. to form the Baptist Joint Committee on Public Affairs (BJC). This organization served all three Baptist bodies in Washington, D.C., representing Baptist opinions on a number of issues — most importantly issues pertaining to the establishment and free-exercise clauses of the first amendment. By the early 1980s, however, inerrantists within the convention became disgruntled with the Baptist Joint Committee's objections to proposed congressional legislation supporting prayer in public schools. The BJC supported the rights of all children to pray in school but not at the request or mandate of teachers or the school in general.[2]

The positions of the BJC directly challenged the positions of the inerrantists in the Southern Baptist Convention, but the inerrantists were unable to take control of the BJC. Over the years, the BJC accumulated more supporting bodies, and the backing from these additional groups meant that the convention did not have enough presence on the BJC's board of trustees to influence the organization as much as some inerrantists desired.

The problem remained, however, that the convention provided a significant portion of the BJC's budget — greater than any other supporting body. Eventually, the inerrantist-appointed trustees of the BJC, known as the Public Affairs Committee of the Southern Baptist Convention, successfully defunded the organization.

Members of the Alliance, committed to the principle of the separation of church and state, believed the BJC was a remarkable institution because of its Baptist ecumenism and its steadfast calling to religious liberty. Maintaining the financial feasibility of the institution was a priority for many. As reflected in the seventh tenet of the Alliance Covenant, members of the Alliance believed that neither the church nor the government ought to use one another for their own purposes. Put another way, Norman Cavender suggested, the church does "not need government to do [its] work, [it does] not want the government doing [its] work, and [it] must *never allow* government to involve itself in any way with the proclamation and ministry of the church, because the government cannot substitute for God."[3]

This chapter addresses the ways in which the Alliance developed its support for the promotion of a free church within a free state. The chapter has been divided into three sections. The first section discusses how the Alliance became a supporting body of the Baptist Joint Committee on Public Affairs, now called the Baptist Joint Committee for Religious Liberty. The second section explains some of the ways in which the Alliance advocated for the separation of church and state and religious liberty. The third section shows how the Alliance advocated for its partnership with the Fraternity of Baptists in Cuba on the grounds of religious freedom and separation of church and state.

Support for the Baptist Joint Committee

When the founding group of twenty-two individuals reconvened two weeks prior to the announcement of the formation of the Southern Baptist Alliance in February 1987, Richard Groves and Lawrence Coleman reported on the status of the organization's ability to support the Baptist Joint Committee on Public Affairs. The two had met with James Dunn, executive director of the BJC, who was hesitant to accept financial aid from a new organization like the Alliance. Dunn explained his desire to maintain ties with the Southern Baptist Convention, since a large portion of his organization's funding came from the convention. He believed that by accepting money from the Alliance, the BJC could become tied to "moderate" issues that did not pertain to its work or to religious liberty.

In some ways, Dunn's rejection might have seemed a major setback for the Alliance, because supporting the work of the BJC was a significant passion about which everyone agreed. Instead, however, as Alan Neely said, "If these were discouraging words for the group, there [was] no evidence of it. Dunn's position was understood and accepted."[4]

The organization remained vigilant in its desire to support the Baptist Joint Committee. In June of 1987, a group of Alliance leaders met with Dunn again at the St. Louis Southern Baptist Convention meeting, with the intention of "meeting in Washington afterwards to determine how the Alliance can relate to the Joint Committee."[5]

Leadership continued to follow and support the work of the BJC on an individual level rather than an organizational level. During the first meeting of the Alliance board of directors in September of 1987, much discussion surrounded religious liberty issues. Jim Strickland, a member of the Issues Committee, reported that there were "two issues which should be addressed immediately, one of which was "support for the Baptist Joint Committee on Public Affairs."[6]

Richard Groves recounted to the board his conversation with Stan Hastey, the future executive director of the Alliance who was then an employee of the Baptist Joint Committee. Hastey explained to Groves that the Southern Baptist Convention was routing BJC money through the Public Affairs Committee (PAC). Hastey believed that the BJC would no longer be funded by the convention as early as 1988. Groves explained to Hastey that "the [Alliance] would not do anything publicly at the moment but would be prepared to do what is necessary in the event that funding is withdrawn."[7]

The Alliance was also aware of the attempts of the convention's Public Affairs Committee to subvert directed funds to the BJC. Members of the PAC were attempting to roll designated gifts into the convention's already budgeted $400,000 for the Baptist Joint Committee. Samuel Currin, chair of the PAC, also began trying to secure a list of all donors to the BJC, including those who requested to be anonymous. Alan Neely suggested that the Alliance become a conduit for designated gifts to reach the BJC. In this way, the Alliance would prevent the PAC from rolling further designated gifts into the convention's pre-approved budget.[8]

At the September board meeting, the Ad Hoc Committee on Issues prompted a discussion about the convention's endorsement of Robert Bork's nomination to the Supreme Court by President Ronald Reagan.[9]

The endorsement marked the first time the Southern Baptist Convention had openly endorsed a candidate for political office. Not only did the endorsement break from the Southern Baptist tradition of not endorsing political candidates, but it also went against the Baptist Joint Committee on Public Affairs' refusal to make political endorsements.

The Alliance adopted a resolution "dealing with the recent Public Affairs Committee endorsement of Robert Bork for the Supreme Court." It cited the convention's historic commitment to not endorse political candidates and stated that a Supreme Court "justiceship is without question a political office." The Alliance also resolved to "express its dismay . . . and . . . remind concerned individuals and groups that the Public Affairs Committee does not speak for all Southern Baptists on this or any other issue." The resolution expressed a desire that "the Public Affairs Committee be requested to withdraw immediately its endorsement of Judge Bork."[10]

In the following years, the Alliance continued to track and follow the actions of the Public Affairs Committee in relation to the Baptist Joint Committee. In September of 1988, the board of directors passed a motion to "express their opposition to the budget request of $75,500 from the Public Affairs Committee of the Southern Baptist Convention." The resolution also called for the SBC Executive Committee "to structure the budget allocation for the Baptist Joint Committee on Public Affairs in a manner consistent with budget increases for other agencies of the Southern Baptist Convention."[11] The convention's funding of the PAC began to pave the way for the Alliance to openly support the Baptist Joint Committee beginning in 1989.

When the convention completely defunded the Baptist Joint Committee in the early 1990s, the BJC lost a large portion of its overall operating budget. By 1992, the BJC recognized that it "must do things differently." The organization needed to "publish materials and spread their message in new and innovative ways."[12] This same year brought some challenging hurdles for the Alliance as well, since the formation of the Cooperative Baptist Fellowship adversely affected the membership and budget of the organization.

In 1992, the BJC requested a renewal of support from the Alliance. A representative of the committee wrote, "In view of the history of the Alliance, and in spite of your budget shortfall, we respectfully request continued support in 1993 in the amount of $12,000, the same level of support that we received in 1992. We request this amount because a reduced gift from one of our few consistent and dependable sources would be extremely difficult to replace."[13] The Alliance was unable to fulfill the request.

In an agreement to avoid financial competition, the Alliance relinquished its funding of the BJC to the larger, more moderate Cooperative Baptist Fellowship. The arrangement lasted only a few years; the Alliance came to realize that supporting the Baptist Joint Committee and having representation on the organization's board of trustees was too valuable. It resumed funding the BJC in the mid-1990s.

Over the years, the Baptist Joint Committee held numerous breakout sessions at Alliance gatherings and board meetings. In 1996, James Dunn and the BJC's general counsel, Brent Walker, attended the Alliance's fall board meeting to discuss school prayer, vouchers, and challenges to the Religious Freedom and Restoration Act.[14] The relationship between the two organizations was greatly aided by the presence of Stan Hastey and Jeannette Holt, former BJC employees, on the Alliance staff. Even after their retirements, however, the Alliance continued a good working relationship with the Baptist Joint Committee into the second decade of the 21st century.

Advocating for Separation of Church and State

Throughout the Alliance's history, members fought in different ways to support the Baptist principle of religious liberty. In her 1999 Covenant Address, Alliance member Nancy Ammerman closed her speech with a discussion of Baptists' contribution to modern society. She explained that Baptists had long fought for the religious rights of minority faith traditions. Drawing attention to the Alliance's identity, she explained that "If despised and outcast Baptists deserved the full and equal participation in society and deserved the freedom to worship without state interference . . . despised and outcast Muslims or American Indians or Branch Davidians deserve those privileges."[15] Ammerman's words resonated with the membership's commitment to the final covenant principle.

When members of Congress proposed the Religious Freedom and Restoration Act (RFRA) in the early 1990s, the Alliance board passed the following resolution: "We express our strong support for the restoration of the compelling interest test as expressed in the Religious Freedom Restoration Act, and we urge all Baptists to advocate passage of the bill with the appropriate Representatives and Senators."[16] The RFRA was passed in response to the Supreme Court's decision in *Employment Division of Oregon vs. Smith*. In this case, the Court ruled that generally applicable laws are not subject to religious exemptions. The RFRA required the government to offer religious exemptions on generally applicable laws, and that laws must seek "the least restrictive means of furthering that compelling governmental interest."[17]

During the 1990s, the Alliance maintained a committee that specifically addressed issues of religious liberty and public policy. The committee went through many name changes over the years but was concerned specifically with issues pertaining to the United States government. In March of 1992, the committee examined the possibility of promoting universal "preventative and curative health care."[18] Such a possibility was further discussed in a board of directors meeting in September 1993 when "Jim Bell of Interfaith IMPACT for Justice and Peace presented information for people of faith concerned about legislation on national health reform, environmental concerns, and hunger."[19] While these individual issues were important to the Alliance on an organizational level, the leadership recognized that they could not be separated from the larger societal and governmental system as a whole.

In 1995, under a new name, the Public Affairs Committee of the Alliance recommended that the group support two organizations — the Interfaith Alliance and Interfaith IMPACT for Justice and Peace. The Interfaith Alliance, discussed in the previous chapter, was "an organization of national mainstream religious leaders who united to speak out against people who use religion as a weapon and to ensure that the religious community continues to have an important voice in the public dialogue."[20] Interfaith IMPACT for Justice and Peace lobbied "Congress on behalf of those who suffer discrimination and/or abuse."[21] The committee also recommended continued support for the "Coalition of the Homeless, which lobbies [on] behalf of homeless people."[22]

Both the Interfaith Alliance and Interfaith IMPACT for Justice and Peace sought to properly locate the religious voice in the public sphere. Strict adherents to the separation of church and state might view these organizations as breaching the concept. For the Alliance, however, these entities represented a rightly positioned religious voice committed to the totality of the individual — mind, body and spirit. The Alliance supported religious liberty but believed that having this freedom could not be separated from an individual's freedom to flourish both economically and physically. Societal poverty and a lack of medical insurance both influence and inhibit one's freedom of conscience, too.

The Alliance did have concerns about religion overstepping political boundaries. In 2002, it endorsed a statement, drafted by the Washington-based grassroots organization called Churches for Middle East Peace, that called for the "recognition of a viable Palestinian state alongside Israel and an end to Israeli occupation in the West Bank and Gaza." The Alliance amended the statement by removing a phrase that expressed encouragement of the diplomatic discussions spurred by the United States government, because some members were wary that it could be open to misinterpretation.[23] Examples like this show that the organization attempted to remain free from becoming entwined in the United States political machinery while still remaining involved in political questions. In this regard, the Alliance both succeeded and failed over the years.

More often than not, the Alliance sided with positions more sympathetic to the Democratic Party. In 2001, the Peace and Justice Committee recommended that the organization "authorize the Executive Director . . . sign the letter . . . written by the Baptist Joint Committee on Public Affairs to President Bush raising concerns about the Administration's charitable choice initiative."[24] Three years later, Stan Hastey celebrated the U.S. Supreme Court decision in *John Geddes Lawrence and Tyron Garner v. State of Texas*, which overturned sodomy laws throughout the nation. Hastey said that "on the side speaking out for those constitutional rights, were no fewer than twenty-nine religious bodies in the United States who joined in a brief *amici curiae* challenging the state of Texas. Heading the list, by virtue of its alphabetical listing, was none other than the Alliance of Baptists."[25] Both of these examples provide positions generally more sympathetic to the Democratic Party.

Its support of such public positions inevitably placed the Alliance in advocacy situations many consider to be outside the sphere of religion. Religious liberty, however, has never meant barring religious individuals from participating in the public sphere. Instead, this deeply engrained Baptist principle means allowing all voices to be heard and respected. A problem emerges, however, when certain religious perspectives are granted privilege over others, and when policies and legislation intentionally prohibit certain religious practices and beliefs. Throughout the history of the Alliance, the organization has tried to embody this distinct Baptist principle in ways deeply committed to life in the public square. In so doing, the organization has understood economic, medical and military issues as religious and moral issues that help to make up one's individual freedom of conscience.

Religious Liberty in Cuba

As mentioned in the previous chapter, the Alliance continued its partnership with the Fraternity of Baptists in Cuba into the second decade of the 21st century. Over the years, the Alliance petitioned the United States government in an attempt to loosen the economic embargo against Cuba. In addition, the membership sought to loosen travel restrictions to Cuba. Since the Alliance understood its relationship with the Fraternity of Baptists as a mutual partnership, many of its petitions took the form of advocating for the religious freedom of organizations in the United States to work, minister and fellowship in Cuba.

While the embargo went through various iterations, it remained in affect into the second decade of the 21st century. The Alliance's opposition to the embargo was spurred on by its relationship with the Fraternity of Baptists. In 2003, the membership passed a Statement on Cuba that read, "We register our objection to the Departments of State, Justice, and Homeland Security for the indignities imposed upon Cuban citizens invited to travel to the United States by groups such as the Alliance of Baptists . . . We object to Cuba's listing as a 'terrorist' state by our government."[26]

In a 2004 *Connections* newsletter article, Stan Hastey informed the organization that Fraternity minister Rev. Raul Suarez was unable to secure a visa to travel to the Alliance's annual convocation. Hastey explained,

> Rev. Suarez is pastor of Ebenezer Baptist Church in Marianao. He is director of the Martin Luther King Jr. Center, which is adjacent to the church. Under his leadership, both church and center have played vital roles in repairing decaying houses in their municipal- ity, in helping residents provide fresh fruits and vegetables in urban organics gardens, and by providing a wide range of social services for older citizens, including the homebound.[27]

Hastey described the United States' decision to deny Rev. Suarez a visa as "disgraceful."[28] Again in 2006, the Alliance issued a statement in response to the government making travel to Cuba "more and more difficult." The resolution was a response to the suspension of the "general license" of the Alliance of Baptists "without cause."[29] Another declaration was adopted the following year that called for ending the ban on travel to Cuba.[30]

The Alliance was affected and in many ways limited by the actions of the U.S. government against Cuba. The Alliance advocated for its partner congregations in Cuba by using its First Amendment rights as religious people in the United States to participate in an integral part of the organi- zation's faith practice — mutual fellowship and encouragement. Religious liberty became the avenue through which the Alliance fought for its right to partner with a fellow Baptist organization in Cuba.

✦

The Alliance has supported religious liberty and the separation of church and state throughout its history. When Stan Hastey was hired as executive director in 1988, he "spoke to the Board on how important religious liberty was to him and the SBA offers him an opportunity to pursue that."[31] Over the years, the actions of the leadership may not have identified the principle of religious liberty as the most important tenet of the Alliance Covenant, but the precept was always significant in grounding the Alliance within Baptist history. The commitment tied the Alliance to the Baptist Joint Committee as well as many historic Baptist leaders.

Perhaps the most tangible action taken by the leadership in support of religious liberty occurred in 2014. For the first time, the Alliance joined a lawsuit with the United Church of Christ against same-sex marriage bans in the state of North Carolina. The plaintiffs argued that North Carolina's marriage laws violated the religious freedom of religious groups and churches that desired to perform same-sex marriages. The North Carolina law prohibited ministers from performing wedding ceremonies without a valid marriage license, which were denied to same-sex couples.[32] Nancy Petty, minister of Pullen Memorial Baptist Church, joined the suit individually and helped to spur the Alliance to join as an organization.

In doing so, the Alliance continued to show its commitment to religious liberty, a commitment that progressed from supporting the Baptist Joint Committee for Religious Liberty to advocating for the right to partner with the Fraternity of Baptists, and on to the 2014 lawsuit. Even without the more tangible examples of supporting this covenant principle, however, the Alliance understood its final covenant value to be one of the most central and sacred parts of what it means to be Baptist. While the other tenets of the covenant also speak to the Alliance's understanding of what it means to be Baptist, perhaps none has the legacy and history as the dedication to a free church in a free state.

Part III: Living Zion

Congregational Studies

The following congregational studies attempt to describe what Alliance congregations look and act like in the second decade of the 21st century. Rather than a primarily text-based methodology, each of these studies uses a more ethnographic methodological approach that combines historical, observational, musical and cultural elements. Since individual congregations comprise the Alliance of Baptists' primary constituency, Alliance congregations and the larger Alliance denominational body influence one another.

Understanding ideas of congregational culture is important. As Mark Chaves writes,

> Congregations' activities and contributions are cultural in two senses. On the one hand, their core activity is the broadly cultural one of expressing and transmitting religious meanings through ritual and religious education. On the other hand, largely but not only because congregations' primary ritual — the worship service — almost always uses music and frequently uses drama, dance, and other art forms, congregational activity is cultural in the narrower sense of facilitating a surprising amount of artistic activity.[1]

Artistic activity and creativity enliven and enrich the Alliance of Baptists. Since the organization understands itself to be in partnership with congregations, the work of each congregation is in essence the work of the Alliance. This is not to say the Alliance takes credit for all of the work of its partner congregations, but it does support, celebrate and encourage each of its congregations in educational, worship, ministry and fellowship endeavors.

As theology professor Dorothy Bass writes, congregations are "bearers of traditions."[2] Each of the following studies attempts to show the various ways in which partner congregations bear the tradition of the Alliance of Baptists. Churches were selected with geographic diversity in mind and represent California, Georgia, Maryland, New York, North Carolina, South Carolina, Tennessee, and Virginia. Some congregations identify more strongly with the Alliance than others, but all represent the perspective of affiliate congregations.

First Baptist Church

Greenville, South Carolina

May 18, 2014

Located only a few miles from the historic downtown sits First Baptist Church of Greenville, South Carolina. Organized in 1831, the church met downtown until the congregation moved to its current location in the 1980s. The present-day "campus" includes three buildings that slightly slope down the church's property and are connected by elevated breezeways. The building at the highest point of the campus is the sanctuary, followed by an educational and fellowship building and the newest building, the Activities and Youth Ministry Center (AYMC), which houses basketball courts and a fitness center. A private preschool meets throughout the week on the first floor of the educational and fellowship building. Also on the church property are two softball fields, a Remembrance Garden, a large playground, and a parking lot looping around the three buildings.

First Baptist Greenville historically was an influential church within Baptist life in the South. According to the church website, an original organizer of the congregation, William Bullein Johnson, served as the first president of the Southern Baptist Convention. Southern Baptist Theological Seminary, the convention's flagship seminary, was also founded and originally housed in the church before moving to Louisville, Kentucky, following the Civil War.

The Alliance held its third convocation at First Baptist in 1989, when the Baptist Theological Seminary at Richmond was founded. By 1999, the congregation was no longer affiliated with the Southern Baptist Convention, and since then the church has continued its support of the Cooperative Baptist Fellowship, which receives a bulk of the congregation's ministry giving. In addition to the CBF, the congregation continues to affiliate with the Alliance of Baptists as well as other Alliance-related organizations, including the Baptist Joint Committee for Religious Liberty and Wake Forest School of Divinity.

Entering the parking lot of First Baptist on a typical Sunday (May 18, 2014) can be confusing because of the one-way lanes. A large, open bell tower and a sign for the visitor's desk provide direction into the sanctuary. Prior to the service, a large, sliding partition opens a space between the narthex and the sanctuary. In the narthex, a cornerstone reveals that the building was constructed in 1984, and a congregant tells me that a church member designed the sanctuary. Bulletins are located on tables throughout the narthex.

Upon entering the sanctuary, one's eyes rise upward as six separate columns of horizontal wood paneling, designed to replicate the "Tree of Life," climb the wall behind the pulpit. These columns expand across the ceiling, rippling out as a wave overhead. The sanctuary is round with no center aisle; a staircase hugs the right wall, curving up toward a small balcony that extends less than half the length around the room. Wooden pews with slightly faded red cushioning and matching carpet accompany the cream walls and wood paneling of the "Tree of Life." A large, bright blue stained-glass mural can be seen on the left wall, as can a series of smaller blue stained-glass windows above the staircase leading to the balcony.

To the left of the pulpit is a choir loft of roughly sixty chairs located beneath a large pipe organ. The instrument is fixed into a section of the wall beside the "Tree of Life." Music serves as an important part of congregational life. The music ministry at First Baptist has a deep-seated connection to Greenville's Furman University, which has a strong Baptist heritage. Many leaders of the music ministry teach at, attend, or attended Furman. The church has at least nine choirs, six of which are for children from preschool to fifth grade. On this day, the middle school and high school choirs combined to lead in worship.

Congregants trickle into the sanctuary while the organist begins to play the prelude at 10:30. After a brief greeting and "Prayer for Worship," most congregants are seated. Those in attendance are nicely dressed, with a majority of women wearing dresses or skirts and a majority of men wearing a coat and tie. Younger members of the congregation are dressed more casually. The minister of activities, AYMC and interim minister to young adults greets me and tells me that on a typical Sunday attendance is anywhere from 600 to 700, but he wishes that number were higher. The congregation is currently two years into a search for a senior minister, which undoubtedly affects attendance. As congregants take their seats, the combined youth choir sings an *a cappella* arrangement of a 16th-century hymn as the "Call to Worship."

The processional hymn titled "Partners in Ministry" serves as the opening and closing hymn. During the first singing of the hymn, two acolytes and the ministers and deacons process to the front of the sanctuary. The ministers wear robes with white matching stoles for the particular season of Eastertide. The theme of the hymn proves fitting, as a local minister from Nicholtown Missionary Baptist Church delivers the sermon as a guest preacher. Nicholtown Missionary Baptist Church is an African American congregation which First Baptist partners with on a number of community initiatives.

This Sunday is "Foundation Sunday," and the service focuses on the congregation's ministry endowment called "The Foundation." According to the bulletin, since its establishment in 1992 this endowment fund has distributed nearly $1.5 million. In her children's sermon, the missions coordinator explains how the endowment works to the more than thirty children gathered on the chancel steps.

After the children's sermon, the youth choir, accompanied by a percussionist on bongos, sings a traditional Zambian song, "Bonsa Aba." Following the song, the guest minister delivers his message. Recognizing that his preaching style is far different from what the church is used to, he asks the congregation to high-five one another and speak to "their neighbor." The congregation obliges with smiles and laughter at what obviously seems to be something not usually asked of them. The minister preaches from the passage of the Good Samaritan and focuses on how Christians should seek to help people have a better life. After twenty-five minutes, the message concludes, and the congregation gives the speaker a standing ovation.

The service transitions to an offertory collection during which a video appears on a screen to the right of the pulpit. The short film shows some of the congregation's ministry partners discussing their work and thanking the church for the financial support provided through the Foundation. After the video, the minister of neighborhood partnerships and Christian fellowship presents to the congregation a tenth-grade girl who has made a profession of faith and seeks membership into the church. The minister asks the church to respond with a collective "Amen." After a benediction, the acolytes lead the recessional as the organist plays the postlude.

First Baptist Church of Greenville has hosted the annual Alliance convocation three times. Ann Quattlebaum, a member of the congregation who served as Alliance president from 1992-1994, says the church has many congregants who support the Alliance as well as some who do not. Of those who do not, she speculates it is over LGBT issues, but she remains hopeful that the congregation may soon begin more productive discussions regarding issues pertaining to sexuality. First Baptist does support and participate in the Alliance's partnership with the Fraternity of Baptist Churches of Cuba and partners with *Iglesia Bautista del Camino* in Guanajay, Cuba.

A historic church in the history of the Alliance, First Baptist Church of Greenville, South Carolina, provides one example of the diversity present within the Alliance of Baptists.

Glendale Baptist Church

Nashville, Tennessee

May 25, 2014

Nashville, Tennessee, known as the Athens of the South, is home to Glendale Baptist Church. Located a few miles from Vanderbilt, Belmont and Lipscomb universities, the church sits on a hill just off of Glendale Lane. A long driveway winds up a green lawn toward a parking lot located predominantly behind the church building.

Glendale was a Southern Baptist church plant in the early 1950s from Belmont Heights Baptist Church, only a few miles away. Because of this, Glendale's building follows the Southern Baptist model for church planting as instituted by the denomination's Sunday School Board. The small steeple identifies the building's original brick chapel. As the church grew, educational space was added to the right of the chapel, and eventually a larger sanctuary was added to the left of the chapel, which was then converted into office space.

Nashville is home to many offices of the Southern Baptist Convention, including the Executive Committee and the Sunday School Board, now known as LifeWay. Because of Glendale's origins as a Southern Baptist church plant as well as its proximity to many of the convention's offices, its membership over the years included employees and former employees of both offices. It was not until the early 1970s, however, that Glendale first attempted to shake up the *status quo* of Baptist life in the city. At the time, pastor Richard Smith was the only Baptist minister in Nashville in favor of desegregation. In response, some members of the congregation attempted to remove him from the church's pastorate. Their attempt failed, but many people left the church.

After this "mass exodus," as one congregant describes the event, Glendale began to develop an identity as a Southern Baptist church on the margins of Southern Baptist life. In 1974, Glendale became the first Southern Baptist church in Nashville to ordain women. In the same year, the church adopted a new covenant that has been changed only twice in the past forty years. The covenant encourages individuals to "see where God is at work in the world and to join in this work," as well as "to build an inclusive Christian community that affirms the worth of all persons."

By the late 1980s and early 1990s, Glendale began to make the transition out of Southern Baptist life. In the early 1990s, the church called Mark Caldwell from University Baptist Church in College Park, Maryland.

He believed the congregation was moving toward the possibility of joining the Alliance. Some members participated in early Alliance meetings, like the listening session in the late 1980s at Woodmont Baptist Church. In 2000, the congregation formed a partnership with a church in Santa Clara, Cuba, and many congregants say this solidified Glendale's partnership with the Alliance. Having partnership ministries like the church in Cuba helped replace annual Southern Baptist mission offerings deeply engrained in the minds of many members.

In 2002, Glendale called an associate minister, an event that caused a few members to leave the church because of her sexual orientation. She became co-pastor two years later, when the congregation hired another minister to replace its former senior minister. The church has had this co-pastoring model ever since. Both pastors alternate preaching duties in addition to most other responsibilities within the life of the congregation.

Sunday mornings at Glendale begin with Sunday school at 9:30, followed by 10:30 worship. The sanctuary is a rectangular room with four aisles that separate three sections of pews. During a recent renovation, the walls, formerly pale yellow, were painted a steel gray. White trim throughout the room matches the light wooden pews and thin white fabric banners throughout the sanctuary. Two members of the congregation describe the windows as 1950s Southern Baptist stained glass. The windows, which have almost a tie-dyed quality, were a cheap alternative to authentic stained glass when the church was built.

At the front of the sanctuary, one's eyes are immediately drawn to a stain-glass window enclosing a cutout in the wall for the baptistry. The earthy tones and abstractly shaped pieces of glass surround a thin cross and fish made of more vibrant colors. Beneath the window sit chairs for a nearly eighteen-person choir. On the chancel rests a piano, with two dark wooden podiums on either side of the stage.

The service on May 25, 2014, begins at 10:32 when one of the ministers rises to share in the life of the community. She informs the congregation of prayer requests and makes announcements, most of which are found within the tri-fold bulletin. When she finishes, the congregation transitions into worship with a pealing of bells followed by a moment of silence.

Four notes sound from a piano in the back of the church, and the choir sings an introit in a beautiful, tight harmony. The congregation has a number of members who have connections to the music industry in Nashville, including some who teach at Belmont University. The music minister originally moved to Nashville to work for LifeWay producing church choir music, but now (along with leading music at Glendale) directs Nashville in Harmony, a 120-voice (predominantly gay and lesbian) community chorus. After a "Call to Worship," an acolyte leads the choir down the two inner aisles to the processional hymn "Come, Thou Fount of Every Blessing." The congregation, a mixture of old and young, stands. The acolyte continues the service with a responsive reading from Psalms and then sings a duet with another member of the children's program, accompanied by the minister of music.

The service moves seamlessly through a pastoral prayer, congregational response, moment of silence, hymn, gospel reading, and choral anthem. This Sunday, the former associate minister offers a sermon in which she speaks from the passage in Acts where Paul goes to Athens and sees the statue to an unknown god. She makes the comparison between the Athens of Paul's generation and Nashville, the Athens of the South. Her sermon remains grounded in the biblical narrative as she asks whether or not the gospel "can hold its own" in the intellectual environment of "Athens." She reminds the congregation that, despite our intellectual acumen, we are finite beings. In her conclusion, she explains that she is tired of "unknown gods," and that the good news is that "God is in the world — groaning and laboring for the fullness of love."

As the sermon concludes and the service shifts toward the collection of tithes and offerings, one recognizes the generational diversity of the congregation. As a congregant rises to play the offertory music, others bring their tithes and offerings to the front of the church. A majority are older males. A look into the bulletin, however, reveals that congregants can make donations via smartphones.

After the offertory collection, the service moves toward conclusion with the doxology, titled "Praise God, the Giver and the Gift." Throughout the service, readings and hymns embrace inclusive language for humanity as well as God. A unison response and hymn are followed by a joint benediction between the co-pastors. The service lasts just over fifty minutes.

From a history immersed in a city where Southern Baptists were far and away one of the most dominant religious entities, Glendale has solidified its identity as an Alliance congregation. The church also partners with the Cooperative Baptist Fellowship, Baptist Peace Fellowship of North America and the Association of Welcoming and Affirming Baptists. Through these organizations, Glendale provides a progressive Baptist voice in the religious landscape of the Athens of the South.

Ginter Park Baptist Church

Richmond, Virginia

June 8, 2014

Both summer and Pentecost were upon Ginter Park Baptist Church on June 8, 2014. As summer schedules affect the pace of life, especially for children with school, Ginter Park chooses to change its Sunday morning routine. Rather than meeting for worship at 10:30 after Sunday school, during the summer the congregation meets at 9:30 for worship, followed by a brief period of fellowship and educational programming. Not only does the church change meeting times, but instead of worshiping in its main sanctuary, it meets in a different space — a smaller chapel.

The chapel is decorated for the liturgical season of Pentecost, and many members are wearing the color red to match the season. More than fifty people are present, not quite filling the chapel.

Wooden beams in the square chapel break up the white plaster walls and ceiling and match the wooden floors and pews. Three strips of red and orange fabric hang on three ceiling beams and flow from the front to the back of the sanctuary. A miniature organ sits to the right of the pulpit, with a piano to the left.

On the stage, the pulpit stands in front of a bright stained-glass window depicting a lamb and the Christian flag. Stained-glass windows are a significant feature of the church building. The sanctuary at Ginter Park was assembled beginning in 1920 with Tiffany stained-glass windows. The brick-Gothic structure, however, was originally built during Reconstruction as Grace Street Presbyterian Church. When Grace Street Presbyterian merged with Covenant Presbyterian early in the 20th century, the sanctuary was disassembled and put in storage. The Ginter Park congregation formed around 1916, and rather than building a sanctuary from scratch, the congregation purchased the disassembled sanctuary. Over the span of six years, the sanctuary was reassembled without the original balcony or steeple.

The church grew quickly in its early years, which led to multiple additions to the building. Spotting the architectural additions from the outside is tricky, as each shares architectural similarities with the original sanctuary. The inside of the building is also quite tricky to maneuver, as one congregant explains. The numerous additions, while creating a neat and coherent outer façade, have turned the inside into a maze of hallways and educational space once used by the almost 1,500-member congregation. Today, with fewer members, the church looks for creative ways to use its extensive space.

In some ways, holding summer services in the chapel allows the congregation to experience another part of its building, in addition to providing a closer and more intimate space for worship. On this particular Sunday, conversation wafts through the air as congregants enter and take their seats. As the service begins, a younger member, serving as the acolyte, brings in the light of Christ. Conversation slowly dies down as she processes in and lights a candle on a small table beneath the pulpit. After the ringing of three centering chimes, the congregation sits and listens to the prelude — a piano arrangement of "Sweet Hour of Prayer."

Historically, the church had a large ministerial staff, but today it employs one full-time minister. The current pastor, called to Ginter Park in 2013, is the first female minister in the congregation's almost 100-year history. The church fills other positions with part-time employees or with volunteers from the congregation. For instance, lay congregants help lead in worship by filling the position of liturgist on a rotating basis.

Before the call to worship and invocation, today's liturgist, a professor of biblical studies at Randolph-Macon College, welcomes the congregation. He informs those present of announcements as well as prayer requests. The liturgist speaks in a conversational tone as he specifically addresses individual members or asks for clarification on some of the announcements. This tone carries over into the children's sermon, during which the pastor asks children and adults to react to sections of the story of Pentecost with sounds and specific responses. At one point, the liturgist makes a joke by responding at an inappropriate time, eliciting both snickering and laughter from the congregation.

The musical selections for this Sunday carry the theme of Pentecost, as songs focus on the Holy Spirit. Prior to the start of worship, the part-time minister of music leads the congregation in the singing of an unfamiliar song so that when the song appears within the service, they will recognize the tune. The nearly ten-person choir rises from within the congregation and moves behind the piano when it is time for the "special music" — an *a cappella* version of "Bringing in the Sheaves." At the end of the service, the pastor explains that during the summer months, the congregation can begin leaving the chapel during the "parting music" rather than remaining seated until the music is finished. The tradition of remaining seated during the "parting music" is so ingrained within the congregation that few if any move from their seats until the piece is finished.

The sermon follows the musical focus on the theme of Pentecost by centering on the image of breath. The minister explains that defining God and Jesus is fairly easy for most people, but defining the Holy Spirit can be difficult. Drawing on the image of breath, she explains that our breath dissipates into the atmosphere almost immediately, but that the final breath of Christ was different; it lingered and grew until it was "time for God to be born again, not in one body but in many." She encourages the congregation to ask themselves whether or not they still believe in a God who transforms. Leaving the question open, she concludes by further encouraging the congregation to pray and pray often the simple prayer, "Come Holy Spirit, Come."

After the final note of the "parting music," the congregation meets outside for pastry and coffee. During this time, children play on the church lawn, and members mingle and talk. On future Sundays, this time will be an intergenerational period of Christian education. While the congregation includes mostly older members, some younger families attend as well. One reason the church has a larger population of older members is because of its close proximity to three retirement communities. On Sunday mornings, a member of the congregation drives a small bus to pick up members from these communities. A few of these older members were once employees of the Southern Baptist Foreign Mission Board, located in Richmond.

The congregation participates in Passport Kids as well as Baptist Youth Camp. Passport Kids is a predominantly Cooperative Baptist Fellowship camp, while Baptist Youth Camp unofficially serves as an Alliance youth camp. A couple of youth say that they are looking forward to rekindling friendships this summer with friends from fellow Alliance churches such as Glendale Baptist, Binkley Memorial and Pullen Memorial.

Ginter Park also supports four seminary students from Baptist Theological Seminary at Richmond by providing housing for them at "The Farley House," located on the church property. The home once housed furloughed missionaries, but now provides housing for seminary students in return for participation in the life of the congregation.

The church partners with the Cooperative Baptist Fellowship, the Richmond Baptist Association and the Alliance of Baptists. In 2012, the Baptist General Association of Virginia voted to disfellowship Ginter Park after the congregation ordained an openly gay man. Moving on from this painful experience, the congregation remains committed to the ministry of its current partners.

Woodbrook Baptist Church

Baltimore, Maryland

June 15, 2014

Praise and laughter are the themes at Woodbrook Baptist Church on June 15, 2014 (Father's Day) as the children's choir leads in worship. As I arrive, a congregational greeter talks baseball — specifically the Baltimore Orioles' victory the previous night. Meanwhile, a ten-member children's choir puts the finishing touches on a musical program to be held in lieu of a sermon this Sunday.

People slowly begin to fill the square sanctuary. One congregant describes the space by emphasizing its simplicity. From the outside of the building, the eyes are drawn from the brown brick up past the sloping and worn metal roofing to a cross atop a geometric glass steeple. Inside, light pours into the sanctuary through a row of clerestory windows that circumvent the room, as well as through the steeple located above the chancel. The wooden chancel and pews complement the brown brick walls and white ceiling. An organ and piano sit to the right of the chancel, with a baptismal pool to the left.

The simplicity of the current church building contrasts with the original downtown structure that now houses an African American congregation. The original church, Eutaw Place Baptist, was constructed after the Civil War in a neo-Gothic style. As the area around the church grew and changed, the congregation made the decision to move outside the city. Rather than allowing its building to be torn down, Woodbrook sold the space to an African American congregation.

During the period in which the congregation was housed at its original location, a number of well-known Southern Baptists were members. Richard Fuller, a president of the Southern Baptist Convention during the Civil War, served as the first pastor. Perhaps even better known, however, was Annie Armstrong, who was the first corresponding secretary of the Woman's Missionary Union. To this day, Southern Baptists collect an offering each Easter named after Annie Armstrong. With such a rich history in the Southern Baptist Convention, in 1962 the congregation was named one of the denomination's historic churches.

Today, Woodbrook identifies most strongly with the Alliance of Baptists, but allows members the option of designating where they would like their missions offerings to go. Congregants may designate to the Alliance, the Cooperative Baptist Fellowship or even the Southern Baptist Convention.

These are not the only organizations with which the congregation partners. The congregation also supports Heifer International, the Salvation Army and the Haitian Literacy Program, among others. In addition, the church helps to support the Woodbrook Early Education School, a preschool that serves as "an extension of the mission and ministry of the Christian education program of" the congregation.

The service begins at 10:30 with roughly fifty people present. The associate pastor opens by informing the congregation of announcements and prayer requests. During this period, another thirty to forty people trickle in. A few members are dressed in suits, but most are dressed casually. Following the gathering period, the liturgy moves through the prelude, processional hymn, call to worship and invocation. Throughout the bulletin, meditations are printed for people to reflect on individually. On this Sunday, the meditations come from hymn lyricists.

After a reading of scripture, a woman rises to offer prayer for the collection of tithes and offerings. The prayer gives thanks and praise for fathers of all kinds — present fathers and distant fathers, divorced fathers and stepfathers, fatherly figures and men with no children. After the prayer, the tithes and offerings are collected and brought forward as the congregation sings a hymn to the tune of Kresmer, rather than the "Old One-Hundredth," or "Doxology," which is used at this point in many Baptist services.

The sanctuary is filled with many children. The "Message to Young Worshippers" is held on the chancel steps but is directed specifically to the children, as the rest of the congregation is encouraged to record their attendance in the friendship registries at the end of each pew.

Just prior to the children's choir program, the congregation sings "Wonderful Grace of Jesus," which has an unusual tune. Most members struggle to read the music, and as the pianist and minister of music move into the second verse, snickers are heard. At the conclusion of the song, laughter is heard throughout the sanctuary, and one gentleman exclaims, "We barely made it through that one." The minister of music whispers to the pastor to let the congregation know she did not pick the song; when he does, everyone erupts into laughter.

The ability to recognize and acknowledge humor is evident even on the congregation's website. A page titled "We're Baptist And Yet" dispels some Baptist stereotypes through a number of statements that begin with the title phrase. Some examples include "We're Baptist and yet . . . we dance," "some of us drink," and "some of us cuss." While the page takes on the serious problem many progressive Baptists face when identifying as Baptist, it does so with an element of humor.[1]

As the children's choir proceeds with its program, momentary lapses of memory are met with laughter and smiles. In between songs, Bible verses and lines are read revolving around the theme of praise. Once the children complete their program, the congregation applauds and the associate pastor rises to thank them.

The associate pastor continues to the moment of invitation, which serves as a time for individuals to make a profession of faith or join the church. The associate pastor is intentional about explaining why this moment in the service exists and the number of ways in which individuals can respond. In the bulletin as well, the invitation is further explained for visitors who may not be familiar with this "typical" liturgical event in Baptist churches. The bulletin explains that the congregation welcomes "committed Christians who have been baptized in other traditions to become full members of Woodbrook Baptist Church without having to be baptized by immersion." This practice educates visitors while reminding current members of their participation within the life of the community.

The associate pastor provides the benediction but asks the children to lead in the parting words. He asks if it would be possible for the children to sing their final song one more time with participation from the congregation. After the song, members move about the sanctuary, thanking the children and talking with family as the postlude plays in the background. Families are encouraged to bid on silent auction items located in the narthex to help raise funds for the children to attend Passport Camp. In this atmosphere of laughter and praise, Woodbrook demonstrates the life and ministry of an Alliance congregation.

Oakhurst Baptist Church

Decatur, Georgia

June 29, 2014

When the formation of the Alliance was announced in 1987, its membership was composed primarily of individuals. One week after the group's formation, however, Oakhurst Baptist Church voted to become the first member congregation in the new movement. Associate pastor Nancy Hastings Sehested and member Walker Knight both served on the Alliance's steering committee. Oakhurst was an influential voice in shaping the identity of the Alliance as it emerged onto the landscape of American Baptist life.

Located in Decatur, a suburb of Atlanta, Oakhurst was founded in 1913, although the congregation's origins can be traced to the formation of a Sunday school class held in the home of Mrs. C.J. Johnson in 1908. Eventually, the class outgrew Mrs. Johnson's home. As it grew, the church acquired a tent as a meeting location; it eventually housed interdenominational revival meetings. These meetings, initiated by a Methodist minister who saw the need for a church in the Oakhurst neighborhood, helped to found multiple churches, including Oakhurst Baptist.

The church met in several locations until the decision was made to build a sanctuary in the early 1930s. Because of the Depression, however, the church was initially unable to erect an auditorium. In 1932, the congregation decided to break ground on a basement; the sanctuary was completed in 1937. The rectangular brick building still serves the congregation today, along with an educational annex (built in 1942) and a separate building with offices and educational space connected to the original sanctuary by an indoor breezeway. By 1993, the church began examining how the building could become more accessible to people with disabilities, which the congregation continues to evaluate.

From its earliest days, Oakhurst placed a heavy emphasis on mission work. In the 1960s, the neighborhood around Oakhurst began to shift from a predominantly white community to an increasingly black community. Rather than catering to their constituency and changing locations, Oakhurst made a conscious effort to remain in the neighborhood and serve the community. While the congregation remains predominantly white, the desire to stay at the original location has informed much of the church's ministry and mission.

The church's emphasis on mission often caused difficulty, particularly with regard to maintaining its facilities. The congregation has a long tradition of individuals who are more willing to create cheap short-term solutions for building needs than to pay for long-term solutions. While these short-term solutions have varied, one in particular included applying tape across cracks in the wall. The renovations that took place in the 1990s included making the facility accessible to persons with disabilities and provided many structural repairs to the original sanctuary.

Both historically and into the present, Oakhurst has been involved in the local struggle to end homelessness and poverty. The church began in the 1980s providing office space to *Seeds* magazine, which was founded by two members of the congregation and seeks to raise awareness about issues related to hunger. In 1991, the Hospitality House, now a nonprofit called the Oakhurst Recovery Program, began providing long-term housing for homeless men with chemical dependency. This ministry has often been supported in the Alliance's annual ministry offering. The church also supports the Decatur Cooperative Ministry, an interdenominational nonprofit that works to help those living in poverty; shares its facilities with a Chinese congregation; and partners with a Cuban congregation within the Fraternity of Baptists.

According to members of the congregation, no two Sundays are alike at Oakhurst Baptist Church. The congregation prides itself on a wide diversity of worship experiences facilitated by two choirs — a "Sanctuary Choir" and a "Gospel Choir." During the summer months, however, the choirs are given time off.

There are two main focal points within the pale yellow sanctuary that features purple, opalescent stained-glass windows. The first is the Jaeckel Organ. This tracker organ made by Dan Jaeckel sits just off to the right of the chancel as a freestanding, fully contained musical instrument. Its placement in the room, along with its wooden frame and cabinet, allows it to resonate throughout the sanctuary in a versatile and unique way. When the organ was purchased and installed in 1990, the congregation was skeptical about spending the church's resources in such a self-serving way. A compromise was made, allowing for the purchase of the organ as long as an equal sum would be raised for missions. Since the organ's instillation, this instrument and, in many ways, aesthetic piece of art has served as both an integral part of worship and as an integral part of the identity and make-up of the sanctuary.

The second focal point within the sanctuary is a large banner hanging to the left of the chancel that contains the congregation's covenant, adopted in

1974 and revised in 1994. The covenant serves as the centerpiece to the life of the congregation. New members are required to attend an "orientation" class centered on the covenant before they may fully enter into the life of the congregation. The covenant addresses participation in worship, study and stewardship, but also covers such issues as the rejection of status of "church office, possessions, education, race, age, gender, sexual orientation, mental ability, physical ability, or other distinctions." Another tenet of the covenant affirms one's willingness to "know and love my sisters and brothers in this fellowship, and ... [willingness] ... to be known and loved by them." Not only does the covenant hang on the wall, but laminated copies are found in the pews.

While each Sunday may reflect a wide array of worship experiences, Sunday, June 29, 2014 focuses on the idea of "welcome." A piano to the right of the chancel, beneath the covenant banner, provides the music. The church operates under a co-pastorate model, but with one minister on sabbatical, today a guest preacher and former church member is present to give the sermon.

The co-pastor in attendance opens the service and delivers a children's sermon to just fewer than ten children. She speaks about the idea of welcoming. At the end of her message, she asks Betty, a sixty-six-year-old member of the congregation with cerebral palsy, to come and be welcomed by the children. Betty has just returned from a trip to the redwood forests in California, a lifelong dream become reality thanks in large part to the financial contributions of fellow members at Oakhurst. The children surround Betty's wheelchair and welcome her back into the congregation after her long trip.

After the children's sermon, a time of "concerns and celebrations" takes place, followed by prayer. One prayer request is offered for the congregation's youth. On this Sunday, close to fifteen youth departed in the early morning to attend Baptist Youth Camp, a weeklong camp funded in part by the Alliance and attended by many Alliance churches.

Following the time of prayer, the guest speaker rises to deliver a sermon that centers upon what it means for a church like Oakhurst Baptist Church to be welcoming. He acknowledges that Oakhurst is already by many standards a church that understands the concept. How can a church be welcoming in this present day? The preacher encourages the congregation to look on the margins of society. This type of welcoming is risky and requires vulnerability, but if Oakhurst is true to its covenant, the risky places are where the congregation is called to go.

Following the sermon, an offertory collection is taken up in silence. The importance of music and sound throughout the service is striking. Music never supplements a part of the service. Instead, music is always an event in and of itself. As the closing piece is played, the congregation remains seated, listening to "Praise, I Will Praise You, Lord." At its conclusion, the congregation rises and begins to mingle and greet one another.

Oakhurst has developed a distinct identity surrounding its understanding of ministry, mission and community. As one of the founding congregations of the Alliance of Baptists, Oakhurst has in turn helped to shape and guide the identity of the organization.

Metro Baptist Church

New York, New York

July 23, 2014

Anyone traveling I-95 North into New York City by way of the Lincoln Tunnel will inevitably see Metro Baptist Church. Located just off the corner of 40th and 9th, the church sits in the neighborhood sometimes referred to as Clinton, but better known as Hell's Kitchen.

The congregation began as a small mission on the Upper West Side of Manhattan in the mid-1970s. Functioning as a "mission fellowship," the congregation helped to sponsor a number of other missions, including East 7th Street Ministry in the Lower East Side of Manhattan — today known as Graffiti Church. Many members of the congregation during these early years remember beginning a soup kitchen that required carrying large pots of soup down numerous flights of stairs and out to a local park where homeless men often gathered.

By 1982, the group officially constituted as Metro Baptist Church of Manhattan and began searching for a new location. The congregation stumbled upon a former Polish Catholic church turned into a rehabilitation center on West 40th Street in Hell's Kitchen, at the time one of New York City's seedier neighborhoods. Upon purchase of the building in 1984, Metro's minister stood across the street, gazing at the neo-Gothic building and praying, "Lord, don't give us this building if we can't put it to use for people who need it 24/7." Metro Baptist Church remains committed to this prayer, as the church strives to use the valuable commodity of space in one of the most densely populated cities in the United States. A few years after purchasing the church, Metro increased its mortgage to acquire the former rectory adjacent to the church, thus further increasing its capacity for service.

The church leased its space to help cover the building costs, while at the same time beginning ministries such as a food pantry and clothes closet. In 1995, the congregation created a nonprofit called Rauschenbusch Metro Ministries (RMM) — named after Walter Rauschenbusch, Baptist minister and father of the Social Gospel. Before writing his most famous works, *Christianity and the Social Crisis* (1907) and *A Theology for the Social Gospel* (1917), Rauschenbusch served as pastor of 2nd German Baptist Church in Hell's Kitchen, only a few blocks from Metro Baptist. By naming its nonprofit Rauschenbusch Metro Ministries, the church sought to draw inspiration from the history of not only its neighborhood but also the Baptist tradition.

As the church progressed into the 21st century, RMM expanded its services to the greater community of Hell's Kitchen and New York City. Now, not only does RMM provide a food pantry and clothing closet, but also an after-school program for children, a teen center, a life skills empowerment program for veterans, and English as a Second Language classes. In 2010, through RMM, Metro Baptist began one of its most creative ministries — the Hell's Kitchen Farm Project. Housed on the roof of the church, the project features around fifty kiddie pools that contain many different varieties of plants. The vegetables harvested from this garden are used to stock the food pantry.

Metro is affiliated with the Alliance of Baptists and the Cooperative Baptist Fellowship. For quite a while, Metro was the only congregation in New York City affiliated with either of these organizations, and thus became a much-visited congregation for individuals and churches who were also part of both groups. The fourth floor of the church contains two dormitory-style rooms and roughly six small apartments for staff and ministry residents. Many churches (often from the Southeast) interested in urban ministry participate in immersion experiences through the church. During the summer months, the congregation partners with the Alliance's Summer Communities of Service to support two individuals to staff a "CLUE Camp" (Children Living the Urban Experience). These individuals plan the overall structure of the camp, while different churches facilitate the content for one week each.

On July 13, 2014, Smoke Rise Baptist Church, a congregation from Georgia, is facilitating the third week of CLUE camp. The sanctuary space is set for worship, with chairs radiating out in a semi-circle from the plain pulpit that sits upon the chancel — a one-step, raised floor that spans the width of the room. Four large square columns, two upon the chancel and two amid the chairs, break up the space. Stained-glass windows and murals on the ceiling from the original Catholic worship space accent the white walls. A short open hallway leads into the worship space, and at the entrance a sound system sits off to the right, with an enclosed hot tub off to the left for baptisms. Coffee and bagels are set out for worshippers as they enter. The worship space transforms, however, depending on the needs of the church. In the summer of 2013, a theatre company used the space to put on a play that ran for two weeks, during which the show's set characterized the space.

At 10:30, the choir slowly begins to trickle in. Instead of meeting on Wednesday night, the choir practices thirty minutes before the service begins. They congregate around a piano to the left of the center pulpit.

Metro's location in Hell's Kitchen is only a few blocks from New York's Theatre District, and many members of the congregation are trained musicians and vocalists. The eight-person choir begins to practice as other members enter the sanctuary to converse or grab some coffee and a bagel.

The service begins at 11 o'clock and follows the liturgy printed in the bulletin. On this particular Sunday, the congregation is in the middle of a search process for a preaching pastor, and the pastor and director of RMM is on vacation. Various members of the staff and diaconate lead the service, while the visiting minister from Smoke Rise Baptist offers a sermon.

After the scripture reading, the congregation moves into a time referred to as the "Covenant of Concerns." A ministry associate rises and takes prayer requests, which are printed on the back of the bulletin and revisited each week with the community in prayer.

After the prayer requests, the offering is collected and the doxology sung. The choir stands from within the congregation and moves to the chancel to sing the anthem. The piece is "Waiting for the Light to Shine," from Roger Miller's musical *Big River*. The song is arranged by Metro's pianist and sung *a cappella*. Upon finishing, the choir members walk by the piano, setting down their music as they return to their seats.

As the minister from Smoke Rise begins his sermon, he praises the choir. He reads a passage from Romans 8:15-25 and preaches on the idea of "unseen hope." He explains that the scripture declares, "What you see is not what you get." The sermon focuses on our beliefs and hopes despite not being able to see and know everything. The congregation, at the request of one of the ministry residents, applauds the message. Following a hymn of commitment, the congregation is informed of areas and opportunities for service in the coming week, including attending a spaghetti lunch in the basement following the service to support the Teen Center's trip to Passport camps.

Through the many ways that Metro Baptist Church uses its space, the congregation remains committed to serving Hell's Kitchen and the greater city of New York. Through its creativity and hospitality, Metro provides an added element of diversity to the identity of the Alliance within the bustling metropolis of New York.

Pullen Memorial Baptist Church

Raleigh, North Carolina

July 28, 2014

Located just off of North Carolina State University's campus in Raleigh, North Carolina, is Pullen Memorial Baptist Church. The congregation was founded as Fayetteville Street Baptist Church in 1884, but renamed itself Pullen Memorial Baptist Church in 1913 in honor and memory of John T. Pullen, a powerful lay leader.

The congregation at Pullen has a long history of pushing boundaries. In 1927, it appointed four female deacons. Although no more women were appointed until 1950, the initial action was a radically progressive move for a Southern Baptist congregation. Ministers at Pullen, in a similar way, have always been outspoken regarding ecumenism, race relations and war, among other things. According to the church's website, upon the death of longtime pastor Edwin McNeill Poteat, the congregation called W.W. Finlator to the pastorate and solidified its reputation as a "liberal" church.

Because of the church's reputation, the Baptist State Convention of North Carolina began working to disfellowship with Pullen as early as the 1970s. However, Pullen retained its membership within the state convention until the early 1990s, when, under the leadership of pastor Mahan Siler, it moved to endorse the unqualified acceptance of gay and lesbian Christians. Within a year, Pullen was disfellowshipped from the Raleigh Baptist Association, the Baptist State Convention and the Southern Baptist Convention. Pullen continued its mission and ministry through the Alliance of Baptists and the American Baptists.

Today, Pullen Memorial also partners with many other organizations. It supports the work of the Association of Welcoming and Affirming Baptists as well as the Baptist Peace Fellowship of North America. It enjoys ecumenical partnerships with Bread for the World, Church Women United and Community of the Cross of Nails. Edwin McNeill Poteat and a Pullen member, Alan Neely, helped begin the North Carolina Council of Churches and the Triangle Interfaith Alliance, respectively. Abroad, Pullen maintains ties to First Baptist Church of Matanzas, Cuba, the Zimbabwe Theological Seminary, Peace Cathedral in the Republic of Georgia, and Project AMOS in Nicaragua.

Within the congregation, Pullen has a number of active ministries. A "Back Door Ministry" offers lunches each week to homeless or low-income members of the Raleigh community. Pullen members also tutor students from a local elementary school. Pullen Mission Women is composed of multiple "circles" of women who help raise money and collect other items for local, national and international ministries.

In addition to these ministries, in 2008 the congregation began a nonprofit called The Hope Center at Pullen. It serves as a homelessness prevention program that seeks to provide individuals with resources and skills "focused on employment, career, and housing goals." In addition, the Hope Center provides a "Foster Youth Academy" tailored to youth who have been in the foster care system. The Hope Center and Pullen's other partnerships and ministries provide only a glimpse into the many different ways in which the church seeks to embody the love of Christ in the world.

On the Sunday of July 28, 2014, the congregation gathers for worship at 11 o'clock. The brick, Romanesque sanctuary sits on the corner of Hillsborough Street and Cox Avenue amid a number of trees and plants. The building was completed in 1950 with a dedication sermon delivered by Harry Emerson Fosdick, the famed liberal Protestant minister of Riverside Church in New York City. Also on the property is a more recently built chapel with a modern, eco-friendly architectural design.

The sanctuary was designed with a cruciform plan, with a deep chancel that contains bright stained-glass windows. At the start of the service, a thirteen-member orchestra begins lightly playing as the pastor speaks from the rear of the sanctuary the congregation's statement on radical community. This statement welcomes all into worship: "The Certain and the Doubtful; The Excluded and the Included; Rich, Poor and In Between; Divorced, Partnered, Single and Widowed; Atheist, Agnostic, Buddhist, Catholic, Protestant, Islamic, Hindu, Jewish or Nothing; Heterosexual, Homosexual and Transgender; Black, White, Asian, Latino; Citizens and Guests." As the statement is read, the music swells and the congregation responds with the refrain from the hymn "All Are Welcome."

After two young girls serving as acolytes bring in the light to the hymn *Come, Friends, to Join and Sing,* the minister rises to give the invocation and statement of worship. On this particular Sunday, Pullen is celebrating its partnership with Zimbabwe Theological Seminary, and a friend of the Alliance from Zimbabwe is present to give the sermon. The minister proceeds to introduce Dr. Henry Mugabe. She explains in detail Dr. Mugabe's story, from being educated at Southern Baptist Theological Seminary to being fired from his position at Baptist Theological Seminary of Zimbabwe. For members of the congregation who are unfamiliar with the Southern

Baptist Convention, she provides some history that helps explain Dr. Mugabe's story.

After a congregational prayer and hymn, Dr. Mugabe stands to preach on a passage from Luke warning against greed. He prefaces the sermon with a little bit of his story and provides an update on the new Zimbabwe Theological Seminary, which the Alliance supports. He explains that when he was fired in 2011, all but one of the faculty left with him, as did 75 percent of the student body. Dr. Mugabe says that the new school was created because they "wanted to be free." As he proceeds with his sermon, Dr. Mugabe explains that there are many different kinds of greed, not just monetary. He suggests: "In God's economy, we are blessed so we can be a blessing to others."

Upon the completion of his sermon, the congregation moves into a time of offertory. The orchestra provides music as the offering is collected, and a gender-inclusive version of the doxology is sung as the ushers bring the offering forward. The closing hymn is titled "We Are Walking," known in Zulu as *Siyahamba*. Pullen's minister asks Dr. Mugabe if he would explain the pronunciations. The orchestra, along with a djembe, brings to life the song's African rhythms, and although many within the congregation have trouble with the lyrics, there are smiles all around.

The service concludes with a benediction offered by Dr. Mugabe in his native tongue, after which the congregation moves into the fellowship hall for refreshments. Dr. Mugabe and the Pullen minister greet individuals as they leave.

Pullen Memorial Baptist Church has a long history of radical inclusion as a Baptist church in North Carolina. Through its work and ministry, it continues its legacy of radical community. This identity in turn also informs the identity of the Alliance of Baptists.

Lakeshore Avenue Baptist Church

Oakland, California

August 10, 2014

Lakeshore Avenue Baptist Church is situated in the Grand-Lakeshore district of Oakland, California. Residing on a tree-lined street just beyond a stretch of small shops, restaurants and other businesses, the large, white church building sits off the road with the name of the congregation above the entrance, beneath a long, narrow, rectangular window. Similar windows line the side of the sanctuary, and a slim steeple rises from above the church's entrance.

The congregation traces its history to 1860, when it was chartered as First Baptist Church of Brooklyn. Founded near Lake Merritt, which was eventually annexed into the city of Oakland, Lakeshore moved to its current location in 1945. In 1972, the congregation purchased the next-door building, which now serves as the location for the Lakeshore Children's Center and the church offices. Although a nonreligious school, the Lakeshore Children's Center is affiliated with the congregation and includes both a preschool and after-school care for children up to fifth grade.

Lakeshore was one of the four churches expelled from the American Baptist Churches of the West in 1996. While it continued to be a part of the ABCUSA, by 1999 it was required to join a regional American Baptist body to remain within the national organization. During the summer of 1999, Stan Hastey brought greetings from the Alliance to the congregation, which began the process of affiliating with the organization and soon became one of the first West Coast churches to join the Alliance. Lakeshore chose in 2000 to begin partnering with the Metro New York region of the ABCUSA, the Alliance of Baptists and the Baptist Peace Fellowship of North America. In addition to these affiliations, the congregation was also a charter congregation for the Association of Welcoming and Affirming Baptists. According to Lakeshore Avenue's pastor, the Alliance provided the congregation a national religious Baptist body that offered endorsement and recognition of LGBT clergy.

Upon walking into the sanctuary, one notices the high vaulted ceiling and the long center aisle leading to the chancel. Narrow rectangular windows with a deep purple hue line the sanctuary. The purple from these windows is complemented by the wooden pews and crossbeams in the ceiling, as well as by white walls. Beneath the baptismal pool on the back wall of the chancel is a stone marble altar. Above the baptismal pool hangs "The Living Tree," a metallic sculpture of a tree formed out of vines and roots, incorporating shades of brown, green and blue. The purchase of this sculpture created much discussion within the congregation about its necessity and cost, but the work of art filled what was once a large blank wall above the baptistry.

On Sunday, August 10, 2014, prior to the service, a group of roughly ten individuals prepare the "special music" for worship. The choir, diverse in age and ethnicity, recently served as the choir for the church's annual congregational retreat. They practice a version of "Walking Up the King's Highway."

By the start of the service, roughly 150 people are present. After the prelude, the congregation stands for the ringing of the chimes and sings "God Has Smiled on Me." Lakeshore uses two hymnals, *The African American Heritage Hymnal* and *Chalice Hymnal*. These hymnals express some of the identity of the congregation. According to one member, Lakeshore is 45 percent white, 45 percent African American, and 10 percent Asian American.

After the opening hymn and Lord's Prayer, the congregation enters into a time of "Passing the Peace." This lasts for roughly five minutes as individuals walk around the sanctuary greeting one another. This tradition is followed by the "Children's Story" and the "Work of the Church," where the pastor discusses what is going on at Lakeshore.

The sermon is a dialogue between the Lakeshore pastor and the former pastor of First Baptist Church in Oakland. First Baptist Oakland stopped meeting in its church building in 2010 and began attending Lakeshore. The congregation was aging and dwindling, so they decided to give their building to a Burmese congregation.

The sermon is titled "The Path on Which God Leads Us," and the conversation lasts for nearly fifteen minutes. One of the themes that arises is that the "good news is 'good.'" The visiting pastor explains that for many people, the gospel functions a lot more like "bad news with an escape clause." The sermon concludes with a discussion of the breadth of God's mercy. The pastor from First Baptist Church Oakland declares, "There is no greater learning than the wideness of God's mercy."

After the sermon is a "Hymn of Commitment," followed by a collection of tithes and offerings. The doxology uses gender-inclusive language, with the following lyrics: "Praise God from whom all blessings flow/ Praise God all creatures here below/ Praise God with all the hosts above/ Praise God in wonder, joy, and love."

At the conclusion of the service, the congregation recognizes a church member and seminary student for his recent placement for field education at another church. Lakeshore Avenue has a longstanding relationship with the American Baptist Theological Seminary of the West, located a few miles away in Berkeley. One member explains that Lakeshore hosts the seminary's graduation every other year. Following the service, a student from the seminary leads the congregation in a discussion on popular culture and today's youth. The forum is part of a summer series that includes the voices of a number of seminary students.

Lakeshore's bulletin mentions many opportunities for service. During the month of August, the congregation collects school supplies to support local teachers who often have to buy their own. In addition, the congregation plans to participate in a local "Walk for Congo" to learn about and raise money to combat the violence to women and children in the Democratic Republic of Congo. According to the congregation's website, the church has a Hunger Task Force to combat hunger and homelessness and provides space for the San Francisco Kashin Baptist Church, Alcoholics Anonymous and Oakland East Bay Gay Men's Chorus, among other groups.

While Lakeshore remains committed to its American Baptist roots, the congregation maintains many organizational partnerships. The church serves as an example of an Alliance church living out its ministry on the West Coast.

Epilogue

The history of the Alliance of Baptists certainly is a history of learning, adapting and changing. Throughout its history, however, the Alliance balanced an identity centered upon the premise of leaving the Southern Baptist Convention as well as reimagining what a Baptist organization could look like. In the process of leaving the convention, the Alliance slowly recognized that supporting the grandeur of a Zion-like denominational structure might have been an idolatrous idea from the beginning. It might be more faithful to come down from the Southern Baptist mountain of established power, wealth and influence to reside on the land. The Alliance strove to imagine what Zion would look like among the secular, the marginalized and the disenfranchised — the nomadic. The organization looked to imagine and create a religious home for the homeless.

In this way, Welton Gaddy may have been most poignantly accurate when he described the Alliance as a "Boundary People." The Alliance resided on the boundaries of society. Certainly, the members maintained the boundary of living between the ideas of leaving Zion and reimagining Zion, but the Alliance also pushed boundaries. When the organization did not have enough money to support missionaries, it pushed boundaries to partner. When the rest of the Baptist community took stands against the LGBT community, the Alliance pushed boundaries to accept, welcome and affirm these persons. As the Alliance became more aware of gender inequality and corrupt power structures, it pushed boundaries to model shared leadership.

Through living as a boundary people, the Alliance learned what it would mean to reimagine Zion. For in the comforts of an idolatrous denominational entity, there is little need for faith in the divine. On the land and on the boundaries, the Alliance learned what it meant to be faithful in a new, reimagined Zion. As the organization matured and grew, it came to learn that perhaps Zion is not an institution at all. Perhaps Zion is wherever the people of God reside.

Appendix

Alliance Timeline

February 12, 1987
The Alliance of Baptists founded
First convocation at Meredith College, Raleigh, North Carolina
Henry Crouch elected president

1988
Annual convocation at Mercer University, Macon, Georgia
John Thomason elected president
Listening session at Woodmont Church, Nashville, Tennessee

1989
Stan Hastey and Jeanette Holt hired
Annual convocation at First Baptist Church, Greenville, South Carolina
Anne Thomas Neil elected president
Baptist Theological Seminary at Richmond founded

1990
Annual convocation at Third Baptist Church, St. Louis, Missouri
Richard Groves elected president
Statement on Racism and Repentance adopted
First Global Missions Offering collected

1991
Annual convocation at Grace Baptist Church, Richmond, Virginia
Partnerships begin with American Baptist Churches USA, Progressive
    National Baptist Inc., and The Fraternity of Baptists in Cuba

1992
Annual convocation at Providence Baptist Church, Charlotte, North
    Carolina
Ann Quattlebaum elected president
Task Force on Human Sexuality appointed

1993
Annual convocation in Daytona Beach, Florida
Partnership begins with the Atlantic Baptist Fellowship

1994
Annual convocation at First Baptist Church, Greenville, South Carolina
John Roberts elected president

1995
Annual convocation at Vienna Baptist Church, Vienna, Virginia
First Christian worship service held in Holocaust Museum
Joint gathering between Alliance and Progressive National Baptist Convention
    in Charlotte, North Carolina
Statement on Jewish Christian Relations adopted

1996
Annual convocation at Myers Park Baptist Church, Charlotte, North
    Carolina
Nancy Hastings Sehested elected president
Partnership begins with Zimbabwe

1997
Annual convocation at Meredith College, Raleigh, North Carolina (host
    congregations Pullen Memorial Baptist Church and Millbrook Baptist
    Church)
10th anniversary celebrated

1998
Annual convocation at Calvary Baptist Church, Washington, D.C.
Welton Gaddy elected president
Mission statement adopted
Partnership begins with Karen and Kevin Smith in Morocco

1999
Annual convocation at Northminster Baptist Church, Richmond, Virginia
Dialogue begins with United Church of Christ

2000
Annual convocation at University Baptist Church, Austin, Texas
Paula Dempsey elected president
Statement on Death Penalty adopted
Rightly Dividing the Word of Truth released

2001

Annual convocation at Oakhurst Baptist Church, Decatur, Georgia

Dialogue continues with United Church of Christ and Christian Church (Disciples of Christ)

Becomes 36th member body of National Council of Churches

2002

Annual convocation at Wake Forest Baptist Church, Winston-Salem, North Carolina

Craig Henry elected president

Partnership begins with Sri Lanka

2003

Annual convocation at Vienna Baptist Church, Vienna, Virginia

Statement on Muslim-Christian Relations adopted

2004

Annual convocation hosted by Cross Creek Community Church and held at First Baptist Church, Dayton, Ohio

Cherie Smith and Chris Copeland elected president and vice president

Statement on same-sex marriage adopted

Partnership begins with Evangelical Baptist Union of Georgia

2005

Annual convocation at Furman University, Greenville, South Carolina

2006

Annual convocation at Baptist Church of the Covenant, Birmingham, Alabama

Jim Hopkins elected president

Partnership begins with Brazil

2007

Annual convocation at Calvary Baptist Church, Washington, D.C.

2008

Annual convocation at St. Charles Avenue Baptist Church, New Orleans, Louisiana (Northminster Church in Monroe also hosts)

Brooks Wicker elected president

2009

Annual convocation at Park Road Baptist Church, Charlotte, North Carolina

2010

Annual convocation at Asilomar Conference Grounds, Pacific Grove, California

Carol Blythe elected president

Statements on Cuba, immigration, and nuclear disarmament adopted

2011

Annual convocation at Crescent Hill Baptist Church, Louisville, Kentucky

Statements on Cuba travel, economic justice, and Gulf oil spill adopted

2012

Annual gathering at Highland Park Baptist Church, Austin, Texas

Statements on gun violence, sex education, violence against transgender persons, torture, immigration, and a faithful budget adopted

2013

Annual gathering at First Baptist Church, Greenville, South Carolina

Statements on Cuba, drone strikes, and food justice adopted

2014

Annual gathering at Williston Immanuel United Church, Portland, Maine

Mike Castle elected president

Statements on Cuba, justice for farmworkers, mass incarceration, military spending, public education, and resisting violence adopted

Alliance*Connect* launched

UCC lawsuit against same-sex marriage ban in North Carolina joined

Endnotes

Introduction

[1]Aaron Douglass Weaver, "Progressive Baptist Dissenters: A History of the Alliance of Baptists" (Term Paper: Baylor University, 2009), 30. Accessed December 3, 2014. http://www.sitemason.com/files/cQ4qR2/Alliance%20of%20Baptists%20History.pdf.

[2]Ibid., 2.

[3]See Rufus Spain, *At Ease in Zion* (Nashville: Vanderbilt University Press, 1961).

[4]Throughout this work, the term "inerrantist" is used rather than "fundamentalist." Moderates often used "fundamentalist" to characterize their adversaries, but the term "inerrantist" characterizes how the conservatives within the Southern Baptist Convention identified themselves.

[5]See Barry Hankins, *Uneasy in Babylon* (Tuscaloosa, AL: Alabama University Press, 2002).

Chapter 1

[1]Martin Marty, "The Protestant Experience and Perspective," in *American Religious Values and the Future of America*, ed. Rodger Van Allen (Philadelphia: Fortress Press, 1978), 46.

[2]See William Estep, *The Anabaptist Story* (Grand Rapids, MI: Wm. B. Eerdmans Publishing Co., 1996); James McClendon, *Ethics: Systematic Theology*, vol. 1 (Nashville: Abingdon Press, 2002).

[3]See Bill Leonard, *Baptist Ways: A History* (Valley Forge, PA: Judson Press, 2003); Robert G. Torbet, *A History of the Baptists*, 3rd ed., (Valley Forge, PA: Judson Press, 1973).

[4]"Propositions and Conclusions Concerning True Christian Religion," in *Baptist Confessions of Faith*, ed. Bill Leonard, 2nd ed. (Valley Forge, PA: Judson Press, 2011), 117.

[5]Ibid., 125.

[6]Ibid., 128.

[7]Thomas Helwys, *A Short Declaration of the Mystery of Iniquity*, ed. Richard Groves (Macon, GA: Mercer University Press, 1998), 24.

[8]Leonard, Baptist Ways, 46-50.

[9]Torbet, *A History of the Baptists*, 45-46. Confessions held the potential to enforce proper belief and practice, but disciplinary measures were rarely used to correct errant congregations or individuals.

[10]I Corinthians 14:34, NRSV.

[11]See Curtis Freeman, *A Company of Women Preachers: Baptist Prophetesses in Seventeenth-Century England* (Waco, TX: Baylor University Press, 2011), 1-45.

[12]Sarah Frances Anders, "Tracing Past and Present," in *The New Has Come: Emerging Roles among Southern Baptist Women*, eds. Anne Thomas Neil and Virginia Garrett Neely (Washington, D.C.: Southern Baptist Alliance, 1989).

[13]Leonard, *Baptists in America* (New York: Columbia University Press, 2005), 13-14; Torbet, A History of the Baptists, 202.

[14]Roger Williams quoted in Leonard, *Baptists in America*, 14.

[15]Pennsylvania was the other colony to provide religious freedom to the same extent as Rhode Island. Maryland and New York offered a form of religious toleration that offered some freedoms to minority religious traditions.

[16]Leonard, *Baptists in America*, 15-18; Torbet, *A History of the Baptists*, 208-220.

[17]Leonard, *Baptist Ways*, 118-120.

[18]Ibid., 129.

[19]Torbet, *A History of the Baptists*, 211-212; Leonard, *Baptist Ways*, 135; Anders, "Tracing Past and Present," in *The New Has Come*, 12.

[20]William H. Brackney, *Baptists in North America* (Malden, MA: Blackwell Publishing, 2006), 28-31; Leonard, Baptist Ways, 132-133.

[21]See Nathan Hatch, *The Democratization of American Christianity* (New Haven: Yale University Press, 1988); Amanda Porterfield, *Conceived in Doubt: Religion and Politics in the New American Nation* (Chicago: The University of Chicago Press, 2012).

[22]Brackney, *Baptists in North America*, 54-61; Leonard, *Baptists in America*, 19-21; Torbet, *A History of the Baptists*, 249-253.

[23]Ibid.

[24]Ibid.

[25]See Christine Leigh Heyrman, *Southern Cross: The Beginnings of the Bible Belt* (New York: Alfred A. Knopf, 1997).

[26]Torbet, *A History of the Baptists*, 288-290.

[27]Leonard, *Baptist Ways*, 185-189.

[28]Torbet, *A History of the Baptists*, 291.

[29]Leonard, *Baptist Ways*, 189-190; Leonard, *Baptists in America*, 28-30.

[30]*Annual Meeting Minutes of the Southern Baptist Convention*, 1861.

[31]Leonard, *Baptist Ways*, 198-199.

[32]*Annual Meeting Minutes of the Southern Baptist Convention*, 1866.

[33]Charles Reagan Wilson, *Baptized in Blood: The Religion of the Lost Cause*, 1865-1920 (Athens, GA: The University of Georgia Press, 1980), 13.

[34]Rufus Spain, *At Ease in Zion: A Social History of Southern Baptists*, 1865-1900 (Nashville: Vanderbilt University Press, 1967), 213-214.

Chapter 2

[1]See Spain, *At Ease in Zion*.

[2]Walter Shurden, "The Southern Baptist Synthesis: Is it Cracking?" in *Not an Easy Journey: Some Transitions in Baptist Life* (Macon, GA: Mercer University Press, 2005), 200-214.

[3]Ibid., 202-209.

[4]One might suggest that the Southern Baptist Alliance spans the differences of the Charleston and Sandy Creek traditions, while paring back the religious and geographic exclusivity of the Tennessee and Georgia traditions.

[5]Proverbs 23:10, KJV.

[6]Shurden, *Not a Silent People: Controversies That Have Shaped Southern Baptists* (Nashville: Broadman Press, 1972), 21-32.

[7]John T. Scopes, a science teacher from Tennessee, was brought to trial for teaching evolution in the high school classroom, which violated Tennessee law. William Jennings Bryan and Clarence Darrow argued the case as prosecutor and defense attorney, respectively, and although the fundamentalists and Bryan won the case, it was a nominal victory for fundamentalists. Edwin Gaustad and Leigh Schmidt, *The Religious History of America* (New York: HarperOne, 2004), 296-298.

[8]John Lee Eighmy, *Churches in Cultural Captivity: A History of the Social Attitudes of Southern Baptists* (Knoxville, TN: The University of Tennessee Press, 1972), 126-127.

[9]Leonard, *Dictionary of Baptists in America* (Downers Grove, IL: Intervarsity Press, 1994), 94.

[10]*Southern Baptist Convention Annual*, 1925.

[11]Leonard, *Dictionary of Baptists in America*, 94.

[12]*Southern Baptist Convention Annual*, 1925.

[13]Ibid., 76.

[14]W.J. McGlothlin, "My Part in the Confession Controversy," *Biblical Recorder*, 2 December 1925.

[15]C.R. Daley, "13 Southern Professors Dismissed by Trustees," *Baptist Press*, 16 June 1958. Accessed January 15, 2015. http://media.sbhla.org.s3.amazonaws.com/718,16-Jun-1958.pdf.

[16]Bill Leonard, "Midwestern Theological Seminary," in *Dictionary of Baptists in America*, 188; Ralph Elliott, *The Genesis Controversy: A Eulogy for a Great Tradition* (Macon, GA: Mercer University Press, 1992).

[17]Elliott, *The Genesis Controversy*, 11.

[18]Ibid., 45; 49.

[19]Theo Sommercamp, *Baptist Press*, 2 June 1962. Accessed January 15, 2015. http://media.sbhla.org.s3.amazonaws.com/1593,02-Jun-1962.pdf.

[20]See Elliott, *The Genesis Controversy*. It should be noted that Elliott was not dismissed from Midwestern Baptist Seminary for the publication of his work or the beliefs that he held. Instead, the seminary board requested that he withdraw the work from publication, which he refused to do. The board then dismissed Elliott for insubordination rather than for holding "heretical" beliefs.

[21]Leonard, "Baptist Faith and Message," in *Dictionary of Baptists in America*, 46-47.

[22]The Broadman Controversy took place in 1969 after the publication of a commentary that included a British scholar's commentary on Genesis. Eventually, the commentary was withdrawn.

[23]See David T. Morgan, *The New Crusades, the New Holy Land: Conflict in the Southern Baptist Convention 1969-1991* (Tuscaloosa, AL: The University of Alabama Press, 1996).

[24]Todd Starnes, "Longtime conservative leader loses battle to Alzheimer's," *Baptist Press*, 16 March 2000.

[25]Morgan, *The New Crusades*, 30.

[26]See James C. Hefley, *The Truth in Crisis: The Controversy in the Southern Baptist Convention*, vol. 5 (Richmond, VA: Hannibal Books, 1990), 23-25.

[27]Nancy Tatom Ammerman, *Baptist Battles: Social Change and Religious Conflict in the Southern Baptist Convention* (New Brunswick, NJ: Rutgers University Press, 1990), 169.

[28]Morgan, *The New Crusades*, 40.

[29]Leonard, *God's Last and Only Hope: The Fragmentation of the Southern Baptist Convention* (Grand Rapids, MI: William B. Eerdmans Publishing Company, 1990), 137.

[30]Ibid., 138.

[31]Tom Miller, "Pressler 'Goes for Jugular' In Fight to Win Convention," *Baptist Press*, 19 September 1980.

[32]Cecil Sherman, "An Overview of the Moderate Movement," in *The Struggle for the Soul of the SBC: Moderate Responses to the Fundamentalist Movement*, ed. Walter Shurden (Macon, GA: Mercer University Press, 1993), 19-23; "North Carolina Pastors Discuss SBC Concerns," *Baptist Press*, 3 November 1980.

[33]Shurden, *Struggle for the Soul of the SBC*, xi.

[34]Ibid., xii.

[35]"Conservatism Sweeps SBC In Resolutions, Election," *Baptist Press*, 17 June 1982.

[36]Stan Hastey, "The Southern Baptist Convention, 1979-1993: What Happened and Why?" in *Baptist History and Heritage* 28, no. 4, October 1993, 23.

[37]Ibid.

[38]See Ellen M. Rosenberg, *The Southern Baptists: A Subculture in Transition* (Knoxville, TN: The University of Tennessee Press, 1989), 189-193.

[39]Aaron Douglas Weaver, *James M. Dunn and Soul Freedom* (Macon, GA: Smyth and Helwys, 2011), 113-117.

[40]Ibid; Shurden, *Struggle for the Soul of the SBC*, xiii.

[41]Roy Honeycutt, "To Your Tents, O Israel," audio film, The Boyce Digital Library. Accessed June 21, 2014. http://digital.library.sbts.edu/handle/10392/2988.

[42]Ammerman, *Baptist Battles*, 3.

[43]Shurden, *Struggle for the Soul of the SBC*, xii.

[44]Ammerman, *Baptist Battles*, 10-11.

[45]Sherman, "An Overview of the Moderate Movement," in *The Struggle for the Soul of the SBC*, 27. Sherman suggests that the decision to start something new came out of the August 1986 meeting in Macon, Georgia. It might be more accurate to suggest that those still interested in combating the inerrantists blessed those who might create something new. To be sure, it was the first inkling that a new organization might be emerging, but formation of the Southern Baptist Alliance can hardly be attributed to the August 1986 meeting.

[46]Libby Bellinger, "More Hidden than Revealed: The History of Southern Baptist Women in Ministry," in *Struggle for the Soul of the SBC*, 138.

[47]"The Glorieta Statement," October 22, 1986.

[48]"Meeting of Concerned Southern Baptists at Meredith College, Raleigh, N.C. September 23, 1986," Box 2 Alliance of Baptist Records, MS 588, Z. Smith Reynolds Library Special Collections and Archives, Wake Forest University, Winston-Salem, NC. (Abbreviated AA for Alliance Archives); Alan Neely, "The History of the Alliance of Baptists," in *Struggle for the Soul of the SBC*, 106-107.

[49]Ibid.

[50]Barry Hankins, *Uneasy in Babylon: Southern Baptist Conservatives and American Culture* (Tuscaloosa, AL: The University of Alabama Press, 2002), 272-277.

[51]Leonard, "A Moderate Responds," in Baptist History & Heritage 28, no. 4 (October 1993): 16.

Chapter 3

[1]"Southern Baptist Alliance Meeting," December 1-2, 1986. Box 2, *AA*. Alliance of Baptist Records, MS 588, Z. Smith Reynolds Library Special Collections and Archives, Wake Forest University, Winston-Salem, NC. (Abbreviated *AA* for *Alliance Archives*).

[2]"Southern Baptist Alliance Meeting," February 2-3, 1987. Box 2, *AA*.

[3]"Minutes of the Director's Meeting: Southern Baptist Alliance," March 23, 1987. Box 2, *AA*.

[4]"Minutes of the Business Session: Southern Baptist Alliance Convocation," May 15, 1987. Box 2, *AA*.

[5]"Minutes of the Board of Directors Meeting: Southern Baptist Alliance," June 14, 1987. Box 2, *AA*.

[6]"Minutes of the Board of Directors Meeting: Southern Baptist Alliance," September 14-15, 1987. Box 3, *AA*.

[7]"Minutes of the Executive Committee: Southern Baptist Alliance," November 19-20, 1987. Box 3, *AA*.

[8]Ibid.

[9]Ibid.

[10]"Minutes of the Board of Directors Meeting: Southern Baptist Alliance," March 21, 1988. Box 3, *AA*.

[11]"Minutes of the Business Session: Southern Baptist Alliance Convocation," March 22, 1988. Box 3, *AA*.

[12]"Minutes of the Executive Committee: Southern Baptist Alliance," June 14, 1988. Box 3, *AA*.

[13]"Minutes of the Board of Directors Meeting: Southern Baptist Alliance," September 10, 1988. Box 3, *AA*.

[14]"Minutes For the Southern Baptist Alliance," February 10-11, 1989. Box 3, *AA*.

[15]"Minutes of the Southern Baptist Alliance in Annual Session," March 1-3, 1989. Box 3, *AA*.

[16]"Minutes of the Executive Committee: Southern Baptist Alliance," March 8, 1990. Box 3, *AA*.

[17]"Minutes of the Executive Committee: Southern Baptist Alliance," September 27-28, 1990; "Minutes of the Board of Directors," September 20-21, 1991. Box 3, *AA*.

[18]"Minutes of the Board of Directors of the Southern Baptist Alliance," September 27-28, 1990. Box 3, *AA*.

[19]"Board of Directors Meeting: Providence Baptist Church, Charlotte, NC," March 4-5, 1992. Box 4, *AA*.

[20]"Board of Directors Meeting: First Baptist Church, Washington, DC," September 24-26, 1992. Box 4, *AA*.

[21]"Meeting of the Board of Directors, First Baptist Church, Washington, DC," September 30-October 2, 1993. Box 4, *AA*.

[22]"Minutes of the Board of Directors: Hyatt Hotel, Greenville, S.C.," March 2-3, 1994. Box 4, *AA*.

[23]"Annual Meeting, First Baptist Church, Greenville, S.C.," March 4, 1994. Box 4, *AA*.

[24]"Meeting of the Board of Directors, First Baptist Church, Washington D.C.," September 22-24, 1994. Box 4, *AA*.

[25]"The Alliance of Baptists, Meeting of the Board of Directors," August 7-8, 1995. Box 4, *AA*.

[26]"Annual Meeting Myers Park Baptist Church, Charlotte, N.C., "March 15, 1996. Box 5, *AA*.

[27]"Minutes of the Annual Meeting Meredith College, Raleigh, N.C.," March 15, 1997. Box 5, *AA*.

[28]"Meeting of the Board of Directors Washington," March 11-12, 1998. Box 5, *AA*; "Report to the Board of Directors Annual Meeting," March 13, 1998. Box 5, *AA*.

[29]"Minutes of the Annual Meeting," April 28, 2000. Box 5, *AA*.; "Meeting of March 11-12, 1999 Richmond, Virginia." Box 5, *AA*.

[30]Ibid.

[31]"Minutes of the Meeting of the Board of Directors," April 4-5, 2002. Box 5, *AA*.

[32]"The Alliance of Baptists: Strategic Plan, 2004-2006." Box 5, *AA*.

[33]"Minutes of the Annual Meeting, Dayton, Ohio," April 17, 2004. Box 6, *AA*.

[34]"Minutes of the Annual Meeting Southside Baptist Church, Birmingham, Alabama," April 22, 2006. Box 6, *AA*.

[35]Ibid.

[36]"Minutes of the Meeting of the Board of Directors Ginter Park Baptist Church, Richmond, Virginia," September 13-15, 2007. Box 6, *AA*; "Minutes of the Meeting of the Board of Directors St. Paul's United Church of Christ, New Orleans," March 27-28, 2008. Minutes after 2007 were not archived prior to publication. All minutes cited after 2007 were personal copies given to the author for research purposes.

[37]"Alliance Virtual Board Meeting," March 16, 2009.

[38]"Minutes of the Annual Meeting Asilomar Conference Grounds, Pacific Grove, CA," July 30, 2010.

[39]"Minutes of the Alliance of Baptists Board of Directors," April 28, 2011.

[40]"Alliance of Baptists — Board of Directors Meeting," April 11, 2012; "Alliance of Baptists Annual Meeting," April 6, 2013.

[41]Ibid.

Chapter 4

[1]Alan Neely, "Forebears, Siblings, and Offspring: A History of the Alliance of Baptists," Manuscript, 67.

[2]"Southern Baptist Alliance Meeting on December 1-2, 1986." Box 2, *AA*.

[3]Neely, "Forebears, Siblings, and Offspring," 71; "Southern Baptist Alliance Meeting on December 1-2, 1986." Box 2, *AA*.

[4]Mahan Siler, "Fussin With the Covenant . . . Along the Way," Covenant Address, 1997. Box 12, *AA*.

[5]"Southern Baptist Alliance Meeting on December 1-2, 1986." Box 2, *AA*.

[6]Neely, "Forebears, Siblings, and Offspring," 71.

[7]"Southern Baptist Alliance Meeting on February 2-3, 1987." Box 2, *AA*.

[8]Neely, "The History of the Alliance of Baptists," in *Struggle for the Soul of the SBC*, 110.

[9]Ibid., 111.

[10]"Southern Baptist Alliance Meeting on February 2-3, 1987." Box 2, *AA*.

[11]At the time of publication of this work, the Alliance Covenant remained the guiding principle of the Alliance of Baptists.

[12]Anne Thomas Neil, "Life's Greatest Adventure," Covenant Address, 1996. Box 12, *AA*.

[13]Neely, "Forebears, Siblings, and Offspring."

[14]Ibid., 78.

[15]Neely, "Servanthood Revisited," Covenant Address, 2002. Box 14, *AA*.

[16]Walker Knight, "The Covenant: A Dream and Demand," Covenant Address, 1992. Box 10, *AA*.

[17]Ibid.

[18]Ibid.

[19]Neely, "Forebears, Siblings, and Offspring," 18.

[20]"Memorandum from Stan Hastey to Visioning Committee," March 5, 1997, Box 8, *AA*.

[21]Siler, "Fussin with the Covenant ... Along the Way," Covenant Address, 1997, Box 8, *AA*.

[22]"Report of the Visioning Committee," 1997, Box 8, *AA*.

[23]Neely, "A History of the Southern Baptist Alliance," 119.

[24]Stan Hastey, "The Alliance and CBF: Setting the record straight," *Baptists Today*, Box 20, *AA*.

Chapter 5

[1]See James Dunn, *Soul Freedom: Baptist Battle Cry* (Macon, GA: Smyth & Helwys, 2000).

[2]Sherman, "Freedom of the Individual to Interpret the Bible," in *Being Baptist Means Freedom*, ed. by Alan Neely (Charlotte, NC: Southern Baptist Alliance, 1988), 15.

[3]Ibid., 16.

[4]Stan Hastey to Mahan Siler, March 23, 1990. Box 20, *AA*.

[5]Siler to Hastey, March 16, 1990. Box 20, *AA*.

[6]"Southern Baptist Alliance Board of Directors Meeting," March 4-5, 1992. Box 4, *AA*.

[7]"The Alliance of Baptists: Meeting of the Board of Directors," September 30-October 2, 1993. Box 4, *AA*.

[8]"The Alliance of Baptists Minutes of the Board of Directors," March 2-3, 1994. Box 4, *AA*.

[9]J. Daniel Day to Stan Hastey, March 15, 1994. Box 18, *AA*.

[10]Hastey, State of the Alliance Address, March 4, 1994. Box 11, *AA*

[11]"The Alliance of Baptists Meeting of the Board of Directors," September 22-24, 1994. Box 4, *AA*.

[12]Ibid.

[13]Ibid.

[14]William Johnson to Stan Hastey, March 10, 1994. Box 19, *AA*.

[15]Stan Hastey to Jay Casey, December 9, 1992. Box 17, *AA*.

[16]This information comes from a personal conversation with Paula Dempsey, Alliance minister of partnership relations.

[17]Cindy Clanton to Stan Hastey, April 13, 1994. Box 17, *AA*.

[18]Alan Neely to Cecil Sherman, April 22, 1993, Box 22, *AA*.

[19]William Crisp to Stan Hastey, November 14, 1998. Box 17, *AA*; Stan Hastey to William Crisp, May 19, 1999. Box 17, *AA*.

[20]Ken Sehested, email message to Mahan Siler, March 23, 1999, Box 7, *AA*.

[21]Ken Sehested, email message to Millard Eiland, April 12, 1999. Box 7, *AA*; Sehested, email message to Select Contacts, May 13, 1999. Box 7, *AA*.

[22]Ken Sehested, email message to Retreat Participants, September 16, 1999. Box 7, *AA*.

[23]Ken Sehested, email message to LaDayne Polaski, April 12, 1999. Box 7, *AA*.

[24]Herman Greene to Alliance of Baptists, February 21, 1996. Box 18, *AA*.

[25]Greene to Alliance of Baptists, December 8, 1995. Box 18, *AA*.

[26]"The Alliance of Baptists Meeting of the Board of Directors," March 13-14, 1996. Box 5, *AA*.

[27]Bob Allen, "Ecology should be a central concern for churches, study group maintains," *Associated Baptist Press*, 1999.

[28]Rick Goodman to Stan [Hastey] and Jeanette [Holt], April 25, 1999. Box 15, *AA*.

[29]Jeanette Holt to Jay McDaniel, February 24, 2003. Box 15, *AA*.

[30]"A Statement on the Gulf Oil Spill," *Alliance of Baptists*, 2011.

[31]Cherie Smith, email message to Jeanette Holt and Stan Hastey, March 30, 2000. Box 13, *AA*; Bob Allen, "Alliance renews call for end to Cuban embargo," Associated Baptist Press. Box 13, *AA*; Nancy Hastings Sehested, email message to Stan Hastey and Jeanette Holt, May 2, 2000. Box 13, *AA*.

[32]"Alliance of Baptists Special Dialogue on Women's Issues and Meeting of the Gender Equity Task Group," Box 22, *AA*.

[33]Stan Hastey to Jeanette Holt, April 30, 2000. Box 22, *AA*.

[34]Stan Hastey to J. Bennett Mullinax, February 18, 2005. Box 15, *AA*; Mullinax to Hastey, February 11, 2005. Box 15, *AA*.

[35]Mary Jane Gorman, email message to Stan Hastey, January 24, 2005. Box 15, *AA*.

[36]Cherie Smith, email message to Stan Hastey, Jeanette Holt, Chris Copeland, February 7, 2005. Box 15, *AA*; Holt, email message to Cherie Smith, February 9, 2005. Box 15, *AA*

[37]Glendale Baptist Church to First Baptist Church Greenville, South Carolina, February 20, 2005. Box 15, *AA*.

[38]Ken Sehested, email message to Jeanette Holt, April 7, 2005 Box 16, *AA*.

Chapter 6

[1]Richard Groves, "The Freedom of the Local Church," in *Being Baptist Means Freedom*, 25.

[2]Ibid., 34.

[3]Ibid.

[4]Neely, "The History of the Alliance of Baptists," in *Struggle for the Soul of the SBC*, 108

[5]Neely, "Forebears, Siblings, and Offspring," 66.

[6]Ibid; Neely, "The History of the Alliance of Baptists," in *Struggle for the Soul of the SBC*, 107-109.

[7]Ibid.

[8]"Minutes of the Board of Directors Meeting," September 14-15, 1987. Box 3, *AA*.

[9]"Minutes of the Board of Directors," March 1, 1989. Box 3, *AA*.

[10]Neely, "Forebears, Siblings, and Offspring," 19.

[11]Ibid., 23.

[12]Neil to Women's Task Force, August 4, 1987. Box 8, *AA*.

[13]Ibid.

[14]Neil, "Suggestions from Members of the Task Force on Women, SBA." Box 8, *AA*.

[15]"Minutes of the Director's Meeting Southern Baptist Alliance," March 23, 1987. Box 3, *AA*.

[16]Bob Richardson to Henry Crouch, March 25, 1987. Box 8, *AA*; David and Rachel Bishop to Henry Crouch, March 17, 1987. Box 8, *AA*.

[17]Kathleen McClain, "Baptist Group Seeks Donations For Female-Pastored Churches," The Charlotte Observer. Box 9, *AA*.

[18]"Minutes of the Director's Meeting Southern Baptist Alliance," March 23, 1987. Box 2, *AA*.

[19]"Minutes of the Board of Directors Meeting," September 14-15, 1987. Box 3, *AA*.

[20]"Minutes of the Board of Directors Meeting," January 11, 1988. Box 3, *AA*.

[21]Libby Bellinger to Jack Harwell, December 5, 1988. Box 8, *AA*.

[22]Neil, "Life's Greatest Adventure," Covenant Address, 1996. Box 12, *AA*.

[23]"Minutes of the Board of Directors Meeting," September 10, 1988. Box 3, *AA*.

[24]Libby Bellinger to Hardy Clemons, November 30, 1988. Box 8, *AA*.

[25]Rebecca Albritton to unnamed, September 26, 1989. Box 8, *AA*.

[26]Neil, "Life's Greatest Adventure."

[27]Stan Hastey to Libby Bellinger, April 20, 1990. Box 8, *AA*; Becky Albritton to Bellinger, May 8, 1990. Box 8, *AA*.

[28]Neil, "Life's Greatest Adventure."

[29]Ibid.

[30]Ibid.

[31]Ibid.

[32]"The Alliance of Baptists: Meeting of the Board of Directors," September 30-October 2, 1993. Box 4, *AA*.

[33]"The Alliance of Baptists Minutes of the Board of Directors," March 2-3, 1994. Box 4, *AA*.

[34]Nancy Hastings Sehested to Women in the Church Committee, March 9, 1994. Box 8, *AA*.

[35]Neil, "Life's Greatest Adventure"; "Reports of Standing Committee," 1996. Box 12, *AA*.

[36]"Alliance of Baptists: Minutes of the Board of Directors," September 17-19, 1998. Box 5, *AA*

[37]Cherie Smith to Alliance of Baptist Convocation Committee, September 13, 2000. Box 5, *AA*.

[38]"The Alliance of Baptists: Minutes of the Board Meeting," September 19-21, 2002. Box 5, *AA*.

[39]Pamela R. Durso, "The State of Baptist Women." Accessed November 17, 2014. bwim.info/files/State_of_Women_in_Baptist_Life_2010.pdf.

[40]"The Alliance of Baptists: Meeting of the Board Meeting," September 15-17, 2005. Box 6, *AA*.

[41]"The Alliance of Baptists: Minutes of the Meeting of the Board of Directors," September 13-15, 2007. Box 6, *AA*.

[42]Alliance of Baptists, "Communities." Accessed November 17, 2014. allianceofbaptists. org/PCP/communities.

[43]"Southern Baptist Alliance: Minutes of the Board of Directors Meeting," March 13-14, 1991. Box 4, *AA*.

[44]Letter from Stephen Shoemaker to Worship Committee, June 5, 1991. Box 8, *AA*.

[45]Michael Hawn to Stan Hastey, 1989. Box 18, *AA*.

[46]Ann Quattlebaum to Michael Hawn, October 21, 1991. Box 8, *AA*.

[47]Paula Dempsey to Steve Shoemaker, Jeanette Holt, Ann Quattlebaum and Michael Hawn, July 16, 1992. Box 8, *AA*.

[48]"Southern Baptist Alliance: Minutes of the Board of Directors Meeting," September 20-21, 1991. Box 4, *AA*.

[49]"Worship Committee Report," September 19, 1991. Box 8, *AA*.

[50]Hawn, "A Little Reverse Missions: In Search of a Global Perspective in Worship." Box 16, *AA*.

[51]Ibid.

[52]"The Alliance of Baptists: Minutes of the Board Meeting," April 15-16, 2004. Box 6, *AA*.

[53]"The Alliance of Baptists: Meeting of the Board Meeting," March 30-April 1, 2005. Box 6, *AA*.

Chapter 7

[1]Rachel Richardson Smith, "The Freedom to Participate in the Wider Community of Faith," in *Being Baptist Means Freedom*, 41.

[2]Neely, "Forebears, Siblings, and Offspring," 1-3.

[3]Fred Anderson, "Company's Coming," *Religious Herald*, Box 13, *AA*.

[4]Rachel Smith, "The Freedom to Participate in the Wider Community, in *Being Baptist Means Freedom*, 38.

[5]The Canadian Association of Baptist Freedoms, "Objectives and History." Accessed September 10, 2014. http://c-abf.ca/history.html.

[6]The Gathering of Baptists, "Who We Are," accessed September 10, 2014, http://www. gatheringbaptists.ca.

[7]M.R.B. Lovesey to Henry Crouch, April 29, 1987. Box 18, *AA*.

[8]Stan Hastey to Edward Colquhoun, May 19, 1993. Box 18, *AA*.

[9]"The Alliance of Baptists: Meeting of the Board of Directors," September 30-October 2, 1993. Box 4, *AA*.

[10]Hastey, State of the Alliance Address, March 4, 1994. Box 11, *AA*.

[11]Hastey, State of the Alliance Address, March 13, 1998. Box 13, *AA*.

[12]"Alliance of Baptists: Meeting of the Board of Directors," September 16, 2004. Box 6, *AA*.

[13]Stan Hastey to Derrick Marshall, September 2, 1994. Box 18, *AA*.

[14]Hastey, "Greetings to the Atlantic Baptist Fellowship," June 2, 1995. Box 17, *AA*.

[15]Atlantic Baptist Fellowship, "Objectives and History," accessed September 10, 2014, http://c-abf.ca/history.html.

[16]"Minutes of the Alliance of Baptists Board of Directors," November 8-10, 2012.

[17]The Cooperative Baptist Fellowship, "About Us," accessed September 11, 2014, http://www.thefellowship.info/identity/about-us.

[18]Cecil Sherman to Henry Crouch, May 27, 1987. Box 8, *AA*.

[19]Ibid.

[20]Cecil Sherman to Crouch, November 18, 1987. Box 7, *AA*.

[21]"The Southern Baptist Alliance 4th Annual Convocation." Box 9, *AA*.

[22]Hastey, "State of the Alliance Address," March 15, 1991, 8-9. Box 10, *AA*.

[23]Hastey, "State of the Alliance Address," February 26, 1993, Box 10, *AA*.

[24]"Southern Baptist Alliance: Minutes of the Board of Directors Meeting," September 20-21, 1991. Box 4, *AA*.

[25]"Southern Baptist Alliance Board of Directors Meeting," March 4-5, 1992. Box 4, *AA*.

[26]"The Alliance of Baptists: Board of Directors Meeting," September 24-26, 1992. Box 4, *AA*.

[27]Ibid.

[28]Hastey, "State of the Alliance Address," February 26, 1993. Box 10, *AA*.

[29]Hastey, "State of the Alliance Address," March 6, 1992, 11. Box 10, *AA*

[30]"The Alliance of Baptists: Board of Directors Meeting," September 24-26, 1992. Box 4, *AA*.

[31]Alan Neely to Mr. and Mrs. Guyon Phillips, October 2, 1992. Box 7, *AA*.

[32]Hastey, "State of the Alliance Address," February 26, 1993, Box 10, *AA*.

[33]Hastey, "State of the Alliance Address," March 4, 1994. Box 11, *AA*.

[34]Mark Buckner to Stan Hastey, November 16, 1993. Box 17, *AA*.

[35]Molly Marshall to Stan Hastey, October 29, 1996. Box 19, *AA*.

[36]Julie Pennington-Russell to Stan [Hastey] and Jeanette [Holt], July 8, 1992. Box 19, *AA*.

[37]Sharyn E. Dowd to Stan Hastey, November 6, 1991. Box 18, *AA*.

[38]Hastey to Dowd, December 2, 1991. Box 18, *AA*.

[39]Mark Olson to Stan Hastey, 1992. Box 19, *AA*.

[40]Cecil Sherman to Stan Hastey, July 23, 1996. Box 20, *AA*.

[41]Stan Hastey to Walter Shurden, June 6, 1996. Box 20, *AA*.

[42]Daniel Vestal to Stan Hastey, February 17, 1997. Box 12, *AA*.

[43]Daniel Vestal to The Alliance of Baptists, February 24, 1997. Box 12, *AA*.

[44]Stan Hastey to Steward A. Newman, April 23, 1998. Box 19, *AA*.

[45]Bob Allen, "CBF 'welcoming but not affirming' of homosexuals," *Baptist Standard*, 23 October 2000.

[46]"Alliance of Baptists: Minutes of the Meeting of the Board of Directors," April 19-20, 2001. Box 5, *AA*.

[47]Hastey, "The Alliance and CBF: Setting the Record Straight." Box 20, *AA*.

[48]Ibid.

[49]Cecil Sherman to Stan Hastey, October 26, 2002. Box 20, *AA*.

[50]Cecil Sherman to Hastey, May 9, 2003. Box 20, *AA*.

[51]Alan Neely to Cecil Sherman, October 11, 2003. Box 20, *AA*.

[52]Stan Hastey to Cecil Sherman, April 11, 2003. Box 20, *AA*.

[53]Walker Knight, "The Covenant: A Dream and Demand," Covenant Address 1992, Box 10, *AA*.

[54]Letter from Daniel E. Weiss. Box 7, *AA*.

[55]Malcolm Shotwell to Stan Hastey, September 4, 1991. Box 16, *AA*.

[56]Eugene Ton to Stan Hastey, December 19, 1991. Box 20, *AA*.

[57]"Minutes of the Board of Directors of the Southern Baptist Alliance," September 27-28, 1990. Box 3, *AA*.

[58]Robert Dilday, "The Southern Baptist Alliance Votes for Stronger Relations with American Baptist Churches USA," *Capital Baptist*, 1991.

[59]"The Southern Baptist Alliance 4th Annual Convocation," Box 9, *AA*.

[60]Stan Hastey to Daniel Weiss, November 27, 1991. Box 10, *AA*.

[61]Stan Hastey to Walter Parrish II, November 27, 1991. Box 10, *AA*.

[62]Hastey, "State of the Alliance Address," March 4, 1994. Box 11, *AA*.

[63]"The Alliance of Baptists Meeting of the Board of Directors," August 7-8, 1995. Box 4, *AA*.

[64]Bob Mathis to Stan Hastey, February 25, 1991. Box 19, *AA*.

[65]"Together . . . For Freedom's Sake!" Conference Brochure, February 3-5, 1994. Box 11, *AA*.

[66]"Together...For Freedom's Sake," *Baptist Today*, Box 11, *AA*.

[67]Hastey, "State of the Alliance Address," March 4, 1994. Box 11, *AA*.

[68]Dwight Lundgren to Alliance of Baptists, November 2, 1995. Box 21, *AA*.

[69]Hastey, "Baptist groups meet together to discuss Baptist distinctives," Associated Baptist Press, 27 August 1996. Box 21, *AA*.

[70]"Alliance of Baptists: Minutes of the Board of Directors' Meeting" September 18-20, 1997. Box 5, *AA*.

[71]"Alliance of Baptists: Minutes of the Meeting of the Board of Directors," September 21-23, 2000. Box 5, *AA*.

[72]"Board of Directors," March 11-22, 1998. Box 5, *AA*.

[73]Hastey, "State of the Alliance Address," March 13, 1998. Box 13, *AA*.

[74]"Alliance of Baptists: Minutes of the Meeting of the Board of Directors," September 16-18, 1999. Box 5, *AA*.

[75]"The Alliance of Baptists: Minutes of the Board Meeting," September 14-16, 2006. Box 6, *AA*.

[76]Hastey, "State of the Alliance Address," April 22, 2006. Box 16, *AA*.

[77]The United Church of Christ, "UCC-Disciples Ecumenical Partnership," http://www.ucc.org/ecumenical/ucc-disciples-ecumenical.html. Accessed September 13, 2014.

[78]"Alliance of Baptists: Minutes of the Board of Directors," September 19, 1996. Box 5, *AA*.

[79]Hastey, "The United Church of Christ/Alliance of Baptists Dialogue," *Baptists Today*, 17 April 1997. Box 22, *AA*.

[80]Richard Hamm to Stan Hastey, 2000. Box 16, *AA*.

[81]Bob Allen, "Alliance of Baptists revisits its founding 'covenant'," *Associated Baptist Press*, 18 March 1997. Box 12, *AA*.

[82]John Thomas to Stan Hastey, June 20, 1997. Box 22, *AA*.

[83]Hastey, "State of the Alliance Address," March 13, 1998. Box 13, *AA*.

[84]Ibid.

[85]"Conclusion of the Proposed Ecumenical Agreement between the Alliance of Baptists, United Church of Christ, and Christian Church (Disciples of Christ)." Box 15, *AA*.

[86]Hastey, "State of the Alliance Address," April 17, 2004. Box 15, *AA*.

[87]The Progressive National Baptist Convention, "History of the PBNC," accessed September 12, 2014, http://www.pnbc.org/#/about-us/history.

[88]Stan Hastey to Charles G. Adams, March 21, 1990. Box 9, *AA*.

[89]"Summary of First PNBC/SBA Dialogue Session," January 21, 1992. Box 20, *AA*.

[90]"Minutes of the AoB/PNBC Dialogue Team Meeting" March 5, 1992. Box 20, *AA*.

[91]Stan Hastey to Tyrone Pitts, November 27, 1991. Box 10, *AA*.

[92]Hastey, "State of the Alliance Address," March 4, 1994. Box 11, *AA*; "Committee Reports," 1995. Box 11, *AA*.

[93]"An Open Letter to Churches Affiliated with the Alliance and the Cooperative Baptist Fellowship," August 9, 1995. Box 20, *AA*.

[94]Amy Andrews, "Like Family: Clinton urges nation to pull together," *Charlotte Observer*. Box 20, *AA*.

[95]"Alliance of Baptists: Minutes of the Board of Directors' Meeting," September 18-20, 1997. Box 5, *AA*.

[96]"Report of the Ecumenical and Interfaith Relations Committee of the Alliance of Baptists," April 24, 2003. Box 22, *AA*.

[97]The National Council of Churches, "History," accessed January 15, 2015, http://nationalcouncilofchurches.us/about/history.php.

[98]Stan Hastey to Joan Brown Campbell, November 27, 1991. Box 10, *AA*.

[99]"Committee Reports," 1995. Box 11, *AA*.

[100]Ibid.

[101]"Action on Alliance of Baptists Eligibility Postponed," Memo Box 22, *AA*.

[102]Hastey, "State of the Alliance Address," April 17, 2004. Box 15, *AA*.

[103]"Alliance of Baptists: Minutes of the Executive Committee," January 11, 2002. Box 5, *AA*.

[104]"The Alliance of Baptists: Minutes of the Board Meeting," March 30-April 1, 2005. Box 6, *AA*.

Chapter 8

[1]"1988 Resolution on the Priesthood of the Believer," The Southern Baptist Convention, June 14-16, 1988. Resolution no. 5.

[2]William Turner, "The Freedom to Be Servant Leaders," in *Being Baptist Means Freedom*, 46.

[3]Ibid., 48-55.

[4]Ibid., 56.

[5]"Constitution for the Southern Baptist Alliance," 1987. Box 8, *AA*.

[6]"Committees of the Southern Baptist Alliance." Box 9, *AA*.

[7]"Constitution for the Southern Baptist Alliance," 1987. Box 8, *AA*.

[8]Letter from Lee Gallman to John Thomason, July 6, 1988. Box 9, *AA*.

[9]"Minutes of the Board of Directors Meeting," January 11, 1988.

[10]Neely, "The History of the Alliance of Baptists," in *Struggle for the Soul of the SBC*, 111-112.

[11]David Holladay to Stan Hastey, May 2, 1989. Box 18, *AA*.

[12]"Minutes of the Officers Meeting: Southern Baptist Alliance," July 14, 1987. Box 2, *AA*.

[13]"Minutes of the Board of Directors Meeting," January 11, 1988. Box 3, *AA*.

[14]"Minutes of the Board of Directors Meeting," September 14-15, 1987. Box 3, *AA*.

[15]Ibid.

[16]"Minutes of the Board of Directors Meeting," November 28-29, 1988. Box 3, *AA*.

[17]"Confidential Memorandum," December 18, 1992. Box 20, *AA*.

[18]"The Alliance of Baptists Meeting of the Board of Directors," March 2-3, 1995. Box 4, *AA*.

[19]The Alliance of Baptists Meeting of the Board of Directors," August 7-8, 1995. Box 4, *AA*.

[20]"Alliance of Baptists: Minutes of the Board of Directors' Meeting," March 13-14, 1997. Box 5, *AA*.

[21]"Alliance of Baptists: Minutes of the Meeting of the Board of Directors," April 26-27, 2000. Box 5, *AA*.

[22]Ibid.

[23]"Alliance of Baptists: Minutes of the Meeting of the Board of Directors," September 21-23, 2000. Box 5, *AA*.

[24]Ibid.

[25]"Alliance of Baptists: Minutes of the Meeting of the Board of Directors," April 4-5, 2002. Box 5, *AA*.

[26]"The Alliance of Baptists: Minutes of the Board Meeting," September 19-21, 2002. Box 5, *AA*

[27]Ibid.

[28]"The Alliance of Baptists: Minutes of the Board Meeting," April 15-16, 2004. Box 6, *AA*.

[29]"The Alliance of Baptists: Minutes of the Board Meeting," September 16, 2004. Box 6, *AA*.

[30]"The Alliance of Baptists: Minutes of the Board Meeting," April 20, 2006. Box 6, *AA*.

[31]"The Alliance of Baptists: Minutes of the Board Meeting," September 14-16, 2006. Box 6, *AA*.

[32]"The Alliance of Baptists: Minutes of the Meeting of the Board of Directors," April 12-13, 2007. Box 6, *AA*.

[33]Ibid.

[34]"The Alliance of Baptists: Minutes of the Board Meeting," September 14-16, 2006. Box 6, *AA*.

[35]"The Alliance of Baptists: Minutes of the Meeting of the Board of Directors," September 13-15, 2007. Box 6, *AA*.

[36]Ibid.

[37]"The Alliance of Baptists: Minutes of the Meeting of the Board of Directors," September 18-20, 2008.

[38]"Alliance of Baptists — Board of Directors Meeting," September 15, 2011.

[39]Ibid.

[40]Ibid.

[41]"Alliance of Baptists: Minutes of the Board of Directors Meeting," September 17-18, 2009.

[42]"Alliance of Baptists: Minutes of the Board of Directors Meeting," October 15-17, 2010.

[43]Ibid.

[44]"Alliance of Baptists — Board of Directors Meeting" April 11, 2012.

[45]Neely, "The History of the Alliance of Baptists," in *Struggle for the Soul of the SBC*, 114.

[46]Neely, "Forebears, Siblings, and Offspring," 10-12.

[47]Neely, "Forebears, Siblings, and Offspring," 84.

[48]Neely, "The History of the Alliance of Baptists," in *Struggle for the Soul of the SBC*, 115.

[49]Stan Hastey to Barbara Williams, April 3, 1999. Box 17, *AA*.

[50]"Alliance of Baptists 10th Anniversary Alliance Athletic Awards." Box 12, *AA*.

[51]"Alliance of Baptists: Minutes of the Board of Directors' Meeting," September 18-20, 1997. Box 5, *AA*.

[52]"The Alliance of Baptists: Minutes of the Board Meeting," April 15-16, 2004. Box 6, *AA*.

[53]"The Alliance of Baptists: Minutes of the Meeting of the Board of Directors," September 18-20, 2008.

[54]"Alliance of Baptists: Minutes of the Board of Directors Conference Call Meeting," January 4, 2010.

[55]"The Alliance of Baptists: Meeting of the Board Meeting," September 14-16, 2006. Box 6, *AA*

[56]Neely, "The History of the Alliance of Baptists," in *Struggle for the Soul of the SBC*, 122.

[57]"Minutes of the Board of Directors Meeting," November 28-29, 1988. Box 3, *AA*.

[58]"The Alliance of Baptists Executive Committee," March 10-11, 1999. Box 5, *AA*."

[59]"Alliance of Baptists: Minutes of the Board of Directors," March 11-12, 1999. Box 5, *AA*.

[60]"Alliance of Baptists: Minutes of the Board of Directors," September 17-19, 1998. Box 5, *AA*.

[61]"Alliance of Baptists: Minutes of the Board of Directors," March 11-12, 1999. Box 5, *AA*.

[62]Ibid.

[63]"The Alliance of Baptists: Minutes of the Board Meeting," September 18-20, 2003. Box 5, *AA*.

[64]Ibid.

[65]"The Alliance of Baptists: Minutes of the Meeting of the Board of Directors," September 13-15, 2007. Box 6, *AA*.

[66]"Minutes of the Alliance of Baptists Board of Directors," April 28, 2011.

[67]"Alliance of Baptists — Board of Directors Meeting," September 15, 2011.

[68]"The Alliance of Baptists: Minutes of the Board Meeting," September 19-21, 2002. Box 5, *AA*.

[69]"Alliance of Baptists — Executive Committee Conference Call," November 29, 2011.

[70]Neely, "Servanthood Revisited," Covenant Address, 2002. Box 14, *AA.*

[71]Ibid.

[72]Ibid.

[73]Matthew 25:40, NRSV.

Chapter 9

[1]Shurden, "Freedom for Theological Education," in *Being Baptist Means Freedom,* 57-68.

[2]Henry Crouch to Executive Committee, November 4, 1987. Box 7, *AA.*

[3]"Minutes of the Board of Directors Meeting," September 14-15, 1987. Box 3, *AA.*

[4]"Minutes of the Board of Directors Meeting," January 11, 1988. Box 3, *AA.*

[5]"Minutes of the Board of Directors Meeting," March 21, 1988. Box 3, *AA.*

[6]"Progress Report on Our Relationship with the Southern Baptist Alliance." Box 16, *AA.*

[7]"Minutes of the Board of Directors Meeting," November 28-29, 1988. Box 3, *AA.*

[8]"Minutes of the Board of Directors Meeting," September 14-15, 1987. Box 3, *AA.*

[9]"Minutes of the Board of Directors Meeting" September 10, 1988. Box 3, *AA.*

[10]"Minutes of the Board of Directors Meeting," June 13, 1988. Box 3, *AA.*

[11]"Minutes of the Board of Directors of the Southern Baptist Alliance," September 27-28, 1990. Box 3, *AA.*

[12]"The Seminary Task Force Report," January 3, 1989. Box 22, *AA.*

[13]"Minutes of the Board of Directors," March 1, 1989. Box 3, *AA.*

[14]Stan Hastey to Bill Leonard, May 19, 1989. Box 19, *AA.*

[15]Mahan Siler to Stan Hastey," March 24, 1989. Box 9, *AA.*

[16]"Southern Baptist Alliance: Minutes of the Board of Directors Meeting," March 13-14, 1991. Box 3, *AA.*

[17]Hastey, "State of the Alliance Address," March 4, 1995. Box 11, *AA.*

[18]Neely, "The History of the Alliance of Baptists," in *Struggle for the Soul of the SBC,* 122.

[19]"Minutes of the Board of Directors," November 29-30, 1989. Box 3, *AA.*

[20]Mahan Siler to Stan Hastey, March 24, 1989. Box 9, *AA.*

[21]"Southern Baptist Alliance: Minutes of the Board of Directors Meeting," September 20-21, 1991. Box 4, *AA.*

[22]"The Alliance of Baptists Executive Committee," March 10-11, 1999. Box 5, *AA.*

[23]Robert A. Ratcliff to Jeanette Holt, September 20, 1993. Box 17, *AA.*

[24]Jeanette Holt to Robert A. Ratcliff, September 29, 1993. Box 17, *AA.*

[25]Stan Hastey to Douglas Jansen, March 3, 1993. Box 19, *AA.*

[26]"Committee Reports," 1995. Box 11, *AA.*

[27]Nathan Powers to The Alliance of Baptists, April 9, 1998. Box 13, *AA.*

[28]Hastey, "State of the Alliance Address," April 17, 2004. Box 15, *AA.*

[29]Jeanette Holt to Ka'thy Gore Chappell, October 15, 2004. Box 17, *AA.*

[30]Stan Hastey to Michael J. Clingenpeel, September 26, 2000. Box 20, *AA.*

[31]"The Alliance of Baptists Executive Committee," March 10-11, 1999. Box 5, *AA.*

[32]"Alliance of Baptists: Minutes of the Board of Directors," March 11-12, 1999. Box 5, *AA.*

[33]"Alliance of Baptists: Minutes of the Meeting of the Board of Directors," April 26-27, 2000. Box 5, *AA*.

[34]Neely, "The History of the Alliance of Baptists," in *Struggle for the Soul of the SBC*, 111.

[35]Everett Gill to Henry Crouch, August 10, 1987. Box 17, *AA*.

[36]Ibid.

[37]"Minutes of the Board of Directors Meeting," September 14-15, 1987. Box 3, *AA*.

[38]Lloyd Householder to Stan Hastey, January 23, 1989, Box 7, *AA*.

[39]Stan Hastey to SBA Sunday School Literature Study Group, May 18, 1989. Box 7, *AA*.

[40]Robert Fulbright to Jeanette Holt. December 19, 1990. Box 7, *AA*.

[41]Robert Fulbright to Frank Bates, June 20, 1989. Box 7, *AA*.

[42]Frank C. Bates to Welton Seal, July 26, 1989. Box 7, *AA*.

[43]Brooks Wicker to Welton Seal, September 4, 1989. Box 7, *AA*.

[44]"Minutes of the Board of Directors," November 29-30, 1989. Box 3, *AA*.

[45]Robert Fulbright to Curriculum Committee, January 17, 1990. Box 7, *AA*.

[46]Ad Hoc Curriculum Committee to SBA Board of Directors, 1900. Box 7, *AA*.

[47]Robert Fulbright to Curriculum Committee, March 14, 1990. Box 7, *AA*.

[48]"Minutes of the Board of Directors," March 9, 1990. Box 3, *AA*.

[49]Robert Fulbright to Curriculum Committee, December 19, 1990. Box 7, *AA*.

[50]Robert Fulbright to Daniel Vestal, March 6, 1991. Box 7, *AA*.

[51]"Minutes of the Board of Directors Meeting," September 10, 1988. Box 3, *AA*.

[52]Walker Knight to Welton Seal, May 19, 1989. Box 7, *AA*.

[53]"Southern Baptist Alliance: Minutes of the Board of Directors Meeting," March 13-14, 1991. Box 3, *AA*.

[54]Jean B. Kim to Stan Hastey, April 17, 1991. Box 7, *AA*.

[55]"Minutes of the Board of Directors Meeting," November 28-29, 1988. Box 3, *AA*.

[56]"The Alliance of Baptists Meeting of the Board of Directors," March 13-14, 1996. Box 5, *AA*.

[57]"Alliance of Baptists: Minutes of the Board of Directors," September 19, 1996. Box 5, *AA*.

[58]"Alliance of Baptists: Minutes of the Board of Directors' Meeting," March 13-14, 1997. Box 5, *AA*.

[59]"Alliance of Baptists: Minutes of the Board of Directors Meeting," September 17-18, 2009.

[60]"Alliance of Baptists Minutes of the Board Conference Call," January 18, 2011.

[61]"Alliance of Baptists — Board of Directors Meeting," April 11, 2012.

[62]"Minutes of the Alliance of Baptists Board of Directors," November 8-10, 2012.

[63]"Conference Call For Executive Committee Of The Alliance Of Baptists," May 2, 2013.

Chapter 10

[1]Neil, "The Freedom to Work for Global Justice," in *Being Baptist Means Freedom*, 70.

[2]Ibid., 71.

[3]Ibid., 77.

[4]Ibid., 78.

[5]"The Alliance of Baptists Minutes of the Board of Directors," March 2-3, 1994. Box 4, *AA*.

[6]Neely, *A New Call to Missions: Help for Perplexed Churches* (Macon, GA: Smyth and Helwys, 1999), 65. Neely also suggests that the Cooperative Baptist Fellowship was not initially a missions organization; however, a "missions program resulted from a proposal presented by a task force appointed by . . . Daniel Vestal." (55).

[7]Ibid., 68

[8]Ibid.

[9]Ibid., 69.

[10]Ibid.

[11]Ibid., 71

[12]Ibid., 72

[13]"Minutes of the Board of Directors Meeting," January 11, 1988. Box 3, *AA*.

[14]"Minutes of the Board of Directors Meeting," September 10, 1988. Box 3, *AA*.

[15]Ibid.

[16]"Minutes of the Board of Directors Meeting," November 28-29, 1988. Box 3, *AA*.

[17]"Minutes of the Board of Directors Meeting," September 10, 1988. Box 3, *AA*.

[18]"Minutes of the Board of Directors," November 29-30, 1989. Box 3, *AA*.

[19]Ibid.

[20]"Minutes of the Board of Directors," March 9, 1990. Box 3, *AA*.

[21]"Minutes of the Board of Directors of the Southern Baptist Alliance," September 27-28, 1990. Box 3, *AA*.

[22]"The Alliance of Baptists: Board of Directors Meeting," September 24-26, 1992. Box 4, *AA*.

[23]"The Alliance of Baptists Meeting of the Board of Directors," August 7-8, 1995. Box 4, *AA*.

[24]Ibid.

[25]"Alliance of Baptists: Minutes of the Meeting of the Board of Directors," September 16-18, 1999. Box 5, *AA*.

[26]"Committee Reports," 1995. Box 11, *AA*.

[27]Bob Balance to Stan Hastey, June 18, 1990. Box 17, *AA*; Hastey to Balance, August 2, 1990. Box 17, *AA*.

[28]"Minutes of the Board of Directors Meeting," September 10, 1988. Box 3, *AA*.

[29]Rabbi David Kline to Stan Hastey. Box 11, *AA*.

[30]Barbara Kline to Stan Hastey, May 24, 1995. Box 11, *AA*.

[31]"A Statement on Jewish-Christian Relations," 1995. Box 15, *AA*.

[32]"Reports of the Standing Committee," 1996. Box 12, *AA*.

[33]Interfaith Relations Committee Report, September 18, 1998. Box 22, *AA*.

[34]Welton Gaddy to Stan Hastey, December 5, 2000. Box 19, *AA*.

[35]"Alliance of Baptists: Minutes of the Meeting of the Board of Directors," April 19-20, 2001. Box 5, *AA*.

[36]"A Statement on Christian-Muslim Relations," 2003. Box 15, *AA*.

[37]By the time of publication of this work, Hyaets had been renamed The Family Tree.

[38]"Alliance of Baptists: Minutes of the Board of Directors Meeting," September 17-18, 2009.

[39]"Alliance of Baptists: Minutes of the Board of Directors," March 11-12, 1999. Box 5, *AA*.

[40]"The Alliance of Baptists: Minutes of the Board Meeting," September 18-20, 2003. Box 5, *AA*.

[41]"Minutes of the Alliance of Baptists Board of Directors," April 28, 2011.

[42]Stan Hastey to Francisco Rodes G., December 20, 1990. Box 10, *AA*.

[43]Leonard, *Baptist Ways*, 250.

[44]Hastey, "The State of the Alliance," March 15, 1991, 4. Box 10, *AA*.

[45]Hastey, "State of the Alliance Address," March 4, 1994. Box 11, *AA*.

[46]"The Alliance of Baptists: Meeting of the Board of Directors," September 30-October 2, 1993. Box 4, *AA*.

[47]Hastey, "State of the Alliance Address," March 13, 1998. Box 13, *AA*.

[48]"A Statement on Travel Restrictions between the United States and Cuba," April 22, 2006. Box 6, *AA*.

[49]"Statement on Cuba," April 2002. Box 5, *AA*.

[50]Joel E. Richardson to Stan Hastey, May 2, 1997. Box 19, *AA*; Linda Kelley to Stan Hastey, August 10, 1998. Box 19, *AA*.

[51]Hastey, "State of the Alliance Address," April 22, 2006. Box 16, *AA*.

[52]Hastey, "State of the Alliance Address," March 13, 1998. Box 13, *AA*.

[53]"Alliance of Baptists: Minutes of the Board of Directors' Meeting," March 13-14, 1997. Box 5, *AA*.

[54]"Alliance of Baptists: Minutes of the Board of Directors' Meeting," September 18-20, 1997. Box 5, *AA*.

[55]Allen, "Baptist Seminary head wins labor appeal," *Associated Baptist Press*, 12 November 2013, accessed September 26, 2014, http://www.abpnews.com/ministry/people/item/9009-baptist-seminary-head-wins-labor-appeal.

[56]Hastey, "State of the Alliance Address," April 17, 2004. Box 15, *AA*.

[57]"The Alliance of Baptists: Minutes of the Meeting of the Board of Directors," September 13-15, 2007. Box 6, *AA*.

[58]"Minutes of the Alliance of Baptists Board of Directors," April 28, 2011.

[59]Allen, "Baptist Seminary head wins labor appeal."

[60]This information comes through personal conversation with Henry Mugabe in July 2014. Mugabe also mentioned that his initial attempts to receive funding for Baptist Theological Seminary of Zimbabwe through the Cooperative Baptist Fellowship were denied.

[61]Karen Smith, email message to Stan Hastey and Jeanette Holt, March 8, 1997. Box 12, *AA*.

[62]Joe Thomas to Stan Hastey, October 20, 1998. Box 20, *AA*; Hastey to Thomas, October 29, 1998. Box 20, *AA*.

[63]"Karen Thomas Smith: Connecting with Morocco," in *Connections* 3, no 4. April 2000.

[64]Harlan Spurgeon to Kevin and Karen Smith, December 29, 1994. Box 20, *AA*.

[65]"The Alliance of Baptists: Minutes of the Board Meeting," September 19-21, 2002. Box 5, *AA*.

[66]Hastey, "State of the Alliance Address," April 17, 2004. Box 15, *AA*.

[67]"The Alliance of Baptists: Minutes of the Meeting of the Board of Directors," April 12-13, 2007. Box 6, *AA*.

⁶⁸"The Alliance of Baptists: Minutes of the Board Meeting," September 19-21, 2002. Box 5, *AA*.

⁶⁹"The Alliance of Baptists: Minutes of the Board Meeting," April 15-16, 2004. Box 5, *AA*.

⁷⁰Stan Hastey to Roger Crook, February 8, 2001. Box 17, *AA*; Crook to Hastey, January 16, 2001. Box 17, *AA*.

⁷¹"School of Elijah," accessed September 27, 2014. http://www.ebcgeorgia.org/Neue_Dateien/start.html.

⁷²Conference Flyer, "Workshops," Box 15, *AA*.

⁷³"The Alliance of Baptists: Minutes of the Board Meeting," September 15-17, 2005. Box 6, *AA*.

⁷⁴The Alliance of Baptists: Minutes of the Meeting of the Board of Directors," September 18-20, 2008.

⁷⁵Samuel Pagan to Stan Hastey, January 6, 1997. Box 19, *AA*.

⁷⁶"The Alliance of Baptists: Minutes of the Board Meeting," April 20, 2006. Box 6, *AA*.

⁷⁷"Minutes of the Board of Directors of the Southern Baptist Alliance," September 27-28, 1990. Box 3, *AA*.

⁷⁸"Alliance of Baptists: Minutes of the Board of Directors' Meeting," March 13-14, 1997. Box 5, *AA*.

⁷⁹"Alliance of Baptists: Minutes of the Board of Directors' Meeting," September 18-20, 1997. Box 5, *AA*.

⁸⁰"The Alliance of Baptists: Minutes of the Board Meeting," September 16, 2004. Box 6, *AA*.

⁸¹"Alliance of Baptists: Minutes of the Board of Directors Meeting," September 17-18, 2009.

⁸²Hastey, "State of the Alliance Address," 2004. Box 15, *AA*.

⁸³Ken Sehested to Stan Hastey and Jeanette Holt, October 19, 1990. Box 7, *AA*.

⁸⁴Hastey, "State of the Alliance Address," 1996. Box 12, *AA*.

⁸⁵"Mission and Vision," accessed September 27, 2014, http://www.bpfna.org/about-us/mission-vision. See also Paul Dekar, *Building a Culture of Peace: Baptist Peace Fellowship of North America, the First Seventy Years* (Eugene, OR: Wipf and Stock, 2010).

⁸⁶Ken Sehested to Jeanette Holt, January 11, 1993. Box 8, *AA*.

⁸⁷"The Alliance of Baptists Executive Committee," March 10-11, 1999. Box 5, *AA*.

⁸⁸Hastey, "State of the Alliance Address," March 13, 1999. Box 13, *AA*.

⁸⁹"The Alliance of Baptists: Minutes of the Board Meeting," March 30-April 1, 2005. Box 6, *AA*.

⁹⁰"Minutes of the Board of Directors," March 9, 1990. Box 3, *AA*.

⁹¹"A Call to Repentance," March 10, 1990. Box 9, *AA*.

⁹²This information comes through personal conversations with Richard Groves.

⁹³"The Alliance of Baptists: Minutes of the Board Meeting," September 19-21, 2002. Box 5, *AA*.

⁹⁴Hastey, "State of the Alliance Address," April 6, 2002. Box 14, *AA*.

⁹⁵"The Alliance of Baptists: Minutes of the Board Meeting," April 15-16, 2004. Box 6, *AA*.

⁹⁶"A Statement on Racism and Repentance," April 22, 2006. Box 16, *AA*.

[97]"Alliance of Baptists: Minutes of the Meeting of the Board of Directors," April 19-20, 2001. Box 5, *AA*

[98]"Workshops — Session I: A Still More Excellent Way." Box 14, *AA*.

[99]Bob Allen, "Alliance of Baptists revisits its founding 'covenant'," *Associated Baptist Press*, 18 March 1997. Box 12, *AA*.

[100]"Alliance of Baptists: Minutes of the Board of Directors," September 17-19, 1998. Box 5, *AA*.

[101]"Alliance of Baptists: Minutes of the Meeting of the Board of Directors," September 16-18, 1999. Box 5, *AA*

[102]"Alliance of Baptists: Minutes of the Meeting of the Board of Directors," April 26-27, 2000. Box 5, *AA*.

[103]"Alliance of Baptists: Minutes of the Meeting of the Board of Directors," April 4-5, 2002. Box 5, *AA*.

[104]"Statements," accessed September 27, 2014, http://allianceofbaptists.org/OurAlliance/statements.

[105]"The Alliance of Baptists: Minutes of the Board of Directors Meeting," April 16-18, 2009.

[106]"Alliance of Baptists: Minutes of the Board of Directors Meeting," October 15-17, 2010; "Alliance of Baptists — Board of Directors Meeting," April 11, 2012.

[107]"Alliance of Baptists — Board of Directors Meeting," April 11, 2012.

[108]"Alliance of Baptists: Minutes of the Board of Directors Meeting," September 17-18, 2009. G.J. Tarazi is listed as the Alliance's representative for Churches for Middle East Peace, but Paula Dempsey, director of partnership relations, explained that Robert Tiller served as the primary contact with the organization.

Chapter 11

[1]Norman Cavender, "Freedom for the Church in a Free State," in *Being Baptist Means Freedom*, 83.

[2]The Baptist Joint Committee, "History of the Baptist Joint Committee," accessed October 20, 2014, http://bjconline.org/mission-history. .

[3]Cavender, "Freedom for the Church in a Free State," in *Being Baptist Means Freedom*, 86.

[4]Neely, "The History of the Alliance of Baptists," in *Struggle for the Soul of the SBC*, 112.

[5]"Minutes of the Board of Directors Meeting," June 14, 1987. Box 2, *AA*.

[6]"Minutes of the Board of Directors Meeting," September 14-15, 1987. Box 3, *AA*.

[7]Ibid.

[8]Neely, "Be Advised: Helping The Baptist Joint Committee May Be More Difficult Than You Think." Box 16, *AA*.

[9]Neely, "Forebears, Siblings, and Offspring," 23.

[10]"Minutes of the Board of Directors Meeting," September 14-15, 1987. Box 3, *AA*.

[11]"Minutes of the Board of Directors Meeting," September 10, 1988. Box 3, *AA*.

[12]James Dunn to Jeannette Holt, August 7, 1992. Box 17, *AA*.

[13]Patrick Horn to Stan Hastey, September 1, 1992. Box 17, *AA*.

[14]"Alliance of Baptists: Minutes of the Board of Directors," September 19, 1996. Box 5, *AA*.

[15]Ammerman, "To Be a Peculiar People," Covenant Address, March 12, 1999. Box 13, *AA*.

[16]"Southern Baptist Alliance: Minutes of the Board of Directors Meeting," September 20-21, 1991. Box 4, *AA*.

[17]"Supreme Court rules that Religious Freedom Restoration Act exceeds congress' power," accessed October 14, 2014, http://www.civilrights.org/monitor/vol9_no2_3/art6. html.

[18]"Southern Baptist Alliance Board of Directors Meeting," March 4-5, 1992. Box 4, *AA*.

[19]"The Alliance of Baptists: Meeting of the Board of Directors," September 30-October 2, 1993. Box 4, *AA*.

[20] "Committee Report," 1995, Box 11, *AA*.

[21]Ibid.

[22]Ibid.

[23]Bob Allen, "Baptist Group Joins Call for Peace in Mideast," *Associated Baptist Press*, 8 April 2002. Box 14, *AA*.

[24]"Alliance of Baptists: Minutes of the Meeting of the Board of Directors," April 19-20, 2001. Box 5, *AA*.

[25]Hastey, "State of the Alliance Address," April 17, 2004. Box 15, *AA*.

[26]"The Alliance of Baptists Statement on Cuba," April 25, 2003. Box 15, *AA*.

[27]Hastey, "A disgraceful decision," *Connections*, March 2004. Box 15, *AA*.

[28]Ibid.

[29]"A Statement on Travel Restrictions between the United States and Cuba," April 22, 2006, Box 16, *AA*.

[30]"A Statement on Ending the Ban on Travel to Cuba," April 14, 2007. Box 16, *AA*.

[31]"Minutes of the Board of Directors Meeting," November 28-29, 1988. Box 3, *AA*.

[32]Bob Allen, "Alliance of Baptists joins first faith-based challenge to gay-marriage ban," *Associated Baptist Press*, accessed October 21, 2014. http://baptistnews.com/index. php?option=com_k2&view=item&id=28770:alliance-of-baptists-challenges-gay-marriage-ban&Itemid=100184.

Part III Living Zion

[1]Mark Chaves, *Congregations in America* (Cambridge, MA: Harvard University Press, 2004), 5.

[2]Dorothy C. Bass, "Congregations and the Bearing of Traditions," in *American Congregations: vol. 2, New Perspectives in the Study of Congregations*, eds. James P. Wind and James W. Lewis (Chicago: The University of Chicago Press, 1998), 173.

Woodbrook Baptist Church

[1]Woodbrook Baptist Church, "We're Baptist and Yet . . .," accessed January 15, 2015, http://www.woodbrook.org/who_we_are/we_are_baptist_and_yet.htm.

Attendees at the first convocation of the Southern Baptist Alliance in line for a meal at
Meredith College, Raleigh, N.C., May, 1987.

Bill Leonard, professor at Southern Baptist Theological Seminary, and Alliance founder
Nancy Hastings Sehested lead communion at the 1987 convocation in Jones Chapel at
Meredith College, Raleigh, N.C.

Norman Cavender, Claxton, Ga., and Henry Crouch, pastor of Providence Baptist Church, Charlotte, N.C., and first president of the Southern Baptist Alliance, exchange greetings on the Meredith College campus during the first convocation, 1987.

Alan Neely, first interim Executive Director of the Southern Baptist Alliance, photographed during his tenure on the faculty of Princeton Theological Seminary. Neely's wide and far-reaching influence in the life of the Alliance of Baptists continues to be felt today.

Founders of the Alliance are photographed at the 1992 convocation held at Providence Baptist Church, Charlotte, N.C. Front row, left to right: Bill Treadwell, Luther Brewer, John Roberts, Alan Neely, Walker Knight, Nancy Hastings Sehested, Susan Lockwood, Doug Murray, Karen Smith Moore, and Bob Spinks. Second row: Mahan Siler, Jim Strickland, Larry Coleman, Henry Crouch, Richard Groves. Third row: Bill Puckett, Tom Austin, and Tom Conley

Charles Adams, pastor of Hartford Memorial Baptist Church, Detroit, Mich., and president of the Progressive National Baptist Convention, preaches at the 1993 convocation held in Daytona Beach, Fla.

Officers elected at the 1994 convocation in Greenville, S.C., pose with executive director Stan Hastey for a photo. Joann Davis, vice president; Paula Clayton Dempsey, secretary; John E. Roberts, president.

The 1995 convocation at Vienna Baptist Church, Vienna, Va., focused on interfaith relations. Liturgical dance and reading from the Torah are interwoven into the tapestry of worship presided over by Alliance founder, Welton Gaddy.

Even though not among the original list of founders, Anne Thomas Neil's solid leadership was formative in the early years of the Alliance. Here she is pictured preaching at 1996 convocation at Myers Park Baptist Church, Charlotte, N.C.

An Alliance founder and its fourth president, Richard Groves is presented a gift by Stan Hastey at the 1997 convocation in Raleigh, N.C.

John Mazvigadza, executive secretary of the Zimbabwe Baptist Convention from 1995-2006 is photographed with Henry Mugabe, president of Baptist Theological Seminary in Zimbabwe, at the 1998 convocation held at Calvary Baptist Church, Washington, D.C.

Jeanette Holt, associate director of the Alliance and Stan Hastey, executive director of the Alliance at the 1998 convocation at Calvary Baptist Church, Washington, D.C., where they were honored for 10 years of service to the Alliance.

Ken Meyers, associate pastor, Hendricks Avenue Baptist Church, Jacksonville, Fla., and Karen Massey, associate pastor, Northside Drive Baptist Church, Atlanta, Ga., lead communion at Baptist Theological Seminary at Richmond during the 1999 convocation whose theme focused on theological education.

Worship in Wait Chapel on the Wake Forest University campus in Winston-Salem, N.C., was the centerpiece of the 2002 convocation themed *Serving You by Loving All.*

Stan Hastey converses with Robert Welsh, ecumenical officer for the Christian Church (Disciples of Christ) and Lydia Veliko, ecumenical officer for the United Church of Christ, at the convocation held at First Baptist Church, Dayton, Ohio in 2005. Joining them is Stephen W. Lucas (right), pastor of Highland Park Baptist Church, Austin, Texas, 1995-2005, for the annual gathering that highlighted the ecumenical partnership in mission and ministry.

Longtime leaders within the American Baptist Churches USA, (from left to right) Richard "Cranny" Cranford, Tom McKibbens and Sandra Cranford engaged in conversation at the 2007 Alliance of Baptists' annual gathering at Calvary Baptist Church, Washington D.C.

Alliance president Mike Castle and vice president April Baker speak at a press conference for religious liberty at Watts Street Baptist Church, Durham, N.C., in June 2014. Also pictured (left to right): Steve Smith, attorney and member of Pullen Memorial Baptist Church, Raleigh, N.C.; Maria Palmer, Chapel Hill Town Council and member of Binkley Baptist Church, Chapel Hill, N.C.; and Russ Dean and Amy Jacks Dean, co-pastors of Park Road Baptist Church, Charlotte, N.C.